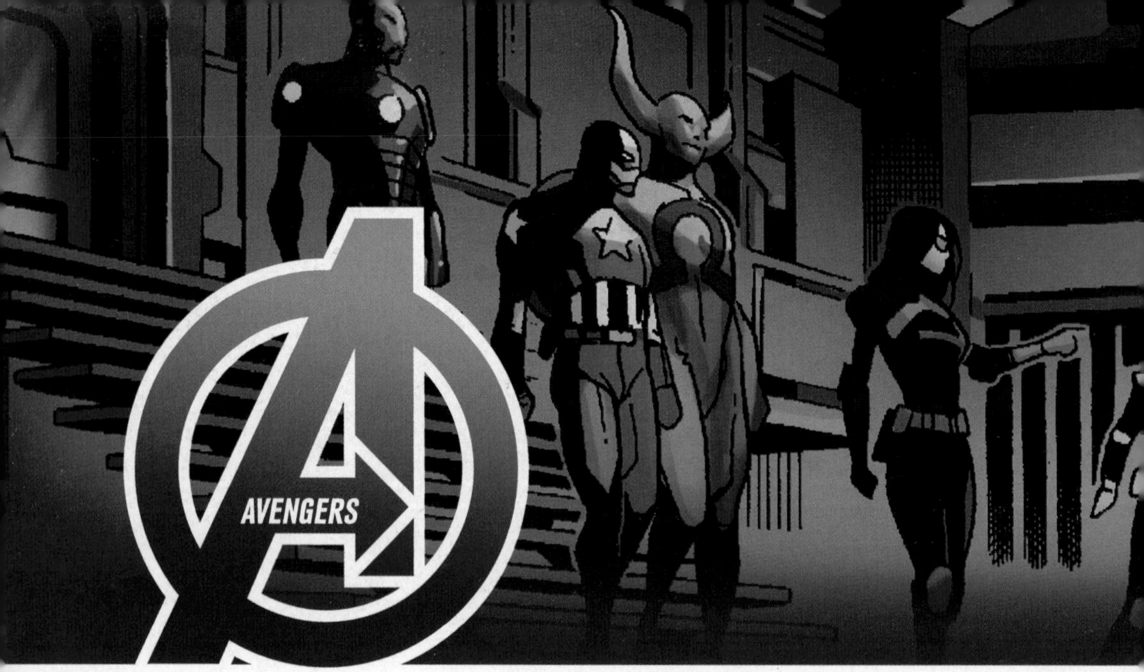
AVENGERS

WRITER: **JONATHAN HICKMAN**
PENCILER: **LEINIL FRANCIS YU**
INKERS: **GERRY ALANGUILAN [#18-22] & LEINIL FRANCIS YU [#23]**
COLORIST, #18-19 & #21-23: **SUNNY GHO WITH DAVID CURIEL [#22] & PAUL MOUNTS [#23]**
COLORIST, #20: **DAVID CURIEL**
LETTERER: **VC'S CORY PETIT**
COVER ART: **LEINIL FRANCIS YU & LAURA MARTIN**
ASSISTANT EDITOR: **JAKE THOMAS**
EDITORS: **TOM BREVOORT WITH LAUREN SANKOVITCH**

COLLECTION EDITOR: **JENNIFER GRÜNWALD**
ASSISTANT EDITORS: **ALEX STARBUCK & NELSON RIBEIRO**
EDITOR, SPECIAL PROJECTS: **MARK D. BEAZLEY**
SENIOR EDITOR, SPECIAL PROJECTS: **JEFF YOUNGQUIST**
SVP OF PRINT & DIGITAL PUBLISHING SALES: **DAVID GABRIEL**

EDITOR IN CHIEF: **AXEL ALONSO**
CHIEF CREATIVE OFFICER: **JOE QUESADA**
PUBLISHER: **DAN BUCKLEY**
EXECUTIVE PRODUCER: **ALAN FINE**

AVENGERS VOL. 4: INFINITY. Contains material originally published in magazine form as AVENGERS #18-23. First printing 2014. ISBN# 978-0-7851-8414-0. Published by MARVEL WORLDWIDE, INC., a s of MARVEL ENTERTAINMENT, LLC. OFFICE OF PUBLICATION: 135 West 50th Street, New York, NY 10020. **Printed in the U.S.A.** ALAN FINE, EVP - Office of the President, Marvel World and EVP & CMO Marvel Characters B.V.; DAN BUCKLEY, Publisher & President - Print, Animation & Digital Divisions; JOE QUESADA, Chief Creative Officer; TOM BREVOORT, SVP of Publishing; DAVID BOGA Operations & Procurement, Publishing; C.B. CEBULSKI, SVP of Creator & Content Development; DAVID GABRIEL, SVP of Print & Digital Publishing Sales; JIM O'KEEFE, VP of Operations & Logistics; DAN CARR, Director of Publishing Technology; SUSAN CRESPI, Editorial Operations Manager; ALEX MORALES, Publishing Operations Manager; STAN LEE, Chairman Emeritus. For information regarding advertising Comics or on Marvel.com, please contact Niza Disla, Director of Marvel Partnerships, at ndisla@marvel.com. For Marvel subscription inquiries, please call 800-217-9158. **Manufactured between 11/15/ 12/30/2013 by R.R. DONNELLEY, INC., SALEM, VA, USA.**

10 9 8 7 6 5 4 3 2 1

"AVENGERS UNIVERSE 1"

PREVIOUSLY IN INFINITY

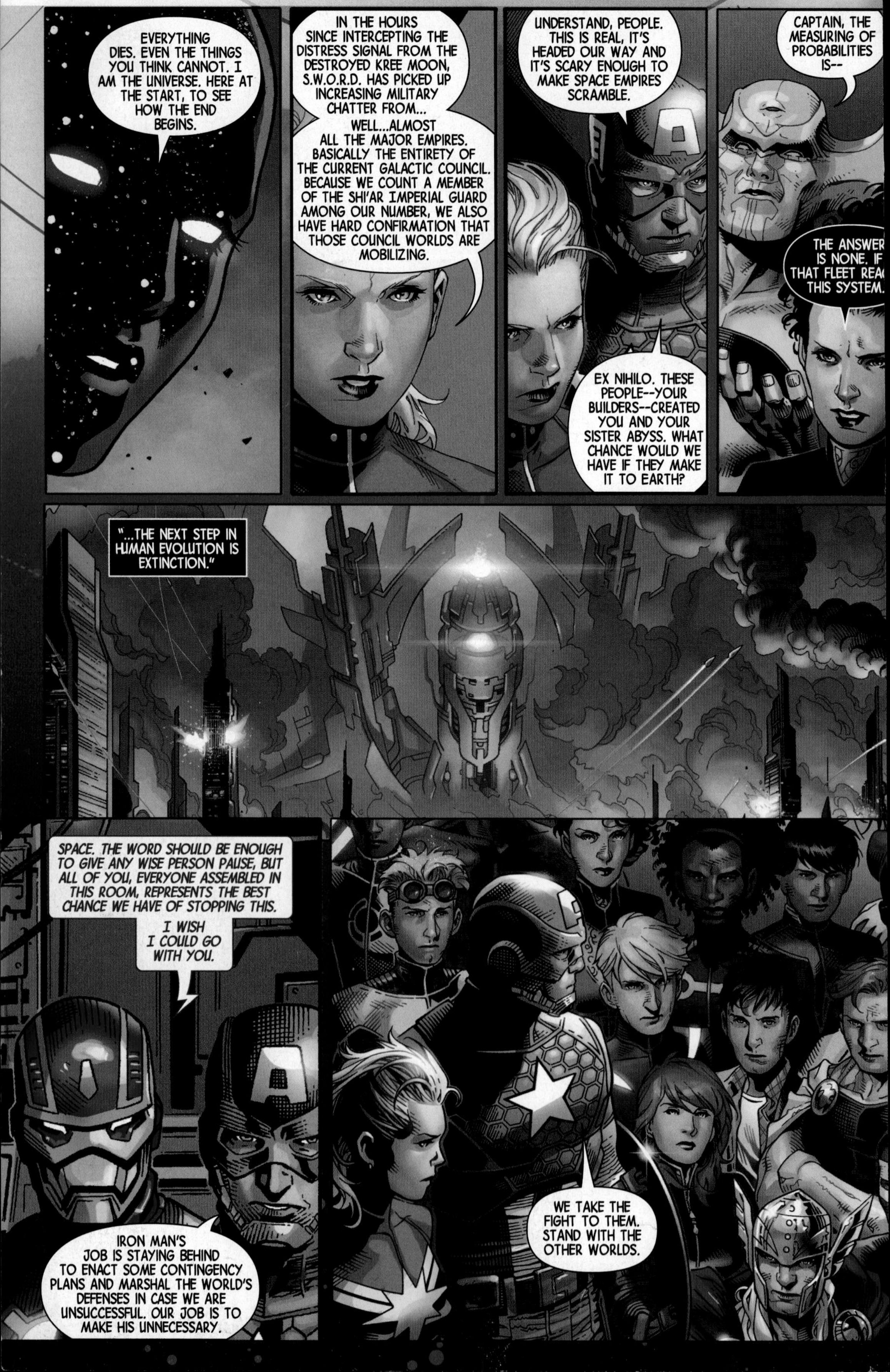

EVERYTHING DIES. EVEN THE THINGS YOU THINK CANNOT. I AM THE UNIVERSE. HERE AT THE START, TO SEE HOW THE END BEGINS.
IN THE HOURS SINCE INTERCEPTING THE DISTRESS SIGNAL FROM THE DESTROYED KREE MOON, S.W.O.R.D. HAS PICKED UP INCREASING MILITARY CHATTER FROM...
WELL...ALMOST ALL THE MAJOR EMPIRES. BASICALLY THE ENTIRETY OF THE CURRENT GALACTIC COUNCIL. BECAUSE WE COUNT A MEMBER OF THE SHI'AR IMPERIAL GUARD AMONG OUR NUMBER, WE ALSO HAVE HARD CONFIRMATION THAT THOSE COUNCIL WORLDS ARE MOBILIZING.
UNDERSTAND, PEOPLE. THIS IS REAL, IT'S HEADED OUR WAY AND IT'S SCARY ENOUGH TO MAKE SPACE EMPIRES SCRAMBLE.
EX NIHILO. THESE PEOPLE--YOUR BUILDERS--CREATED YOU AND YOUR SISTER ABYSS. WHAT CHANCE WOULD WE HAVE IF THEY MAKE IT TO EARTH?
CAPTAIN, THE MEASURING OF PROBABILITIES IS--
THE ANSWER IS NONE. IF THAT FLEET REA THIS SYSTEM.
"...THE NEXT STEP IN HUMAN EVOLUTION IS EXTINCTION."
SPACE. THE WORD SHOULD BE ENOUGH TO GIVE ANY WISE PERSON PAUSE, BUT ALL OF YOU, EVERYONE ASSEMBLED IN THIS ROOM, REPRESENTS THE BEST CHANCE WE HAVE OF STOPPING THIS.
I WISH I COULD GO WITH YOU.
IRON MAN'S JOB IS STAYING BEHIND TO ENACT SOME CONTINGENCY PLANS AND MARSHAL THE WORLD'S DEFENSES IN CASE WE ARE UNSUCCESSFUL. OUR JOB IS TO MAKE HIS UNNECESSARY.
WE TAKE THE FIGHT TO THEM. STAND WITH THE OTHER WORLDS.

CAST

THE AVENGERS

QUINCRUISER 1

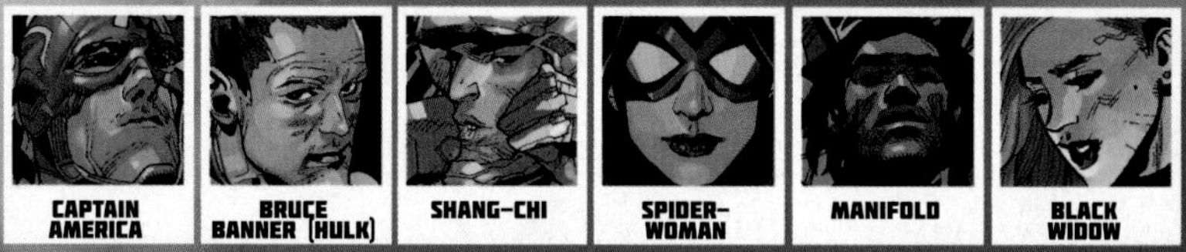
CAPTAIN AMERICA
BRUCE BANNER (HULK)
SHANG-CHI
SPIDER-WOMAN
MANIFOLD
BLACK WIDOW

QUINCRUISER 2

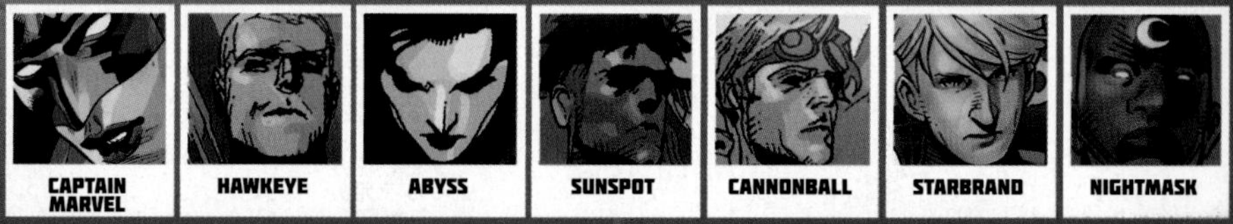
CAPTAIN MARVEL
HAWKEYE
ABYSS
SUNSPOT
CANNONBALL
STARBRAND
NIGHTMASK

FREE-FLYING

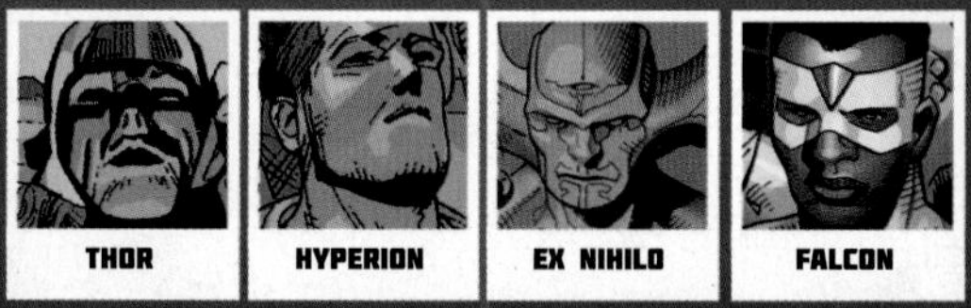
THOR
HYPERION
EX NIHILO
FALCON

THE BUILDERS

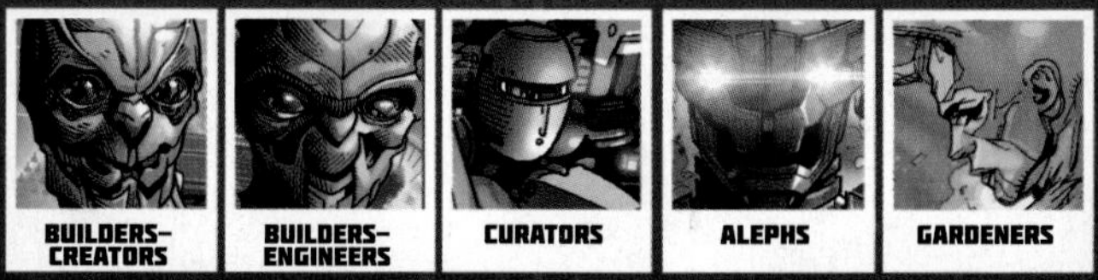
BUILDERS-CREATORS
BUILDERS-ENGINEERS
CURATORS
ALEPHS
GARDENERS

THE GALACTIC COUNCIL

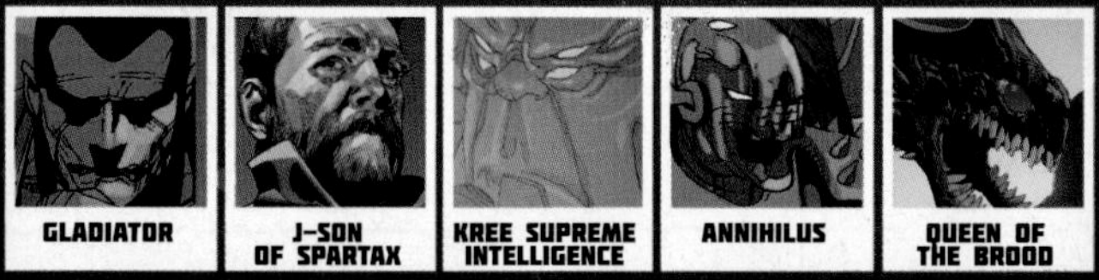
GLADIATOR
J-SON OF SPARTAX
KREE SUPREME INTELLIGENCE
ANNIHILUS
QUEEN OF THE BROOD

SHI'AR IMPERIAL GUARD

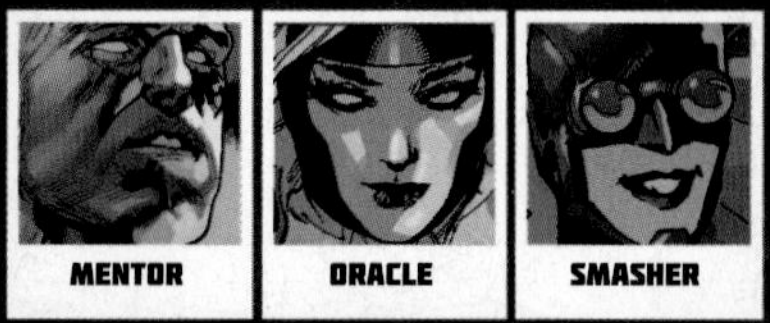
MENTOR
ORACLE
SMASHER

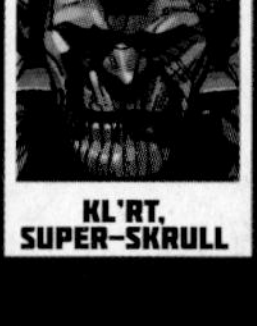
KL'RT, SUPER-SKRULL

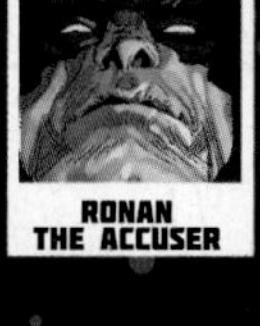
RONAN THE ACCUSER

WORLDS RISE

◆

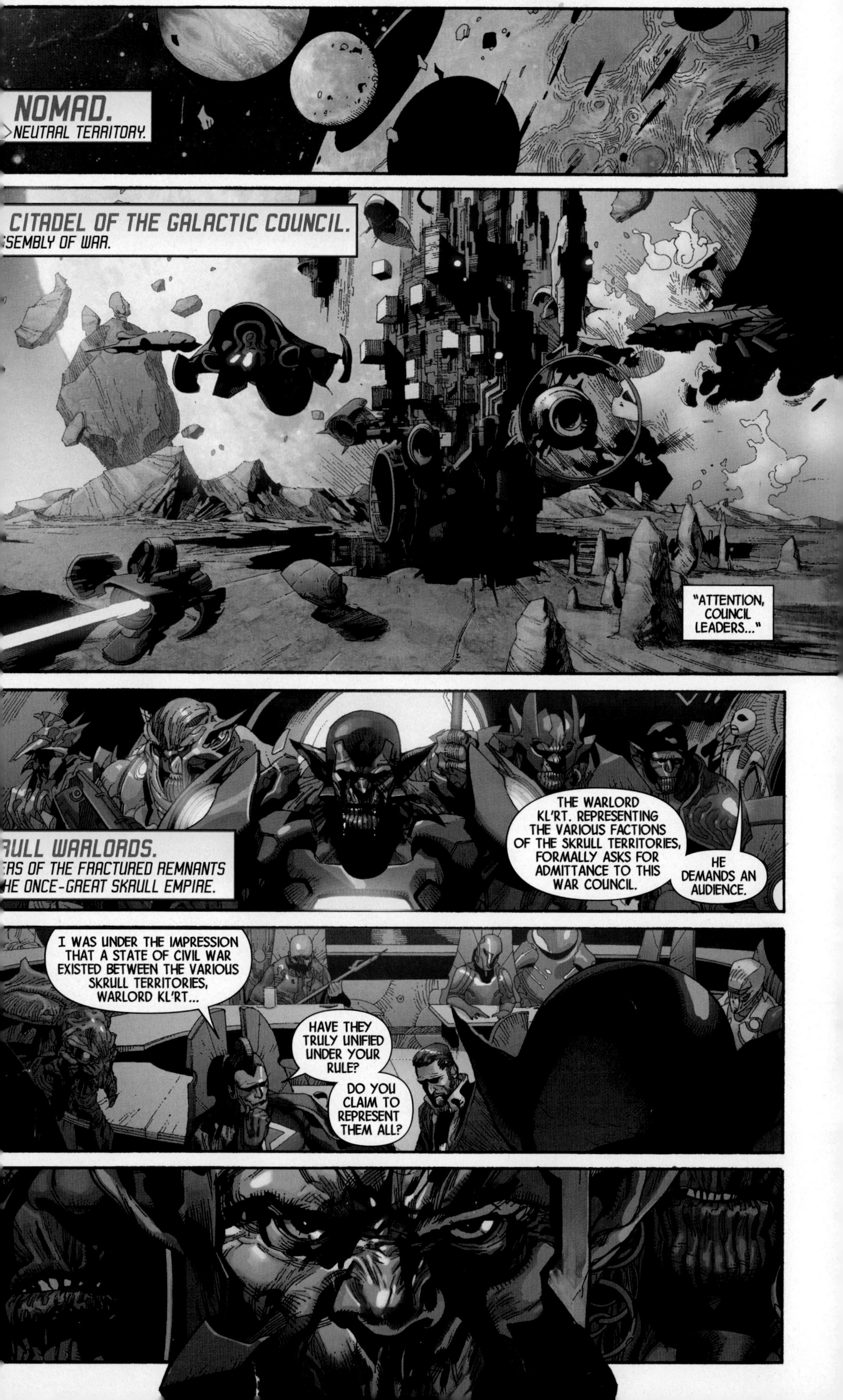
NOMAD.
>NEUTRAL TERRITORY.
CITADEL OF THE GALACTIC COUNCIL.
SEMBLY OF WAR.
"ATTENTION, COUNCIL LEADERS..."
RULL WARLORDS.
ERS OF THE FRACTURED REMNANTS
HE ONCE-GREAT SKRULL EMPIRE.
THE WARLORD KL'RT. REPRESENTING THE VARIOUS FACTIONS OF THE SKRULL TERRITORIES, FORMALLY ASKS FOR ADMITTANCE TO THIS WAR COUNCIL.
HE DEMANDS AN AUDIENCE.
I WAS UNDER THE IMPRESSION THAT A STATE OF CIVIL WAR EXISTED BETWEEN THE VARIOUS SKRULL TERRITORIES, WARLORD KL'RT...
HAVE THEY TRULY UNIFIED UNDER YOUR RULE?
DO YOU CLAIM TO REPRESENT THEM ALL?

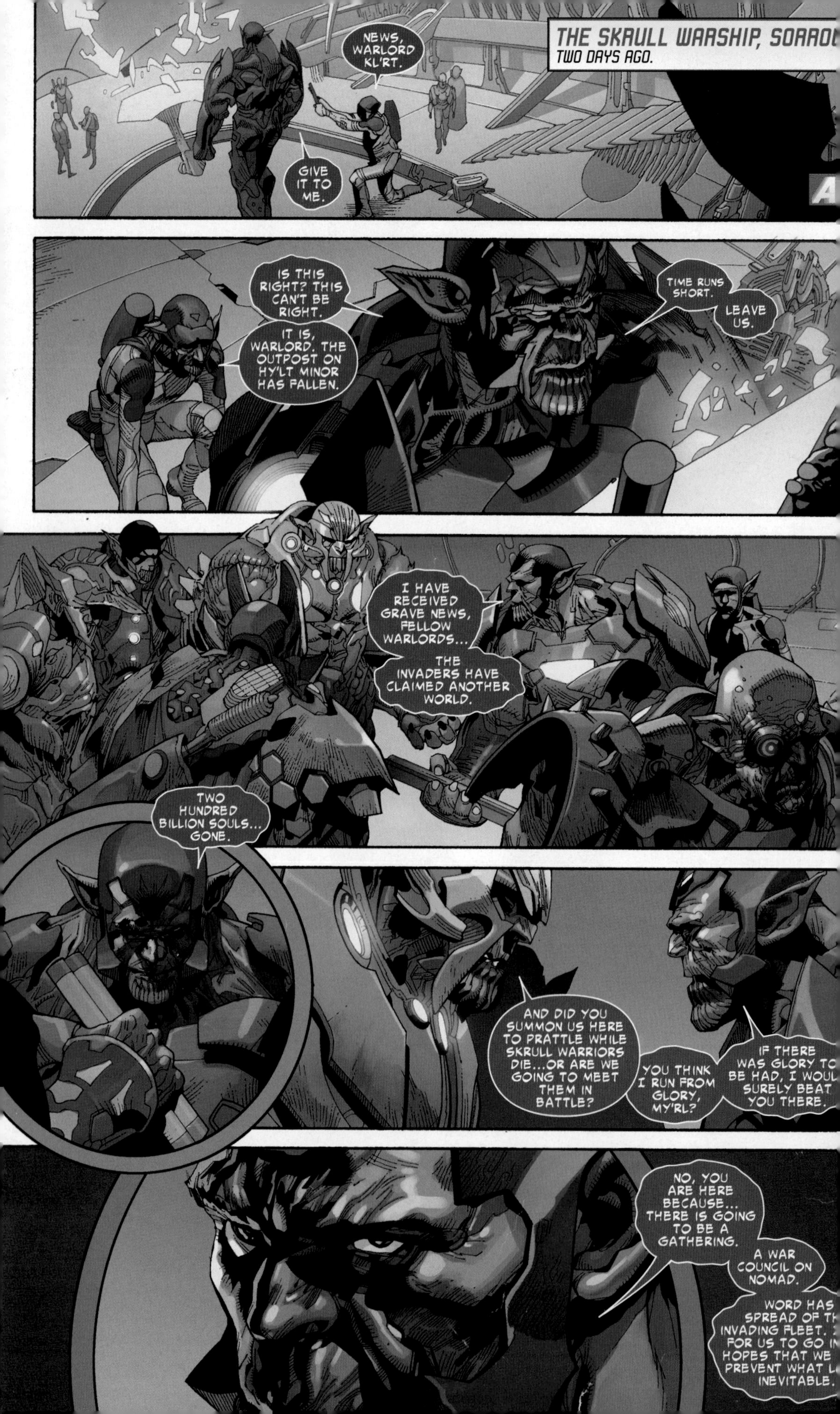
THE SKRULL WARSHIP, SORRO
TWO DAYS AGO.
NEWS, WARLORD KL'RT.
GIVE IT TO ME.
IS THIS RIGHT? THIS CAN'T BE RIGHT.
IT IS, WARLORD. THE OUTPOST ON HY'LT MINOR HAS FALLEN.
TIME RUNS SHORT.
LEAVE US.
I HAVE RECEIVED GRAVE NEWS, FELLOW WARLORDS...
THE INVADERS HAVE CLAIMED ANOTHER WORLD.
TWO HUNDRED BILLION SOULS... GONE.
AND DID YOU SUMMON US HERE TO PRATTLE WHILE SKRULL WARRIORS DIE...OR ARE WE GOING TO MEET THEM IN BATTLE?
YOU THINK I RUN FROM GLORY, MY'RL?
IF THERE WAS GLORY TO BE HAD, I WOUL SURELY BEAT YOU THERE.
NO, YOU ARE HERE BECAUSE... THERE IS GOING TO BE A GATHERING.
A WAR COUNCIL ON NOMAD.
WORD HAS SPREAD OF TH INVADING FLEET. FOR US TO GO IN HOPES THAT WE PREVENT WHAT I INEVITABLE.

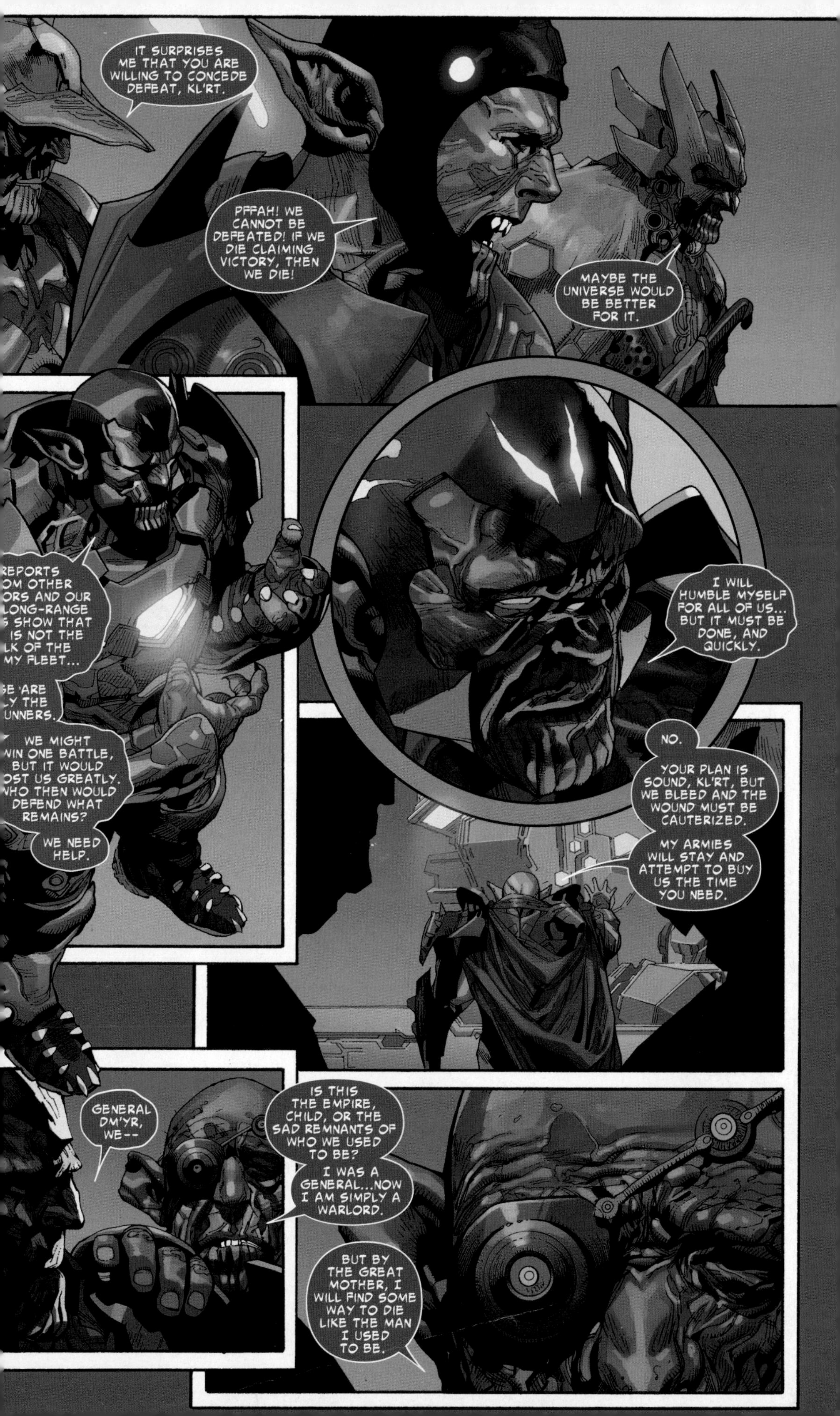
IT SURPRISES ME THAT YOU ARE WILLING TO CONCEDE DEFEAT, KL'RT.
PFFAH! WE CANNOT BE DEFEATED! IF WE DIE CLAIMING VICTORY, THEN WE DIE!
MAYBE THE UNIVERSE WOULD BE BETTER FOR IT.
REPORTS OM OTHER ORS AND OUR LONG-RANGE S SHOW THAT IS NOT THE LK OF THE MY FLEET...
SE ARE Y THE UNNERS.
WE MIGHT WIN ONE BATTLE, BUT IT WOULD OST US GREATLY. WHO THEN WOULD DEFEND WHAT REMAINS?
WE NEED HELP.
I WILL HUMBLE MYSELF FOR ALL OF US... BUT IT MUST BE DONE, AND QUICKLY.
NO.
YOUR PLAN IS SOUND, KL'RT, BUT WE BLEED AND THE WOUND MUST BE CAUTERIZED.
MY ARMIES WILL STAY AND ATTEMPT TO BUY US THE TIME YOU NEED.
GENERAL DM'YR, WE--
IS THIS THE EMPIRE, CHILD, OR THE SAD REMNANTS OF WHO WE USED TO BE?
I WAS A GENERAL...NOW I AM SIMPLY A WARLORD.
BUT BY THE GREAT MOTHER, I WILL FIND SOME WAY TO DIE LIKE THE MAN I USED TO BE.

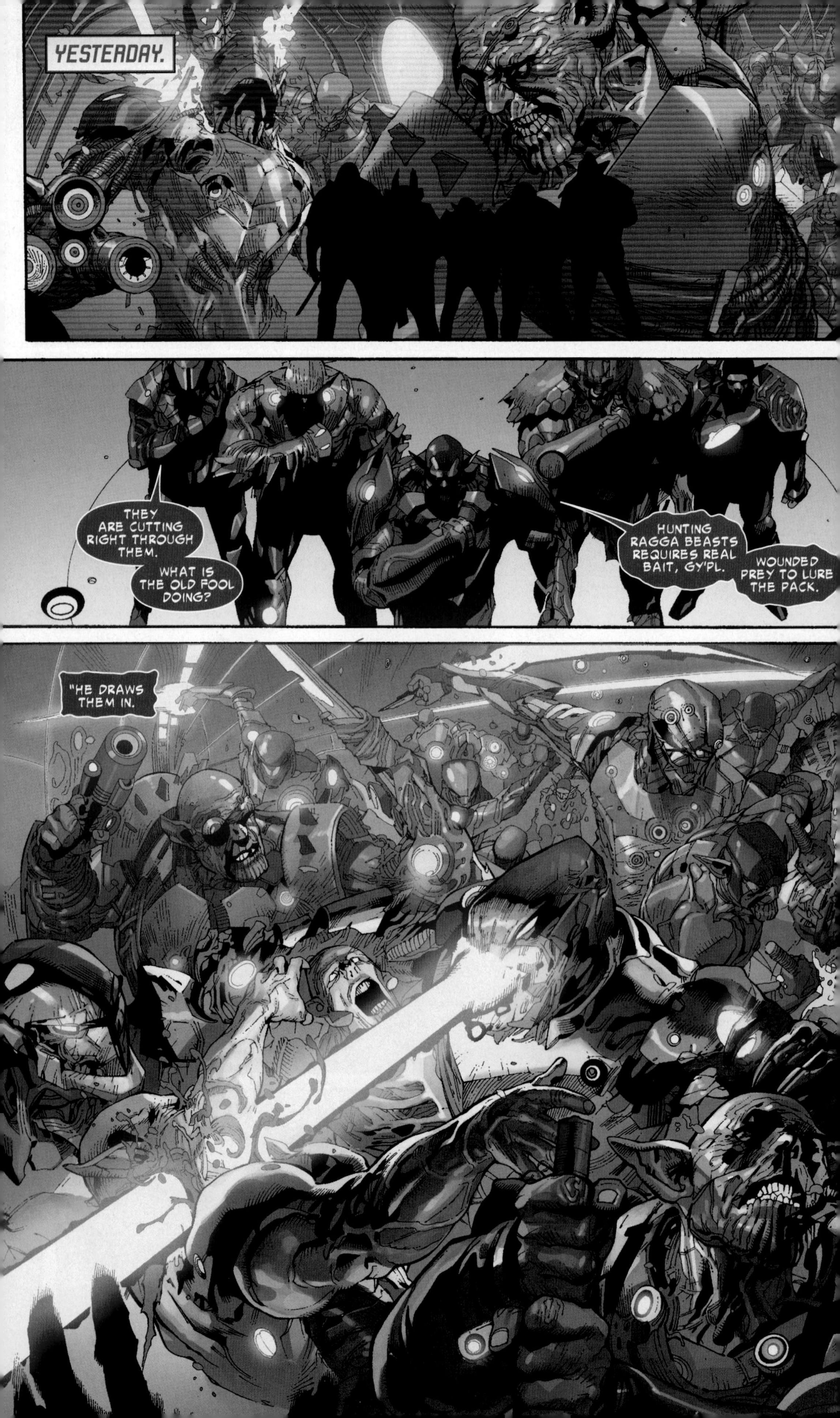
YESTERDAY.
THEY ARE CUTTING RIGHT THROUGH THEM.
WHAT IS THE OLD FOOL DOING?
HUNTING RAGGA BEASTS REQUIRES REAL BAIT, GY'PL.
WOUNDED PREY TO LURE THE PACK.
"HE DRAWS THEM IN.

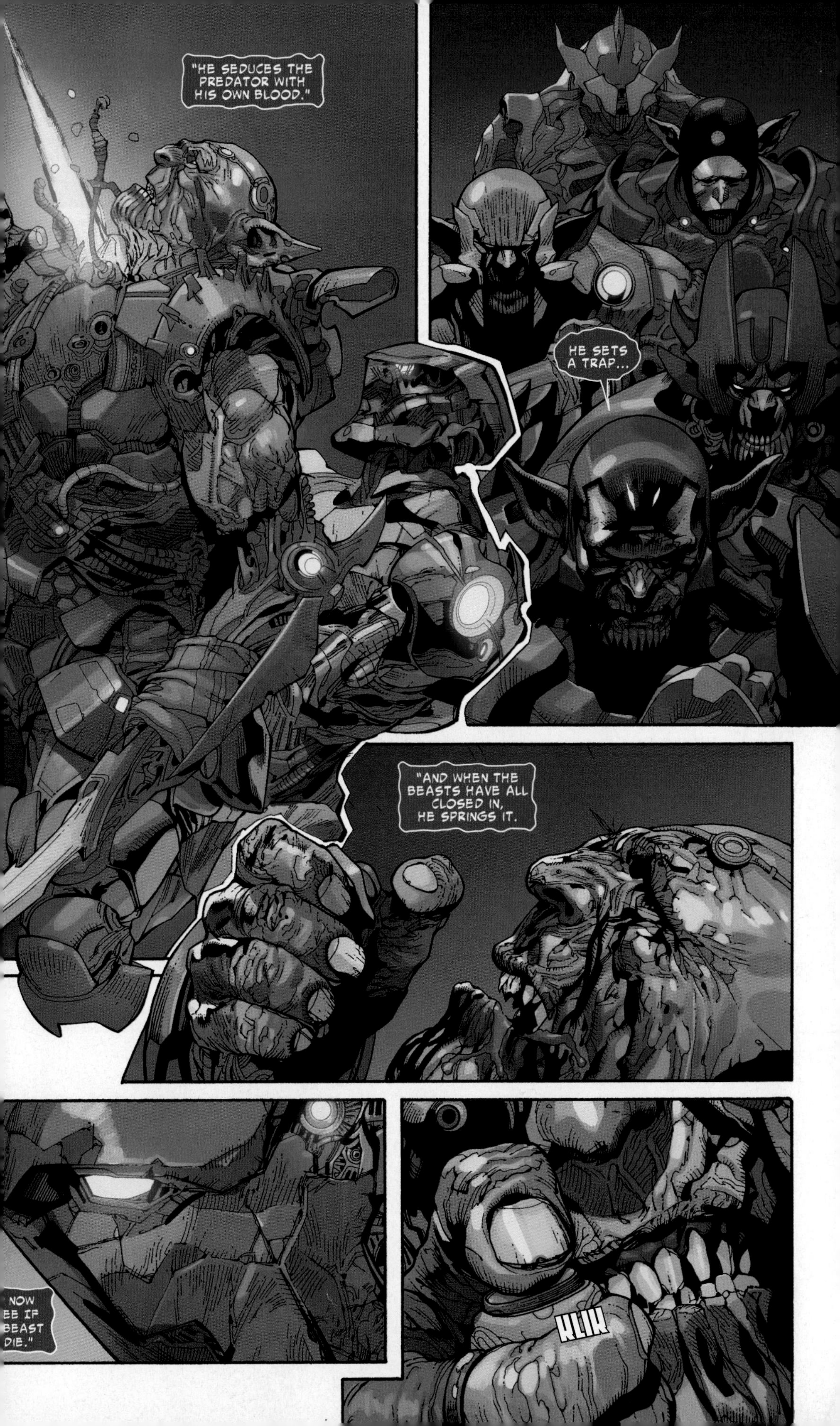
"HE SEDUCES THE PREDATOR WITH HIS OWN BLOOD."
HE SETS A TRAP...
"AND WHEN THE BEASTS HAVE ALL CLOSED IN, HE SPRINGS IT.
NOW EE IF BEAST DIE."
KLIK

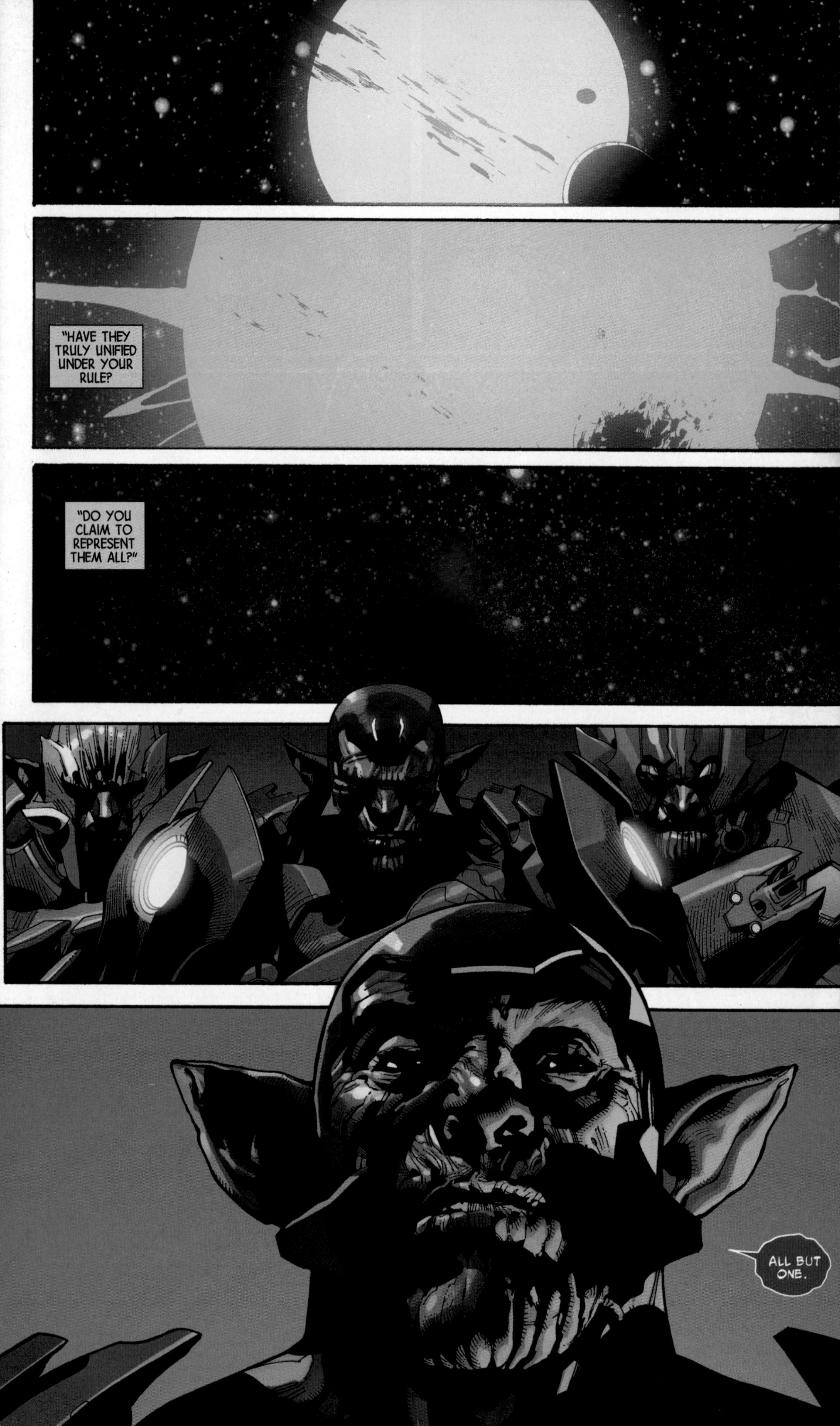
"HAVE THEY TRULY UNIFIED UNDER YOUR RULE?
"DO YOU CLAIM TO REPRESENT THEM ALL?"
ALL BUT ONE.

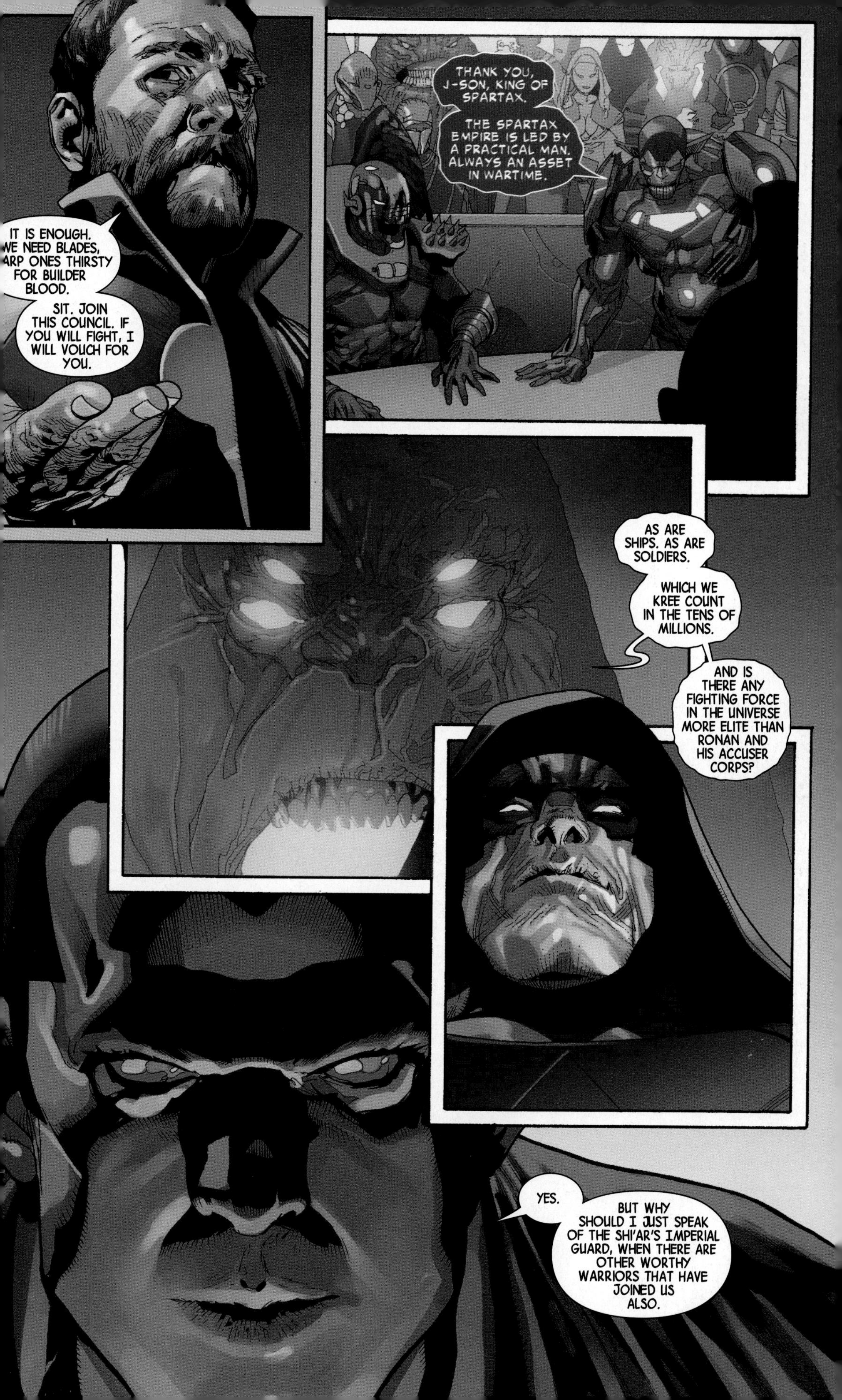
IT IS ENOUGH. WE NEED BLADES, ARP ONES THIRSTY FOR BUILDER BLOOD.
SIT. JOIN THIS COUNCIL. IF YOU WILL FIGHT, I WILL VOUCH FOR YOU.
THANK YOU, J-SON, KING OF SPARTAX.
THE SPARTAX EMPIRE IS LED BY A PRACTICAL MAN. ALWAYS AN ASSET IN WARTIME.
AS ARE SHIPS. AS ARE SOLDIERS.
WHICH WE KREE COUNT IN THE TENS OF MILLIONS.
AND IS THERE ANY FIGHTING FORCE IN THE UNIVERSE MORE ELITE THAN RONAN AND HIS ACCUSER CORPS?
YES.
BUT WHY SHOULD I JUST SPEAK OF THE SHI'AR'S IMPERIAL GUARD, WHEN THERE ARE OTHER WORTHY WARRIORS THAT HAVE JOINED US ALSO.

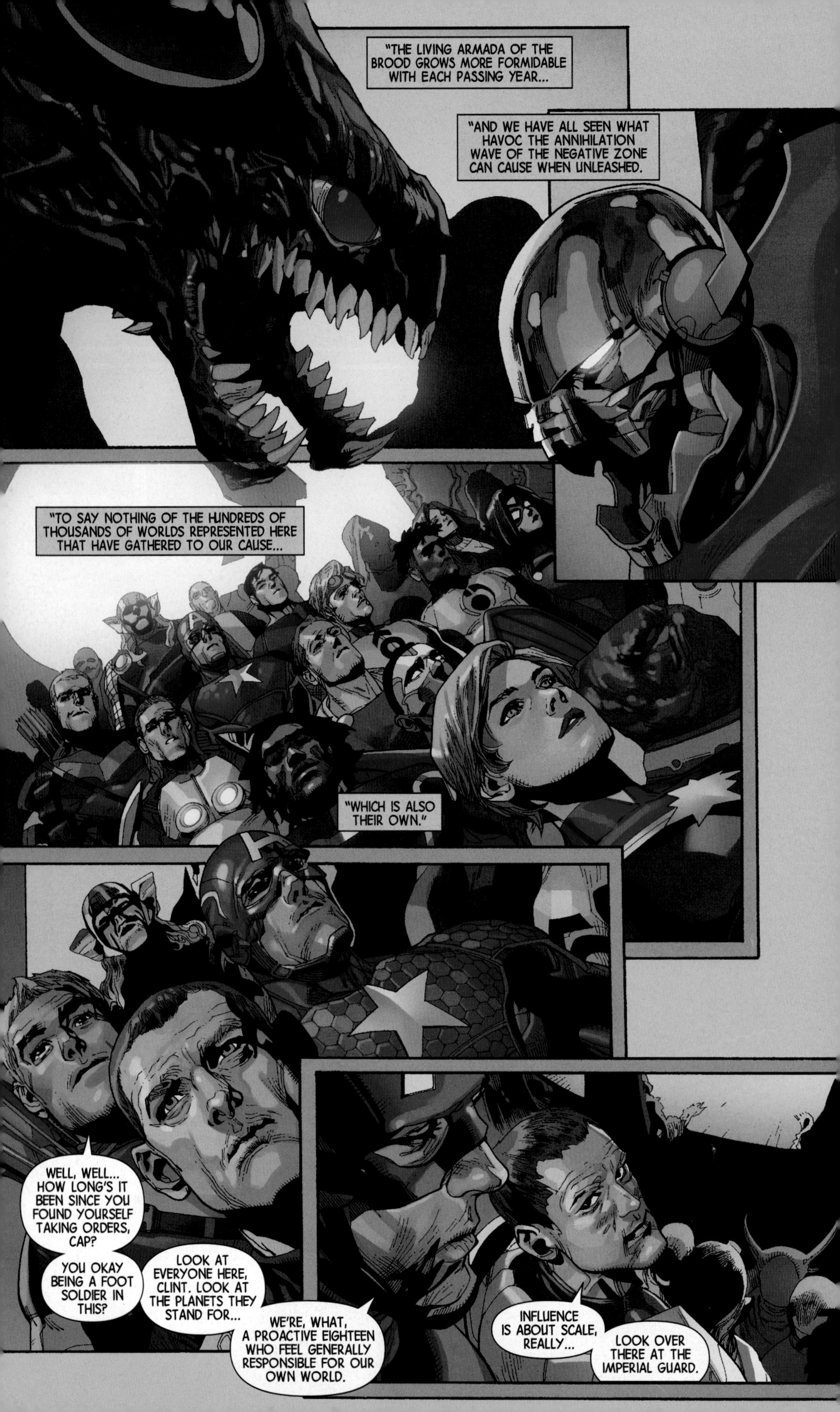
"THE LIVING ARMADA OF THE BROOD GROWS MORE FORMIDABLE WITH EACH PASSING YEAR...
"AND WE HAVE ALL SEEN WHAT HAVOC THE ANNIHILATION WAVE OF THE NEGATIVE ZONE CAN CAUSE WHEN UNLEASHED.
"TO SAY NOTHING OF THE HUNDREDS OF THOUSANDS OF WORLDS REPRESENTED HERE THAT HAVE GATHERED TO OUR CAUSE...
"WHICH IS ALSO THEIR OWN."
WELL, WELL... HOW LONG'S IT BEEN SINCE YOU FOUND YOURSELF TAKING ORDERS, CAP?
YOU OKAY BEING A FOOT SOLDIER IN THIS?
LOOK AT EVERYONE HERE, CLINT. LOOK AT THE PLANETS THEY STAND FOR...
WE'RE, WHAT, A PROACTIVE EIGHTEEN WHO FEEL GENERALLY RESPONSIBLE FOR OUR OWN WORLD.
INFLUENCE IS ABOUT SCALE, REALLY...
LOOK OVER THERE AT THE IMPERIAL GUARD.

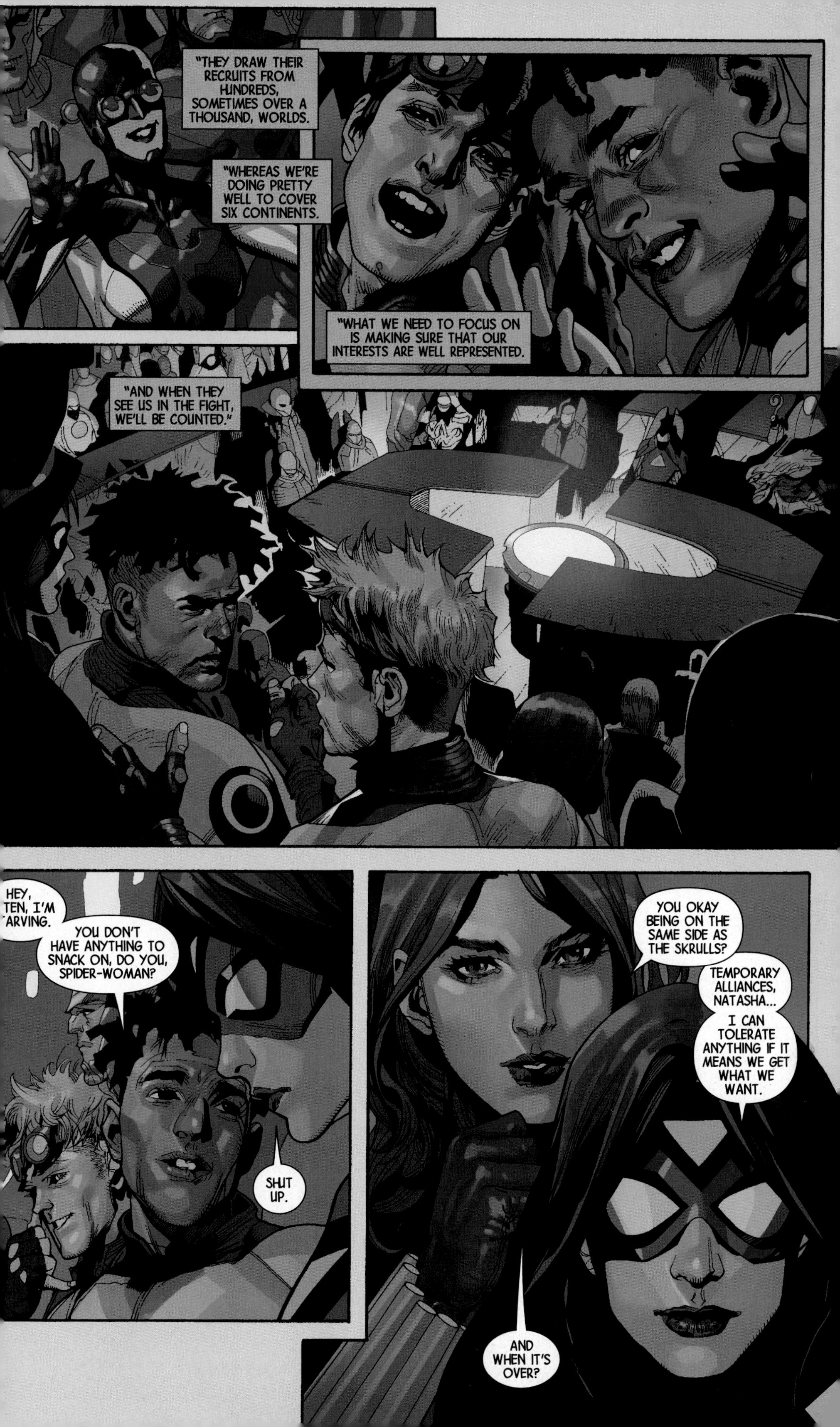
"THEY DRAW THEIR RECRUITS FROM HUNDREDS, SOMETIMES OVER A THOUSAND, WORLDS.
"WHEREAS WE'RE DOING PRETTY WELL TO COVER SIX CONTINENTS.
"WHAT WE NEED TO FOCUS ON IS MAKING SURE THAT OUR INTERESTS ARE WELL REPRESENTED.
"AND WHEN THEY SEE US IN THE FIGHT, WE'LL BE COUNTED."
HEY, TEN, I'M ARVING.
YOU DON'T HAVE ANYTHING TO SNACK ON, DO YOU, SPIDER-WOMAN?
SHUT UP.
YOU OKAY BEING ON THE SAME SIDE AS THE SKRULLS?
TEMPORARY ALLIANCES, NATASHA...
I CAN TOLERATE ANYTHING IF IT MEANS WE GET WHAT WE WANT.
AND WHEN IT'S OVER?

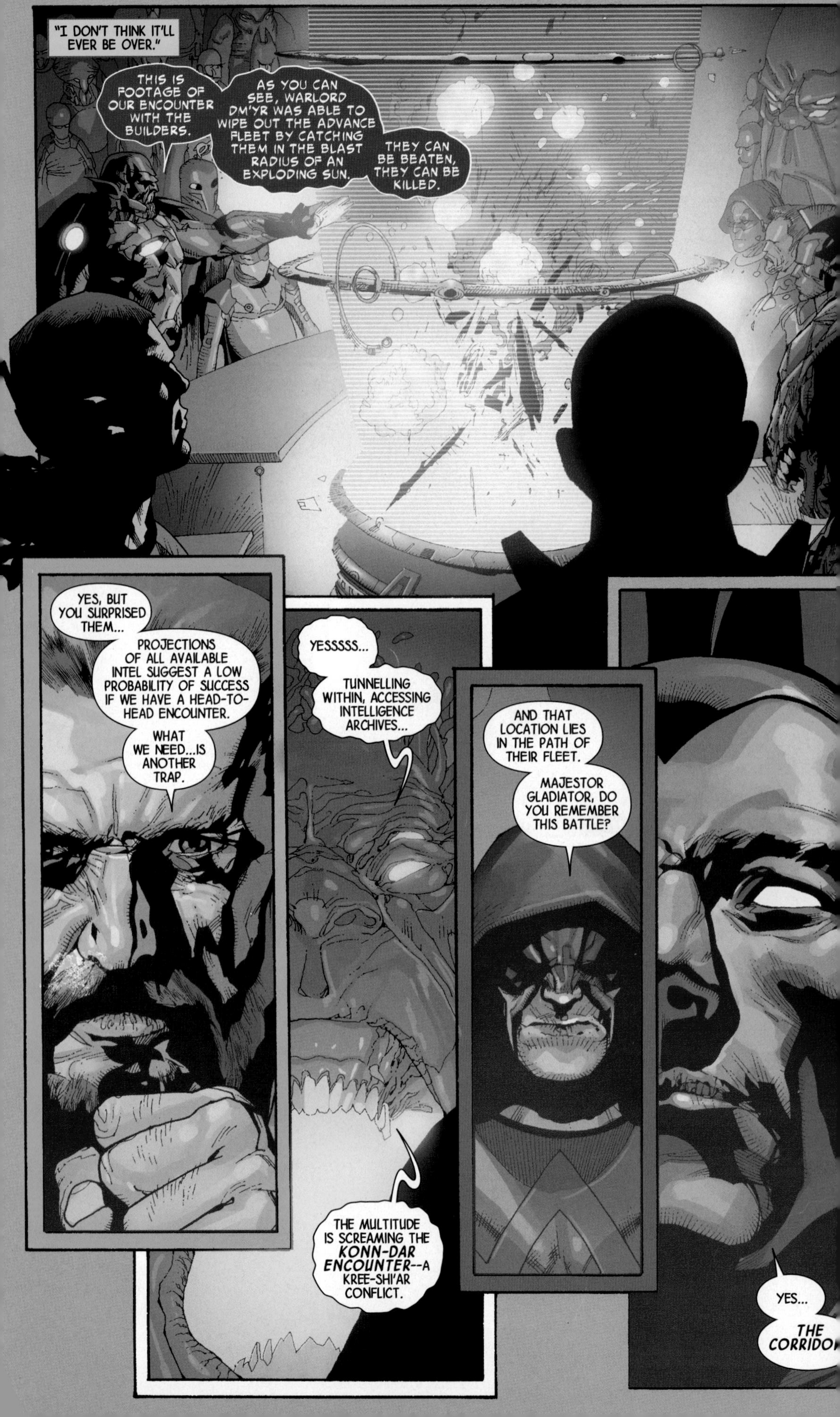
"I DON'T THINK IT'LL EVER BE OVER."
THIS IS FOOTAGE OF OUR ENCOUNTER WITH THE BUILDERS.
AS YOU CAN SEE, WARLORD DM'YR WAS ABLE TO WIPE OUT THE ADVANCE FLEET BY CATCHING THEM IN THE BLAST RADIUS OF AN EXPLODING SUN.
THEY CAN BE BEATEN, THEY CAN BE KILLED.
YES, BUT YOU SURPRISED THEM...
PROJECTIONS OF ALL AVAILABLE INTEL SUGGEST A LOW PROBABILITY OF SUCCESS IF WE HAVE A HEAD-TO-HEAD ENCOUNTER.
WHAT WE NEED...IS ANOTHER TRAP.
YESSSSS...
TUNNELLING WITHIN, ACCESSING INTELLIGENCE ARCHIVES...
THE MULTITUDE IS SCREAMING THE *KONN-DAR ENCOUNTER*--A KREE-SHI'AR CONFLICT.
AND THAT LOCATION LIES IN THE PATH OF THEIR FLEET.
MAJESTOR GLADIATOR, DO YOU REMEMBER THIS BATTLE?
YES...
THE CORRIDO

FALL INTO SINGULARITY

◆

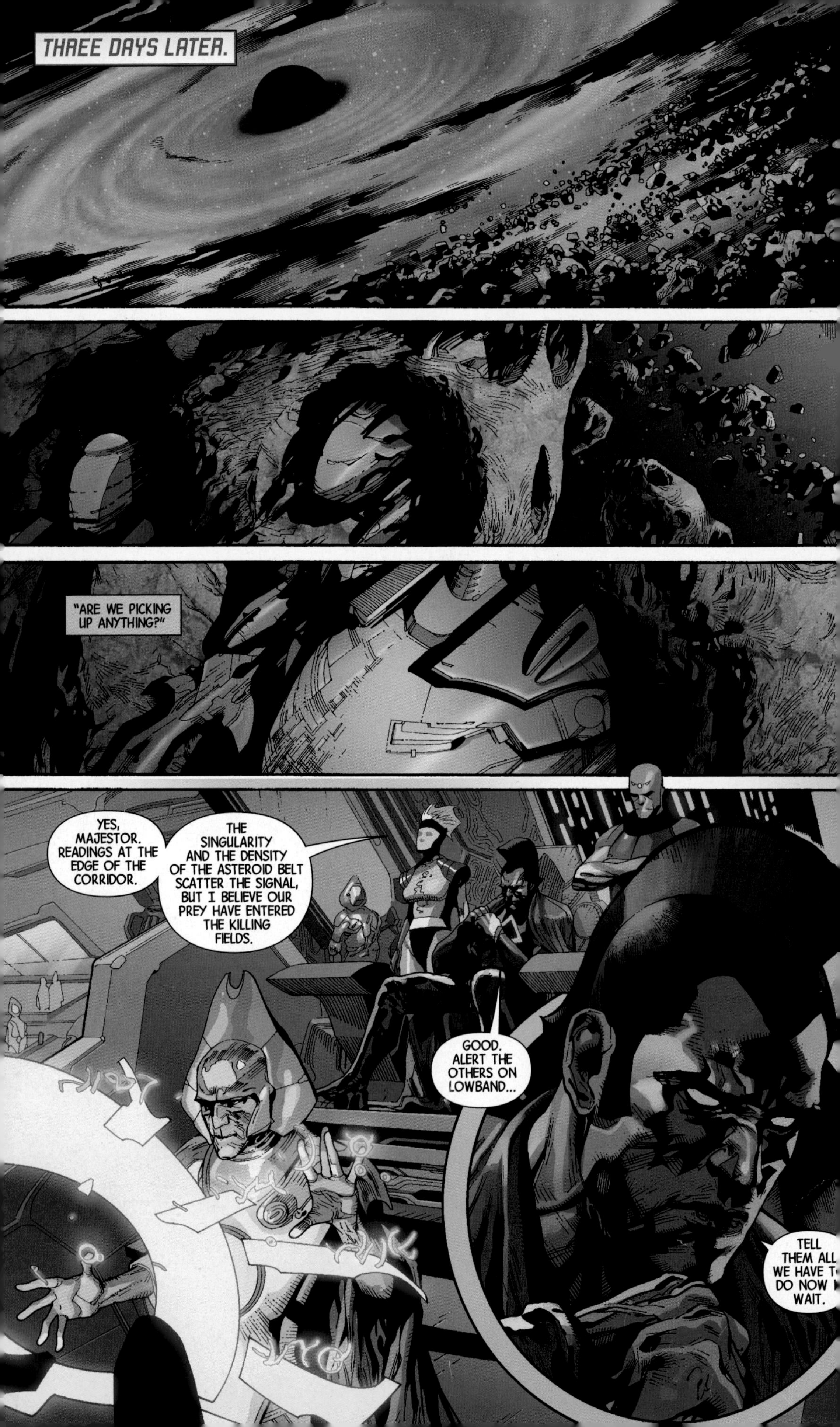
THREE DAYS LATER.
"ARE WE PICKING UP ANYTHING?"
YES, MAJESTOR. READINGS AT THE EDGE OF THE CORRIDOR.
THE SINGULARITY AND THE DENSITY OF THE ASTEROID BELT SCATTER THE SIGNAL, BUT I BELIEVE OUR PREY HAVE ENTERED THE KILLING FIELDS.
GOOD. ALERT THE OTHERS ON LOWBAND...
TELL THEM ALL WE HAVE TO DO NOW IS WAIT.

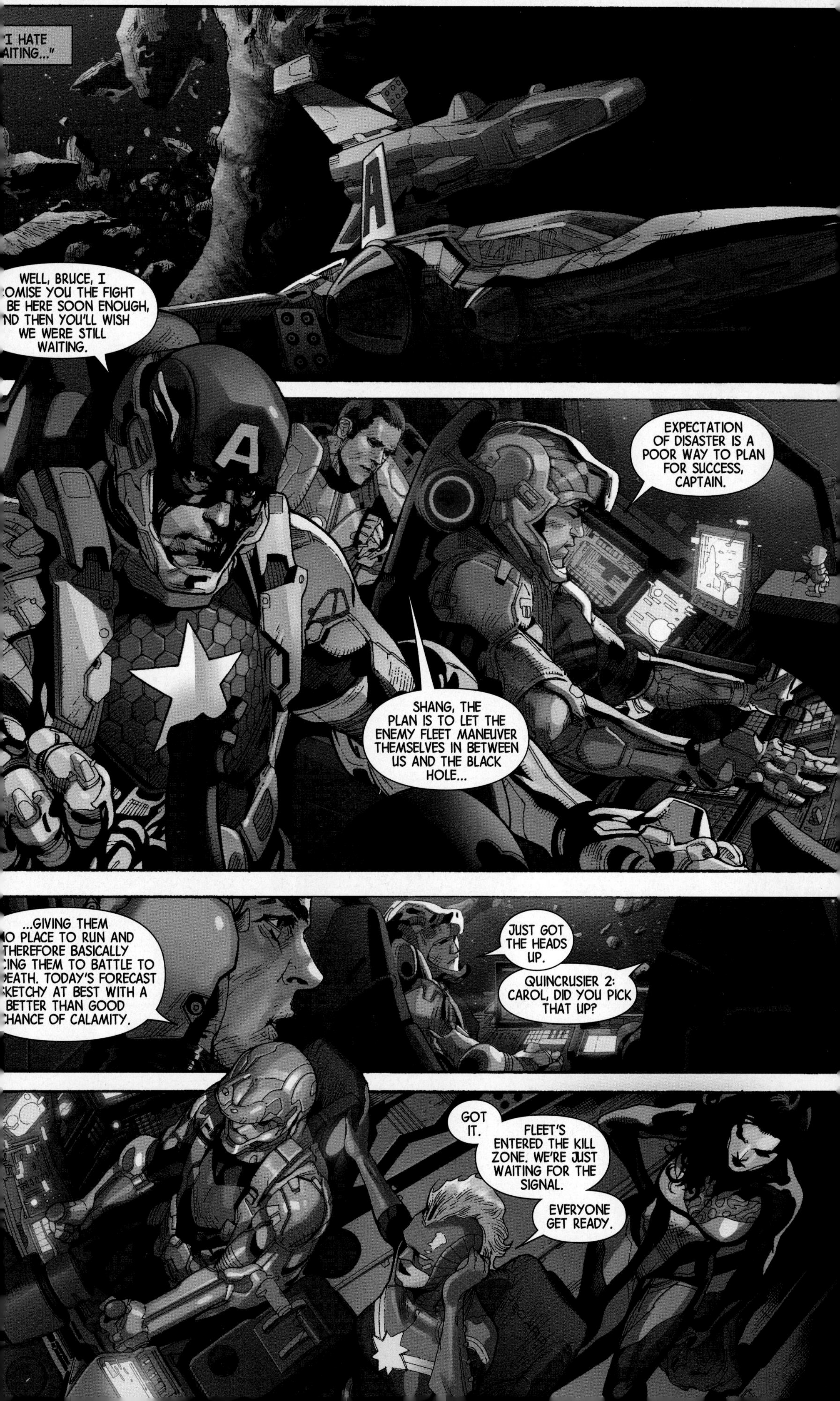

I HATE
AITING..."
WELL, BRUCE, I
OMISE YOU THE FIGHT
BE HERE SOON ENOUGH,
ND THEN YOU'LL WISH
WE WERE STILL
WAITING.
EXPECTATION OF DISASTER IS A POOR WAY TO PLAN FOR SUCCESS, CAPTAIN.
SHANG, THE PLAN IS TO LET THE ENEMY FLEET MANEUVER THEMSELVES IN BETWEEN US AND THE BLACK HOLE...
...GIVING THEM
O PLACE TO RUN AND
THEREFORE BASICALLY
CING THEM TO BATTLE TO
EATH. TODAY'S FORECAST
KETCHY AT BEST WITH A
BETTER THAN GOOD
HANCE OF CALAMITY.
JUST GOT THE HEADS UP.
QUINCRUSIER 2: CAROL, DID YOU PICK THAT UP?
GOT IT.
FLEET'S ENTERED THE KILL ZONE. WE'RE JUST WAITING FOR THE SIGNAL.
EVERYONE GET READY.

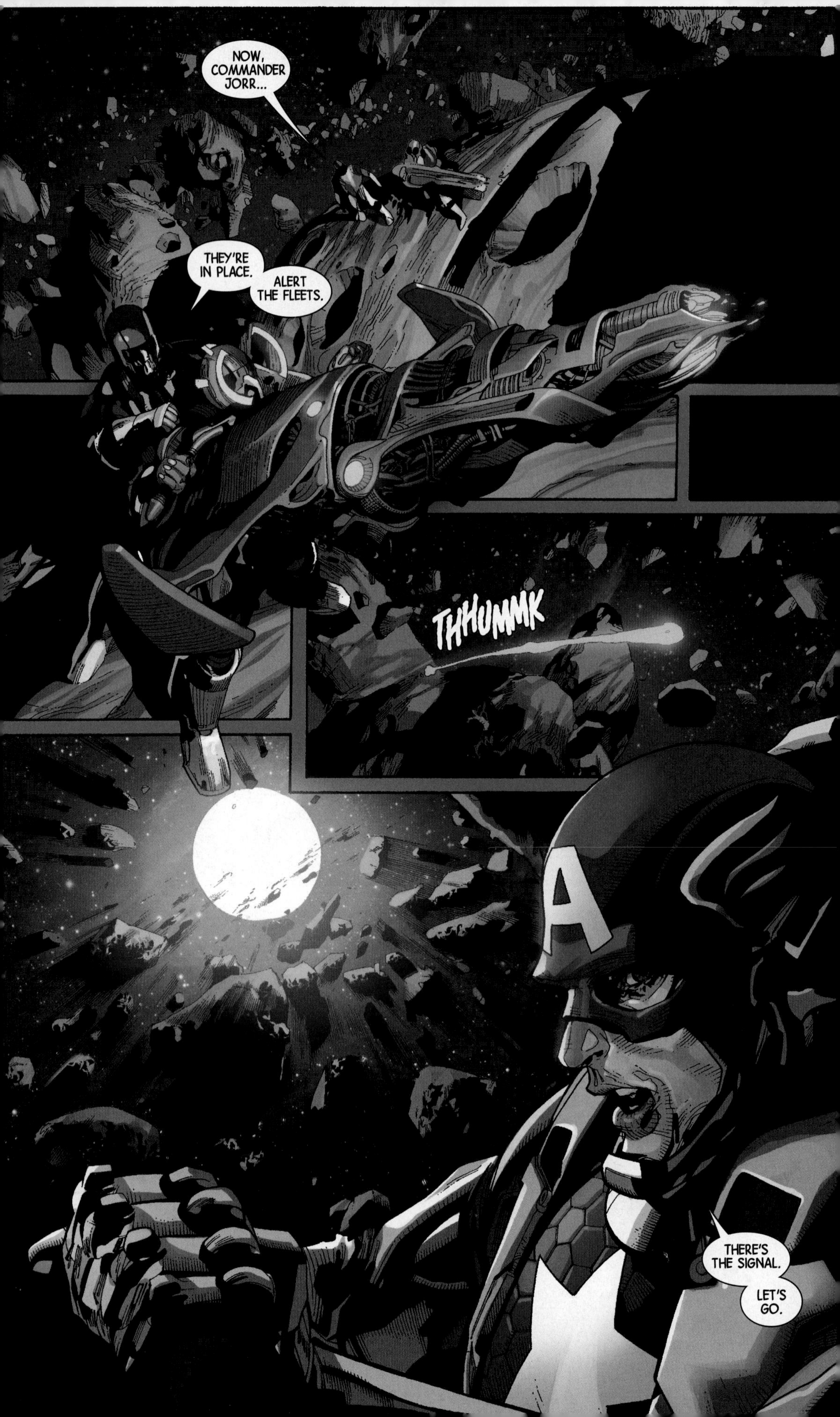
NOW, COMMANDER JORR...
THEY'RE IN PLACE.
ALERT THE FLEETS.
THHUMMK
THERE'S THE SIGNAL.
LET'S GO.

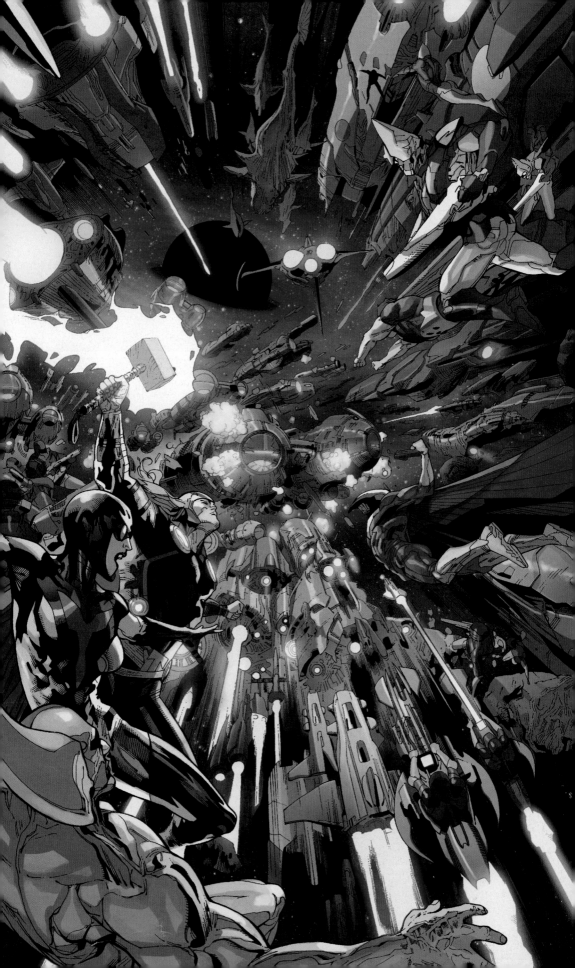

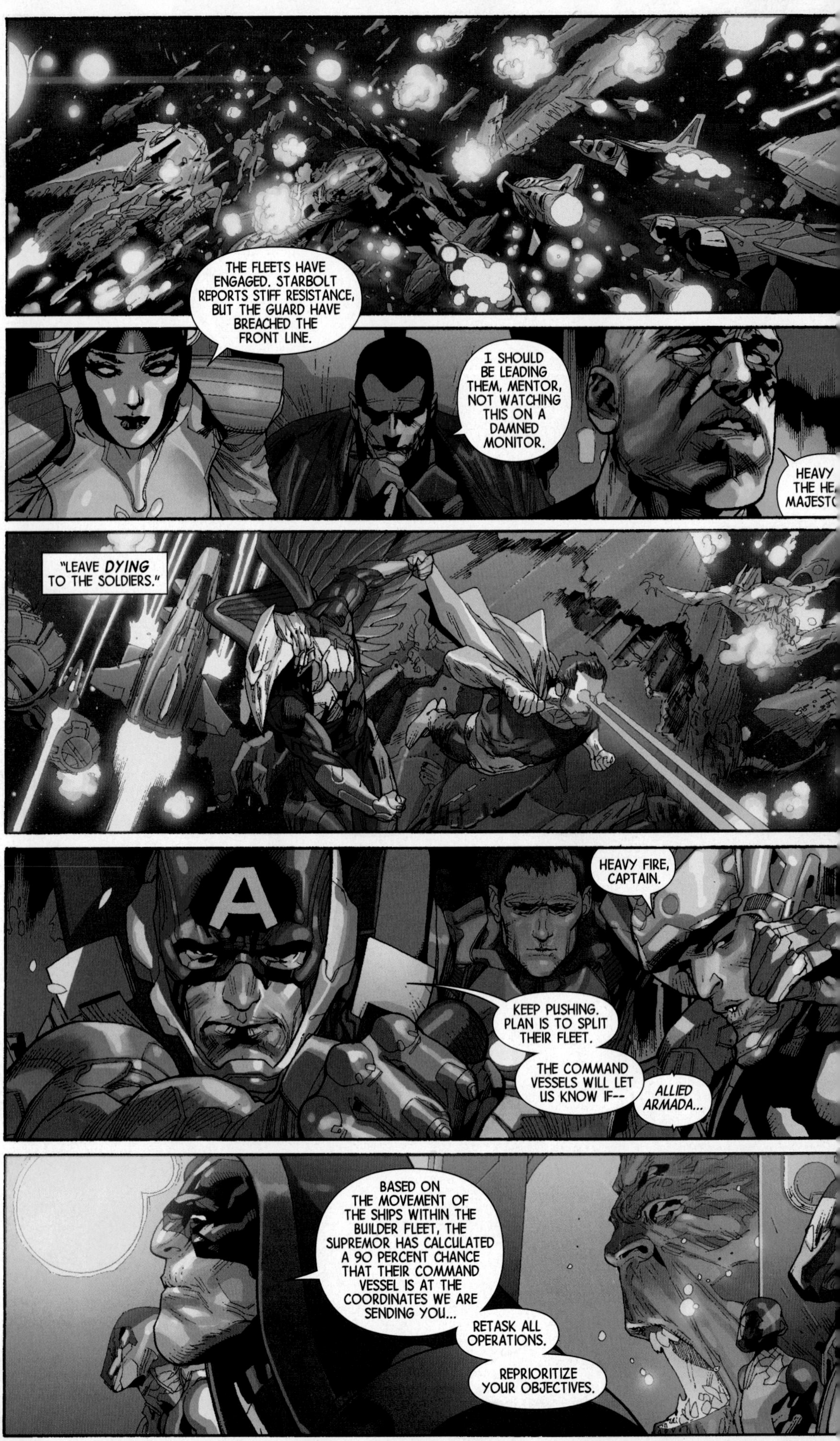
THE FLEETS HAVE ENGAGED. STARBOLT REPORTS STIFF RESISTANCE, BUT THE GUARD HAVE BREACHED THE FRONT LINE.
I SHOULD BE LEADING THEM, MENTOR, NOT WATCHING THIS ON A DAMNED MONITOR.
HEAVY THE HE MAJESTO
"LEAVE *DYING* TO THE SOLDIERS."
HEAVY FIRE, CAPTAIN.
KEEP PUSHING. PLAN IS TO SPLIT THEIR FLEET.
THE COMMAND VESSELS WILL LET US KNOW IF--
ALLIED ARMADA...
BASED ON THE MOVEMENT OF THE SHIPS WITHIN THE BUILDER FLEET, THE SUPREMOR HAS CALCULATED A 90 PERCENT CHANCE THAT THEIR COMMAND VESSEL IS AT THE COORDINATES WE ARE SENDING YOU...
RETASK ALL OPERATIONS.
REPRIORITIZE YOUR OBJECTIVES.

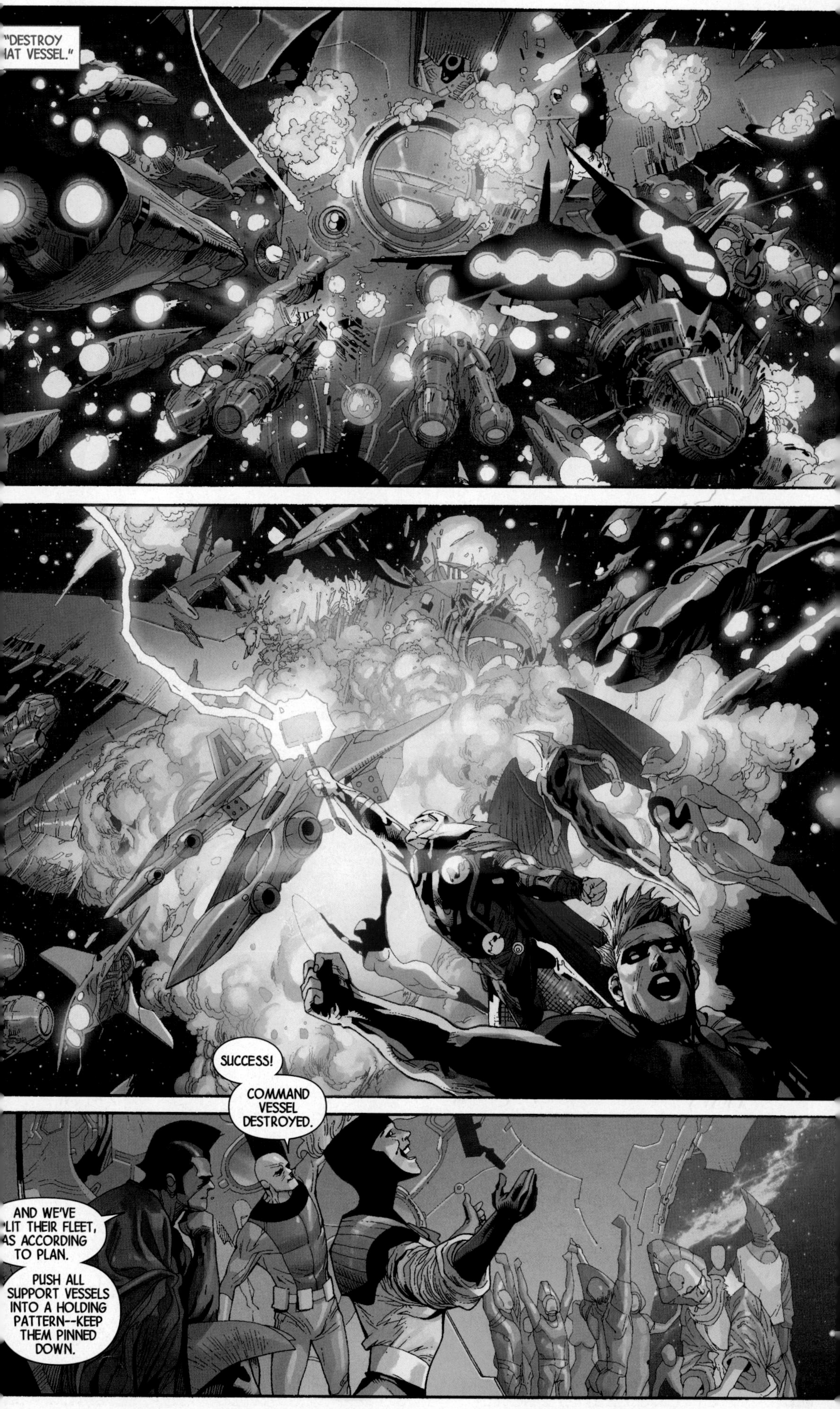
"DESTROY
IAT VESSEL."
SUCCESS!
COMMAND VESSEL DESTROYED.
AND WE'VE 'LIT THEIR FLEET, AS ACCORDING TO PLAN.
PUSH ALL SUPPORT VESSELS INTO A HOLDING PATTERN--KEEP THEM PINNED DOWN.

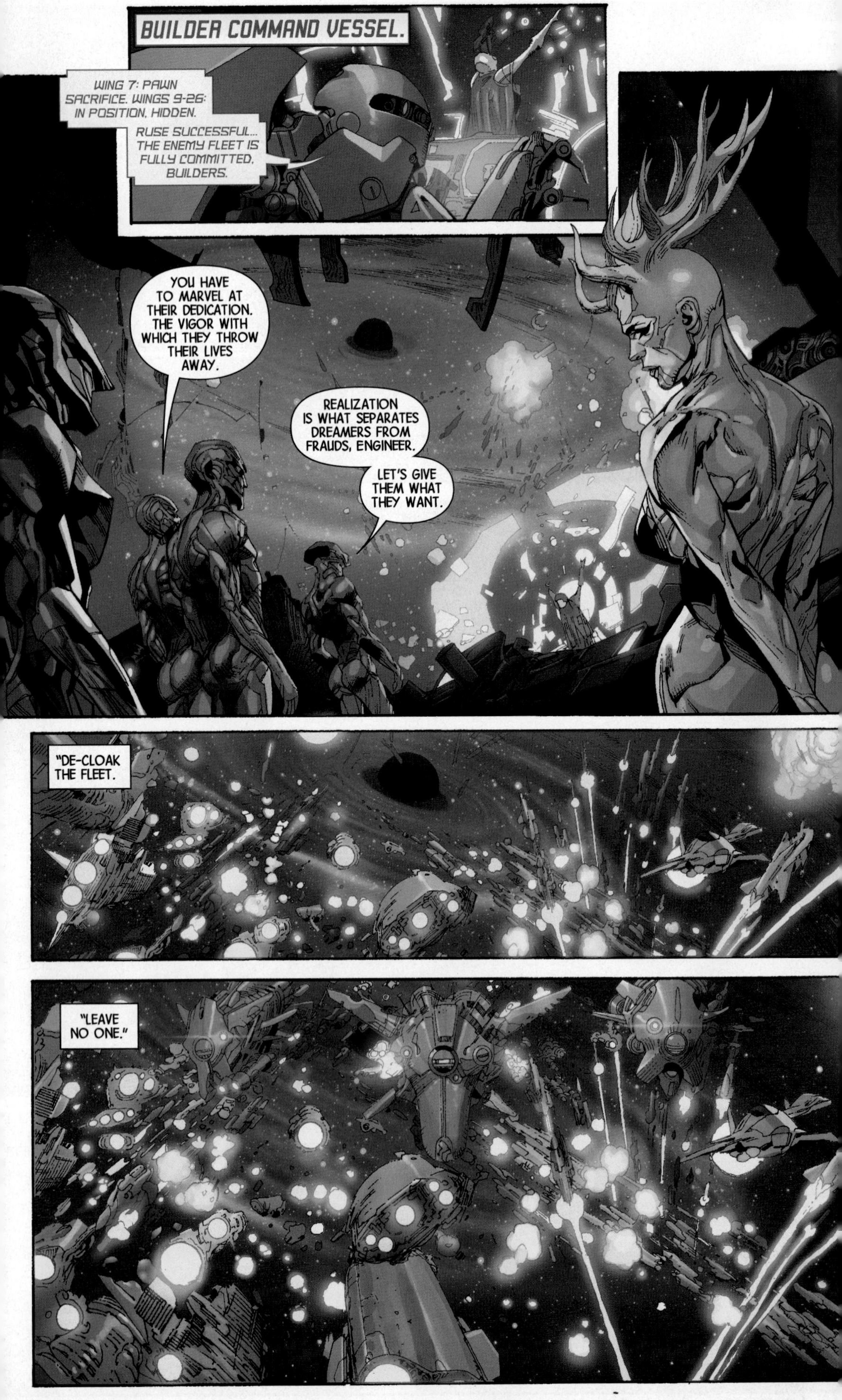
BUILDER COMMAND VESSEL.
WING 7: PAWN SACRIFICE. WINGS 9-26: IN POSITION. HIDDEN.
RUSE SUCCESSFUL... THE ENEMY FLEET IS FULLY COMMITTED, BUILDERS.
YOU HAVE TO MARVEL AT THEIR DEDICATION. THE VIGOR WITH WHICH THEY THROW THEIR LIVES AWAY.
REALIZATION IS WHAT SEPARATES DREAMERS FROM FRAUDS, ENGINEER.
LET'S GIVE THEM WHAT THEY WANT.
"DE-CLOAK THE FLEET.
"LEAVE NO ONE."

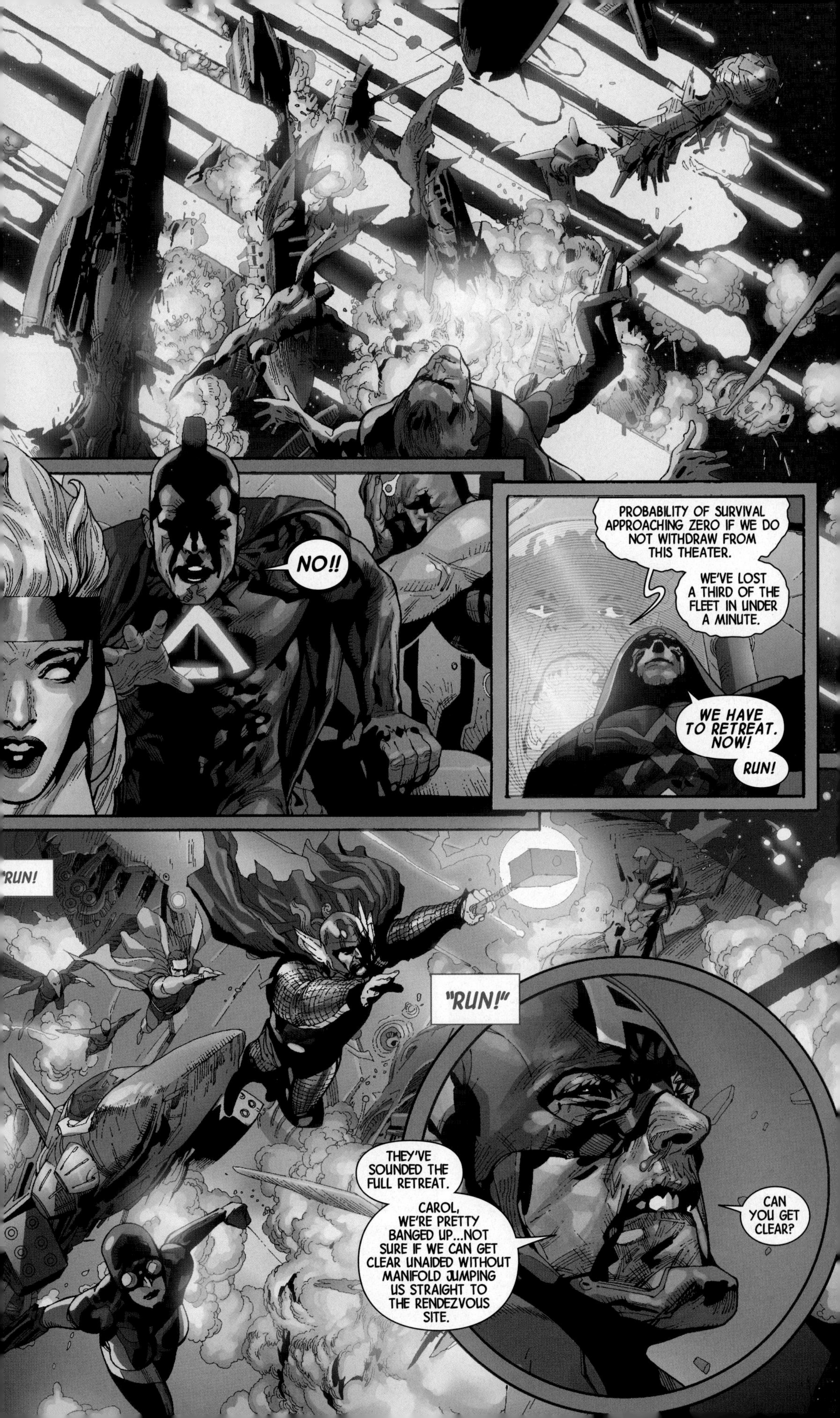
NO!!
PROBABILITY OF SURVIVAL APPROACHING ZERO IF WE DO NOT WITHDRAW FROM THIS THEATER.
WE'VE LOST A THIRD OF THE FLEET IN UNDER A MINUTE.
WE HAVE TO RETREAT. NOW!
RUN!
RUN!
"RUN!"
THEY'VE SOUNDED THE FULL RETREAT.
CAROL, WE'RE PRETTY BANGED UP...NOT SURE IF WE CAN GET CLEAR UNAIDED WITHOUT MANIFOLD JUMPING US STRAIGHT TO THE RENDEZVOUS SITE.
CAN YOU GET CLEAR?

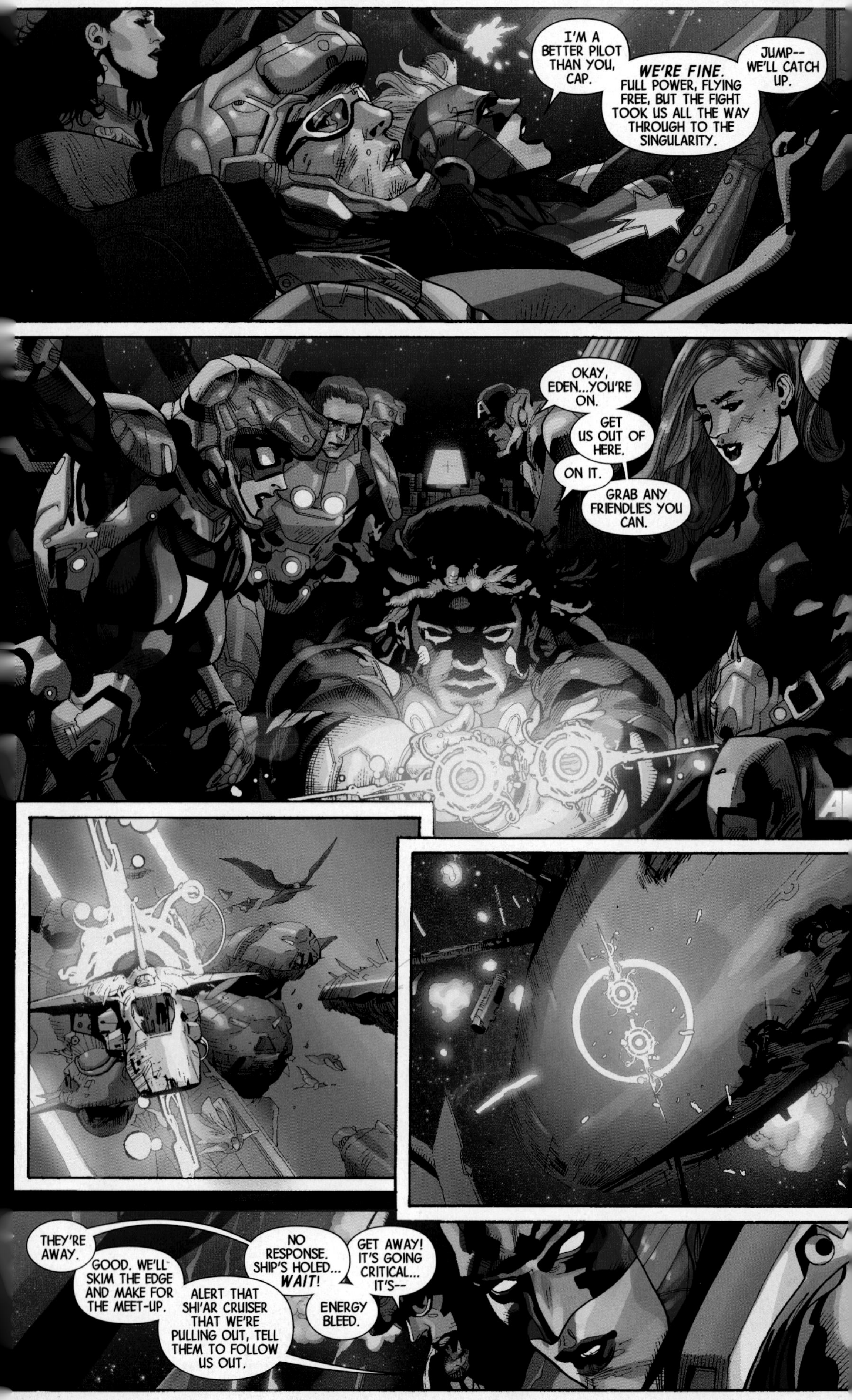
I'M A BETTER PILOT THAN YOU, CAP.
WE'RE FINE. FULL POWER, FLYING FREE, BUT THE FIGHT TOOK US ALL THE WAY THROUGH TO THE SINGULARITY.
JUMP-- WE'LL CATCH UP.
OKAY, EDEN...YOU'RE ON.
GET US OUT OF HERE.
ON IT.
GRAB ANY FRIENDLIES YOU CAN.
THEY'RE AWAY.
GOOD. WE'LL SKIM THE EDGE AND MAKE FOR THE MEET-UP.
ALERT THAT SHI'AR CRUISER THAT WE'RE PULLING OUT, TELL THEM TO FOLLOW US OUT.
NO RESPONSE. SHIP'S HOLED... WAIT!
ENERGY BLEED.
GET AWAY! IT'S GOING CRITICAL... IT'S--

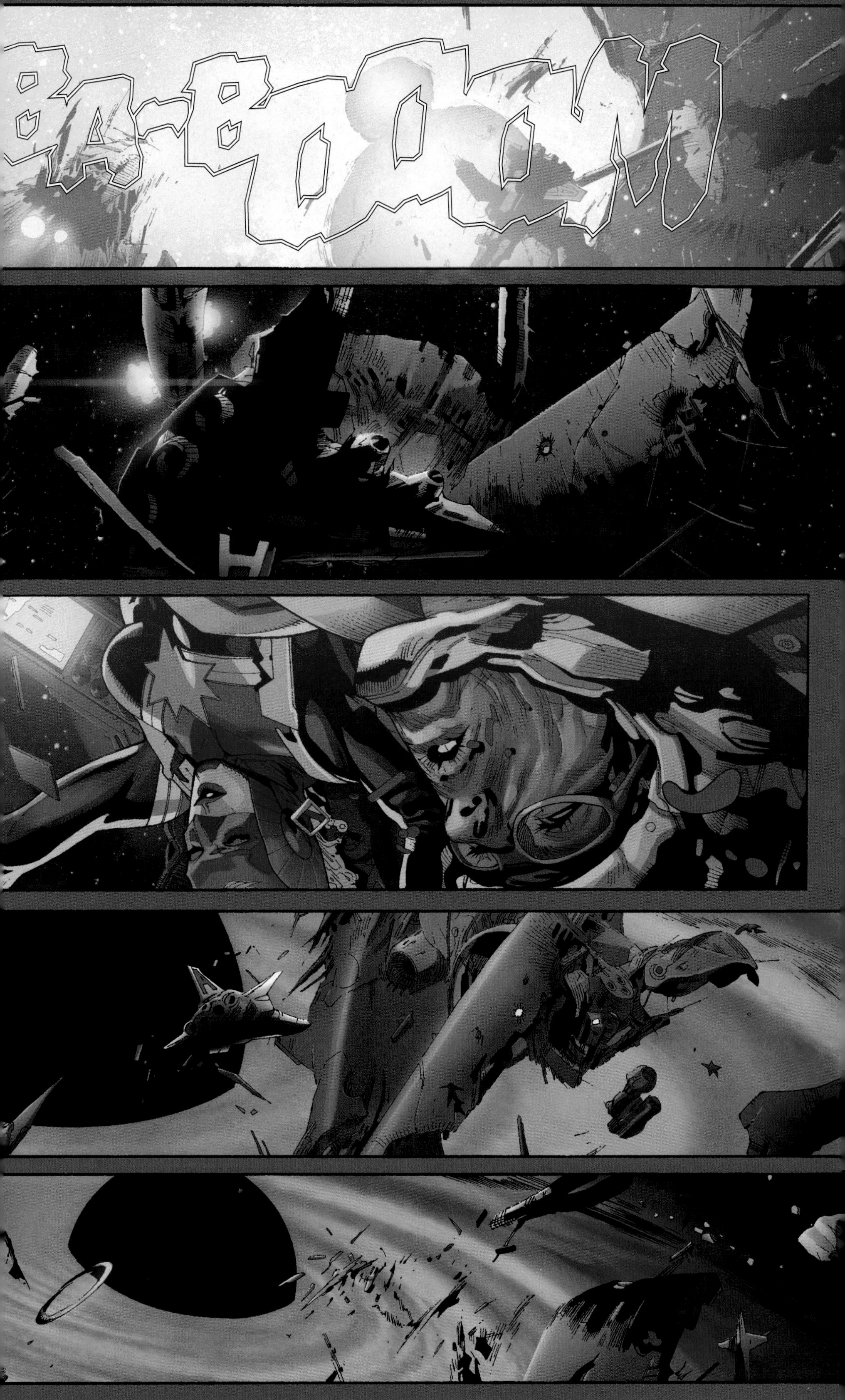
BA-BOOOM

"BUILDING TOWARDS COLLAPSE"

PREVIOUSLY IN INFINITY

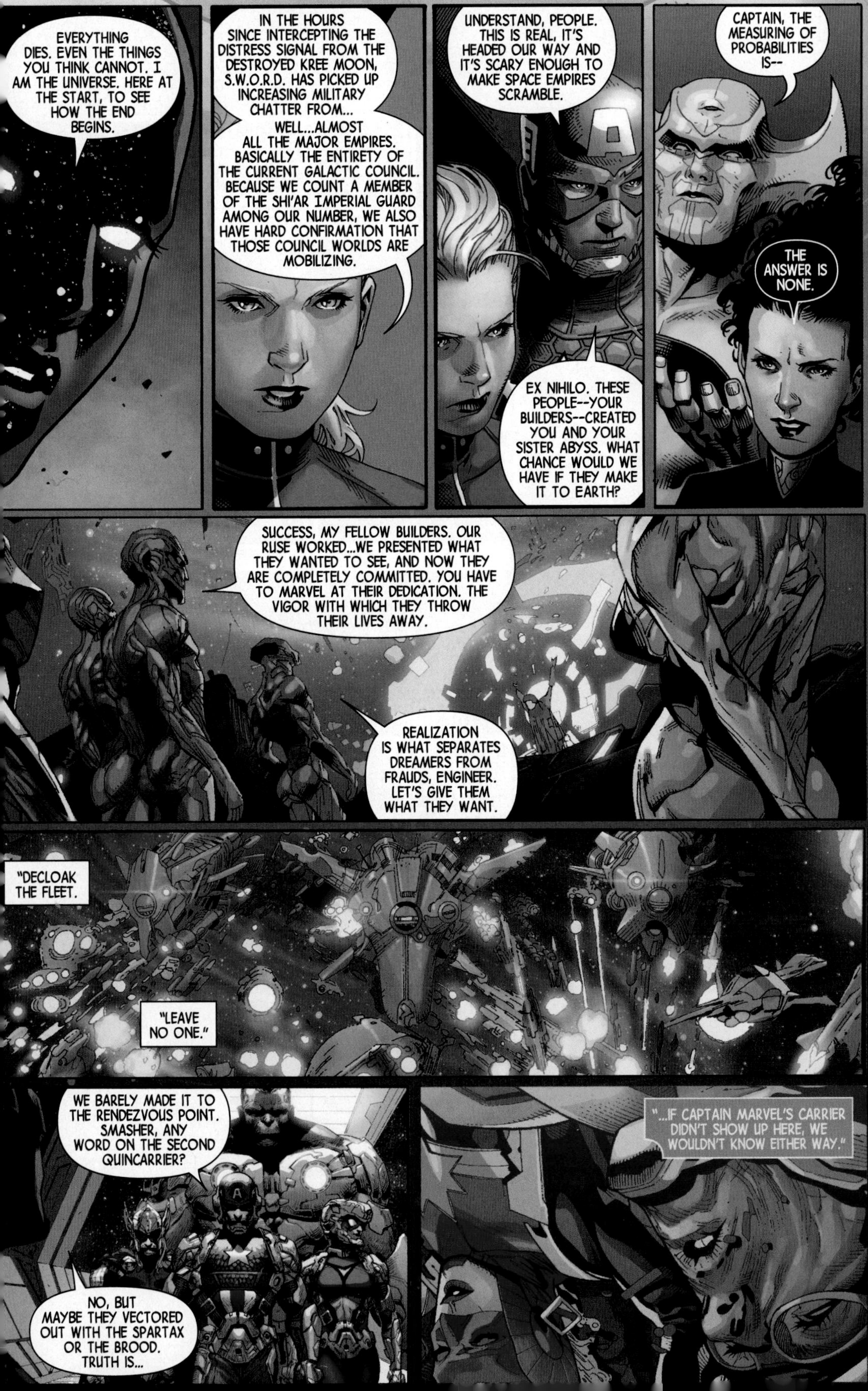

EVERYTHING DIES. EVEN THE THINGS YOU THINK CANNOT. I AM THE UNIVERSE. HERE AT THE START, TO SEE HOW THE END BEGINS.
IN THE HOURS SINCE INTERCEPTING THE DISTRESS SIGNAL FROM THE DESTROYED KREE MOON, S.W.O.R.D. HAS PICKED UP INCREASING MILITARY CHATTER FROM...
WELL...ALMOST ALL THE MAJOR EMPIRES. BASICALLY THE ENTIRETY OF THE CURRENT GALACTIC COUNCIL. BECAUSE WE COUNT A MEMBER OF THE SHI'AR IMPERIAL GUARD AMONG OUR NUMBER, WE ALSO HAVE HARD CONFIRMATION THAT THOSE COUNCIL WORLDS ARE MOBILIZING.
UNDERSTAND, PEOPLE. THIS IS REAL, IT'S HEADED OUR WAY AND IT'S SCARY ENOUGH TO MAKE SPACE EMPIRES SCRAMBLE.
EX NIHILO. THESE PEOPLE--YOUR BUILDERS--CREATED YOU AND YOUR SISTER ABYSS. WHAT CHANCE WOULD WE HAVE IF THEY MAKE IT TO EARTH?
CAPTAIN, THE MEASURING OF PROBABILITIES IS--
THE ANSWER IS NONE.
SUCCESS, MY FELLOW BUILDERS. OUR RUSE WORKED...WE PRESENTED WHAT THEY WANTED TO SEE, AND NOW THEY ARE COMPLETELY COMMITTED. YOU HAVE TO MARVEL AT THEIR DEDICATION. THE VIGOR WITH WHICH THEY THROW THEIR LIVES AWAY.
REALIZATION IS WHAT SEPARATES DREAMERS FROM FRAUDS, ENGINEER. LET'S GIVE THEM WHAT THEY WANT.
"DECLOAK THE FLEET.
"LEAVE NO ONE."
WE BARELY MADE IT TO THE RENDEZVOUS POINT. SMASHER, ANY WORD ON THE SECOND QUINCARRIER?
NO, BUT MAYBE THEY VECTORED OUT WITH THE SPARTAX OR THE BROOD. TRUTH IS...
"...IF CAPTAIN MARVEL'S CARRIER DIDN'T SHOW UP HERE, WE WOULDN'T KNOW EITHER WAY."

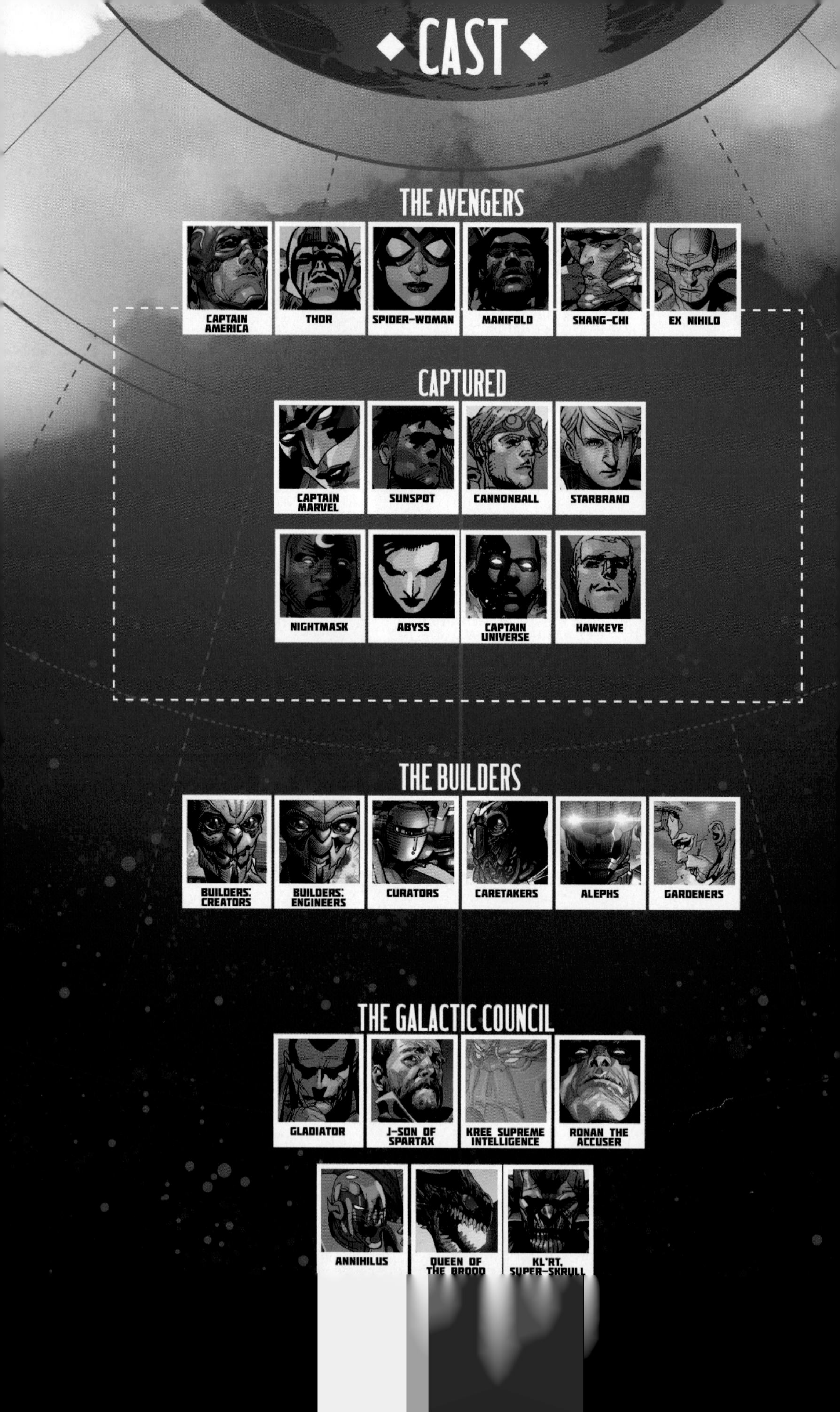
CAST
THE AVENGERS
CAPTAIN AMERICA
THOR
SPIDER-WOMAN
MANIFOLD
SHANG-CHI
EX NIHILO
CAPTURED
CAPTAIN MARVEL
SUNSPOT
CANNONBALL
STARBRAND
NIGHTMASK
ABYSS
CAPTAIN UNIVERSE
HAWKEYE
THE BUILDERS
BUILDERS: CREATORS
BUILDERS: ENGINEERS
CURATORS
CARETAKERS
ALEPHS
GARDENERS
THE GALACTIC COUNCIL
GLADIATOR
J-SON OF SPARTAX
KREE SUPREME INTELLIGENCE
RONAN THE ACCUSER
ANNIHILUS
QUEEN OF THE BROOD
KL'RT, SUPER-SKRULL

BINARY COLLAPSE

◆

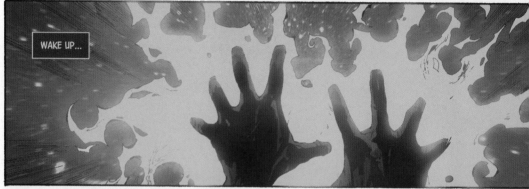

WAKE UP...

WAKE UP, CAROL...

THEY'RE COMING BACK.

PSSHH

ASSESSING: MUTATE, HUMAN MALE. CONTAINED.

ASSESSING: MUTATE, HUMAN MALE. CONTAINED.

ASSESSING: ...SETYPE, ...MAN MALE. ...NTAINED.

...EEP ...NKING ...HAT, ...AL.

ASSESSING: ENHANCED, HUMAN-KREE HYBRID FEMALE.

POWER LEVELS... IN FLUX.

REALLY? A HALF-BREED DYNAMO...

THE UNIVERSE ...SUCH A CHAOTIC AND WONDERFUL PLACE....

TELL ME, CHILD...

WHAT BROUGHT YOU TO THIS?

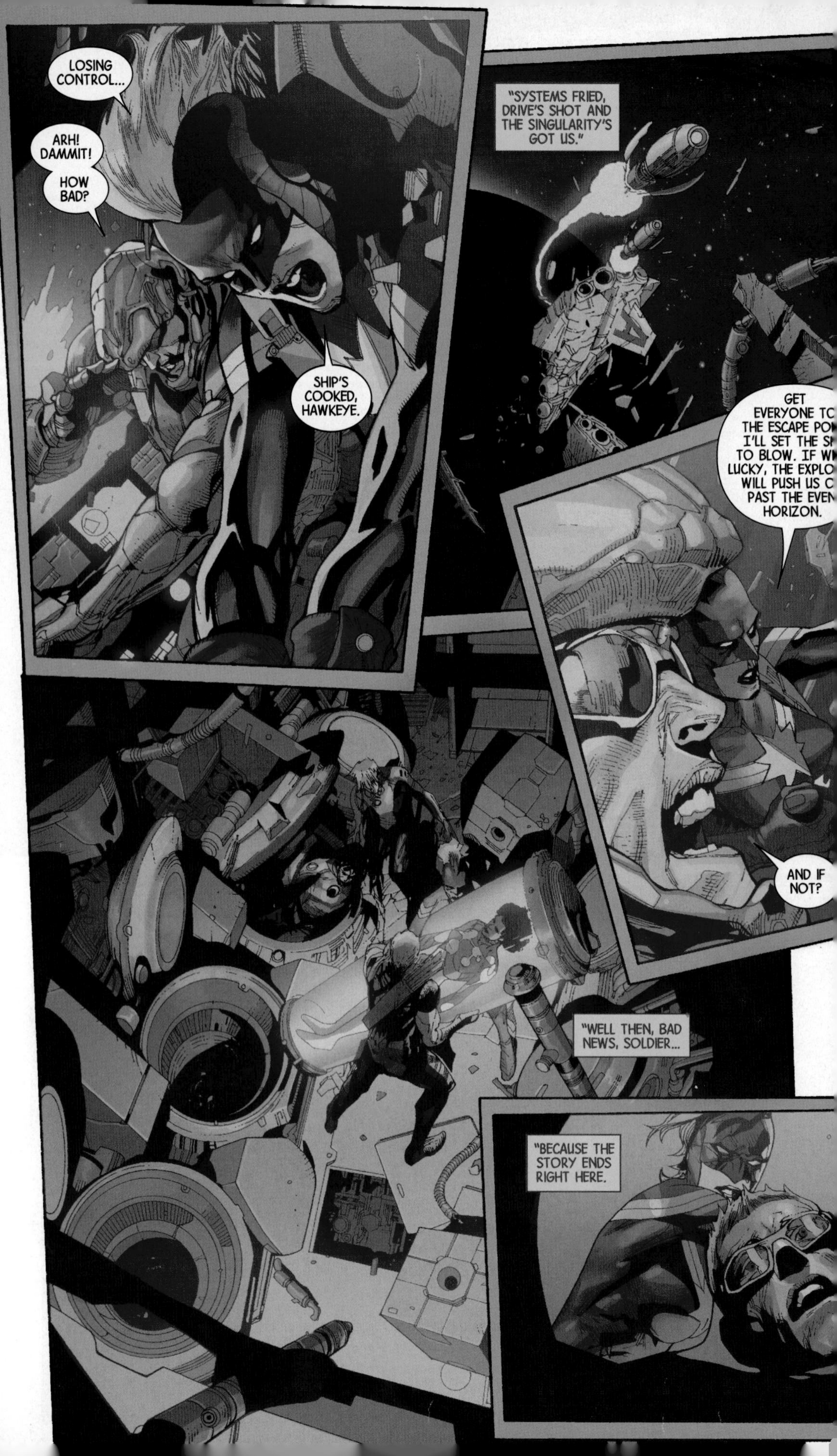
LOSING CONTROL...
ARH! DAMMIT!
HOW BAD?
SHIP'S COOKED, HAWKEYE.
"SYSTEMS FRIED, DRIVE'S SHOT AND THE SINGULARITY'S GOT US."
GET EVERYONE TC THE ESCAPE PO I'LL SET THE S TO BLOW. IF W LUCKY, THE EXPLO WILL PUSH US C PAST THE EVEN HORIZON.
AND IF NOT?
"WELL THEN, BAD NEWS, SOLDIER...
"BECAUSE THE STORY ENDS RIGHT HERE.

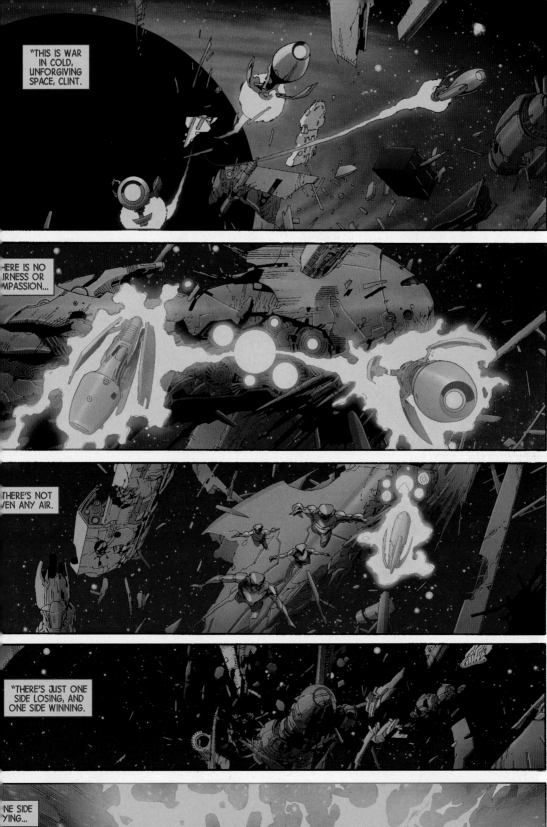

"THIS IS WAR IN COLD, UNFORGIVING SPACE, CLINT.

HERE IS NO IRNESS OR MPASSION...

THERE'S NOT EN ANY AIR.

"THERE'S JUST ONE SIDE LOSING, AND ONE SIDE WINNING.

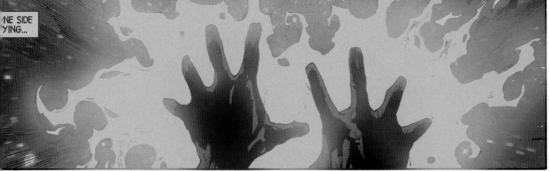

NE SIDE YING...

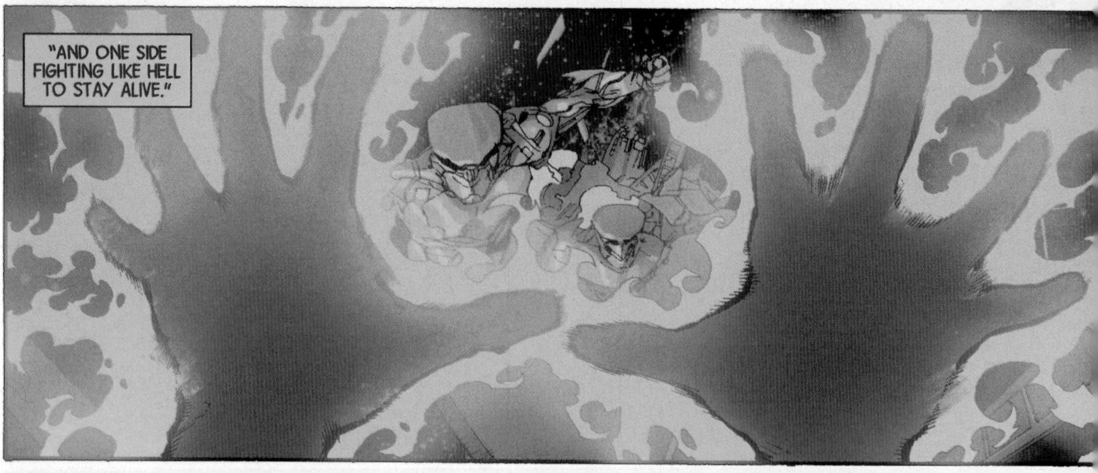
"AND ONE SIDE FIGHTING LIKE HELL TO STAY ALIVE."

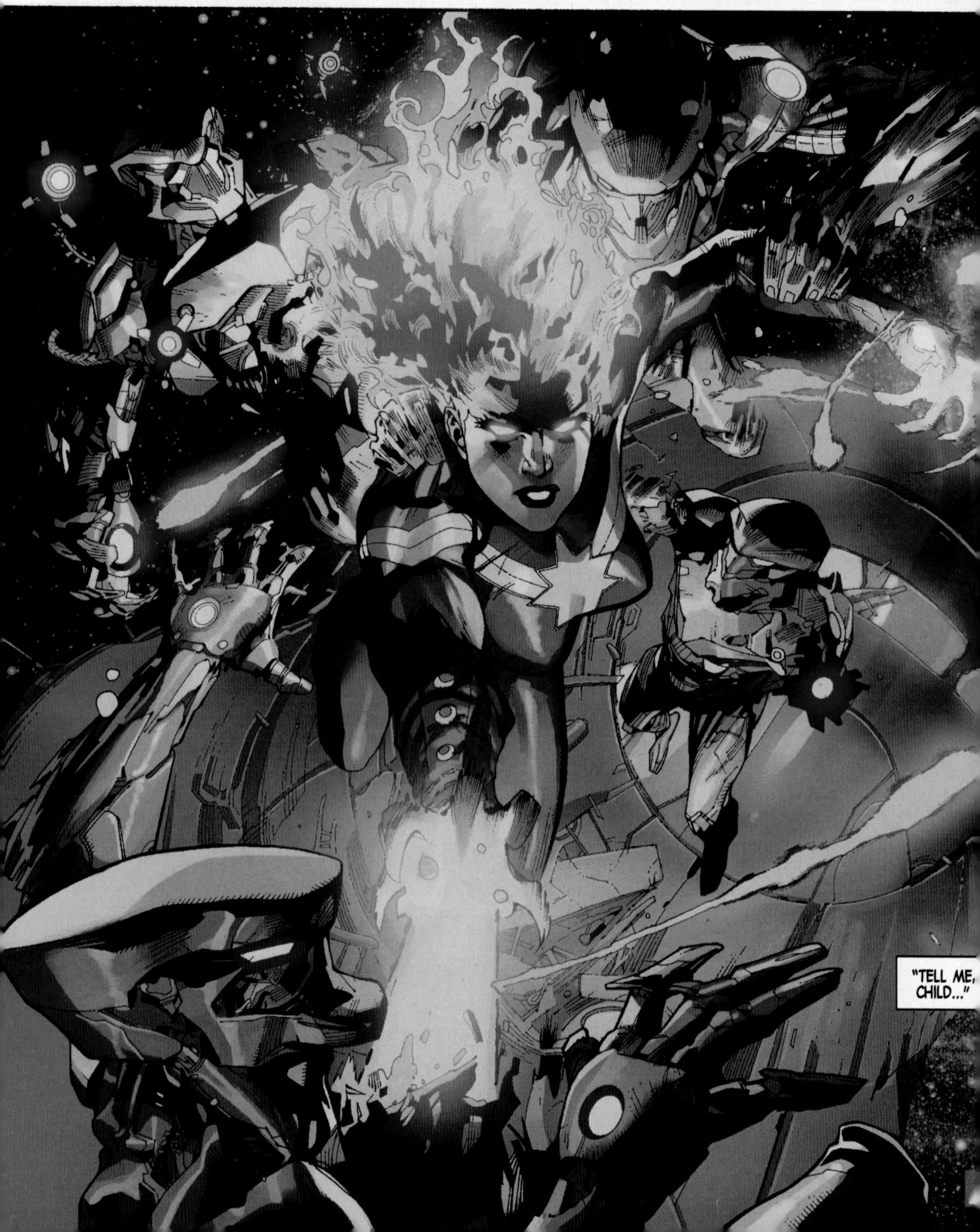
"TELL ME, CHILD..."

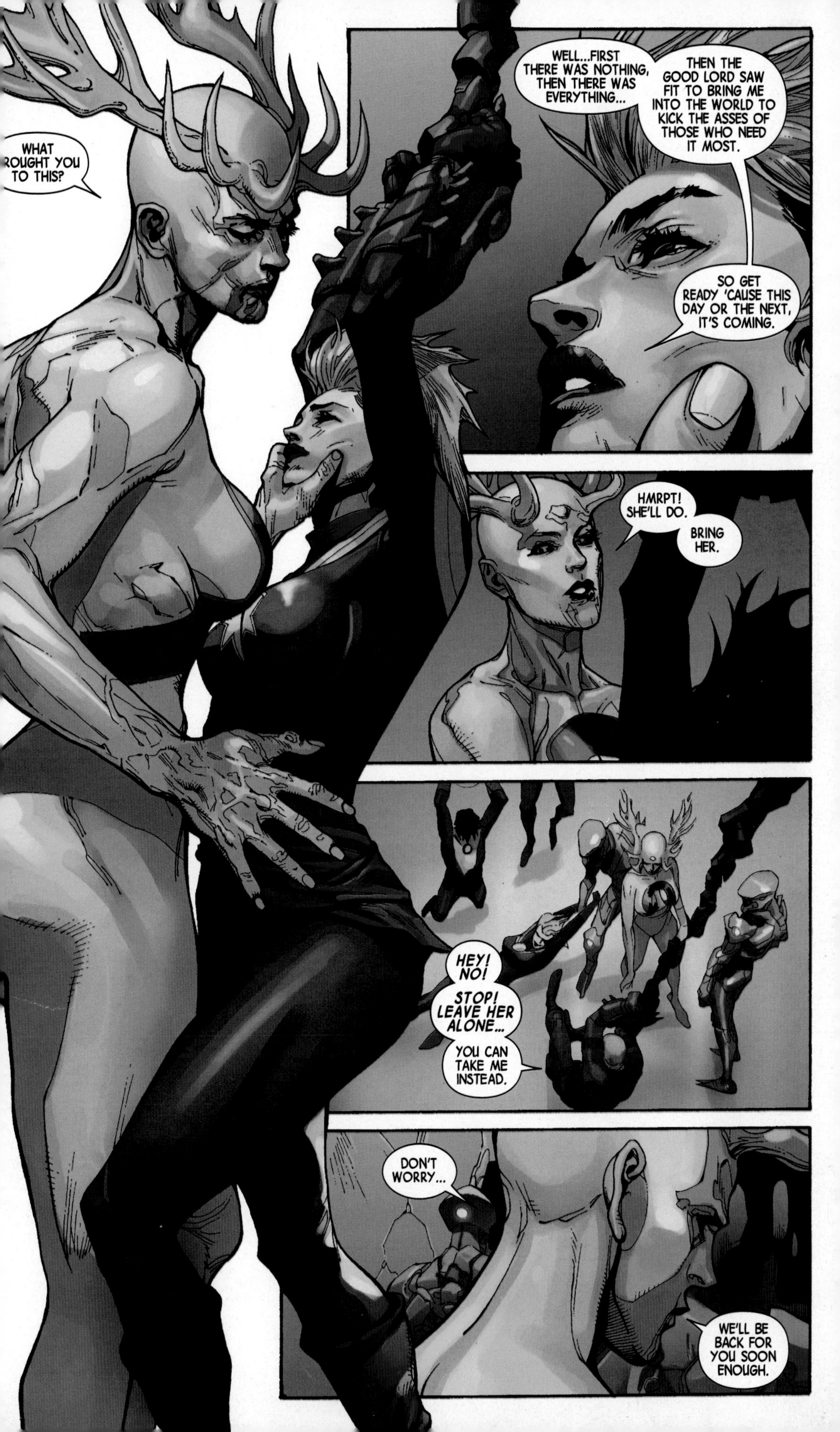
WHAT
ROUGHT YOU
TO THIS?
WELL...FIRST THERE WAS NOTHING, THEN THERE WAS EVERYTHING...
THEN THE GOOD LORD SAW FIT TO BRING ME INTO THE WORLD TO KICK THE ASSES OF THOSE WHO NEED IT MOST.
SO GET READY 'CAUSE THIS DAY OR THE NEXT, IT'S COMING.
HMRPT! SHE'LL DO.
BRING HER.
HEY! NO!
STOP! LEAVE HER ALONE...
YOU CAN TAKE ME INSTEAD.
DON'T WORRY...
WE'LL BE BACK FOR YOU SOON ENOUGH.

BEHEMOTH

◆

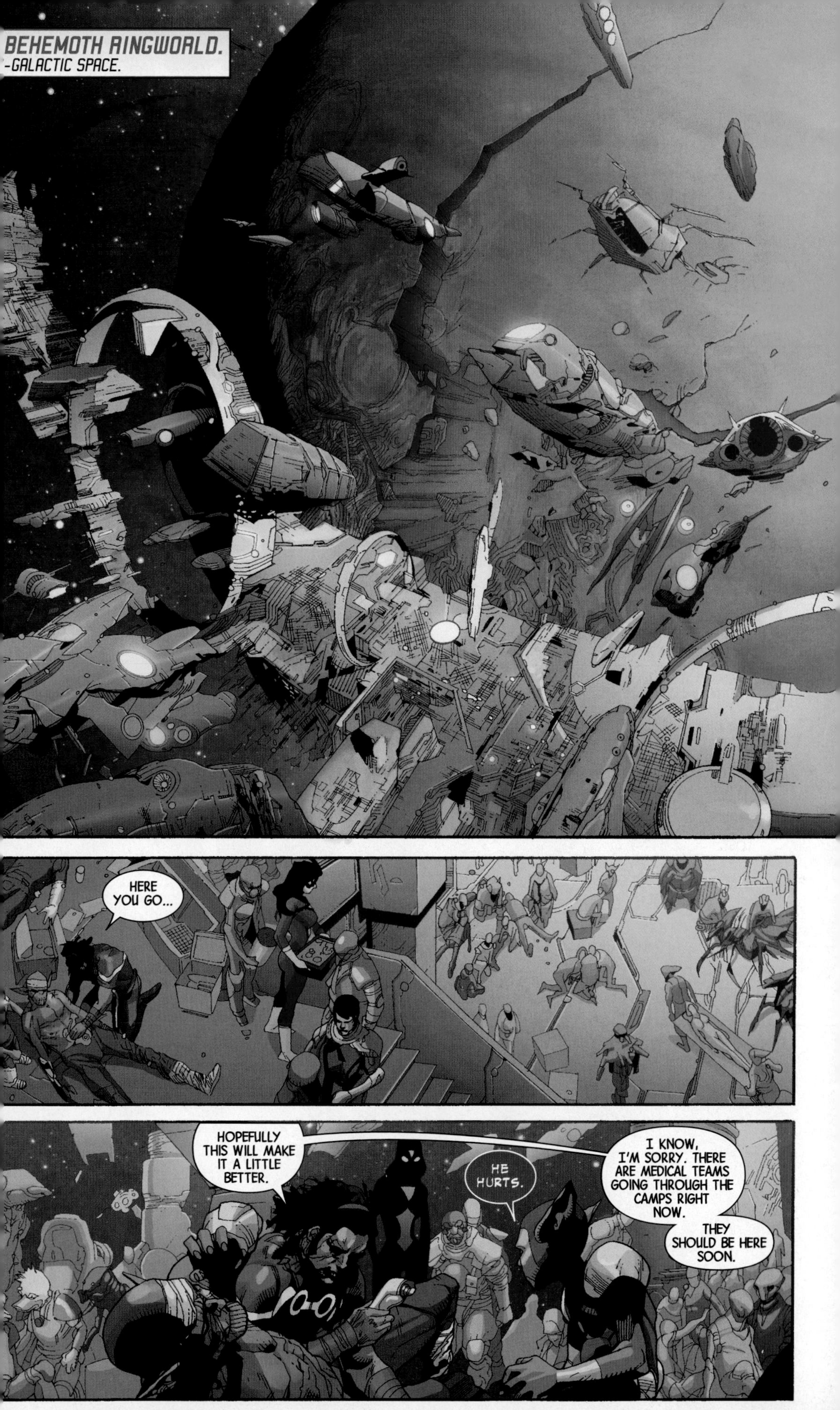
BEHEMOTH RINGWORLD.
-GALACTIC SPACE.
HERE YOU GO...
HOPEFULLY THIS WILL MAKE IT A LITTLE BETTER.
HE HURTS.
I KNOW, I'M SORRY. THERE ARE MEDICAL TEAMS GOING THROUGH THE CAMPS RIGHT NOW.
THEY SHOULD BE HERE SOON.

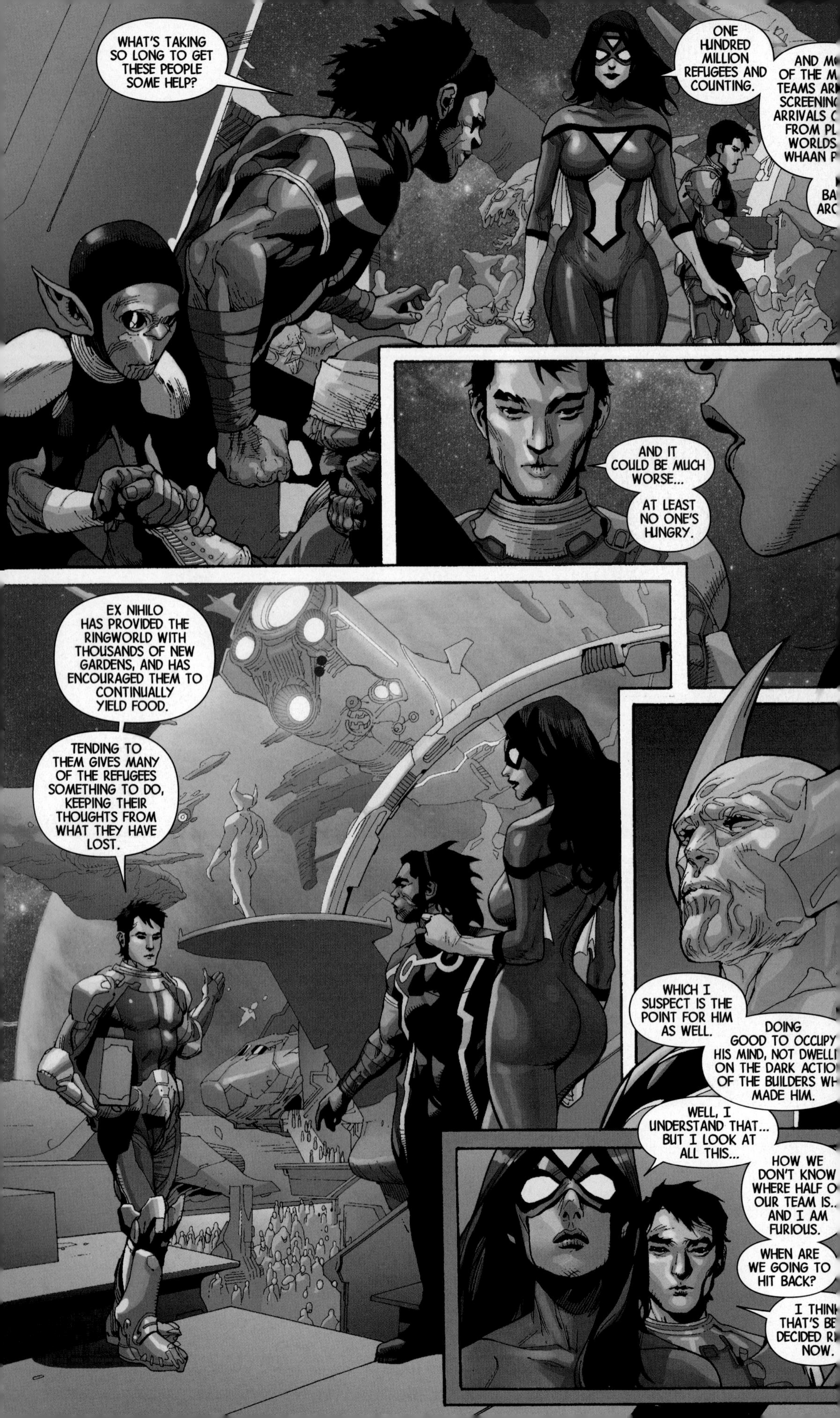
WHAT'S TAKING SO LONG TO GET THESE PEOPLE SOME HELP?
ONE HUNDRED MILLION REFUGEES AND COUNTING.
AND IT COULD BE MUCH WORSE...
AT LEAST NO ONE'S HUNGRY.
EX NIHILO HAS PROVIDED THE RINGWORLD WITH THOUSANDS OF NEW GARDENS, AND HAS ENCOURAGED THEM TO CONTINUALLY YIELD FOOD.
TENDING TO THEM GIVES MANY OF THE REFUGEES SOMETHING TO DO, KEEPING THEIR THOUGHTS FROM WHAT THEY HAVE LOST.
WHICH I SUSPECT IS THE POINT FOR HIM AS WELL.
WELL, I UNDERSTAND THAT... BUT I LOOK AT ALL THIS...
WHEN ARE WE GOING TO HIT BACK?

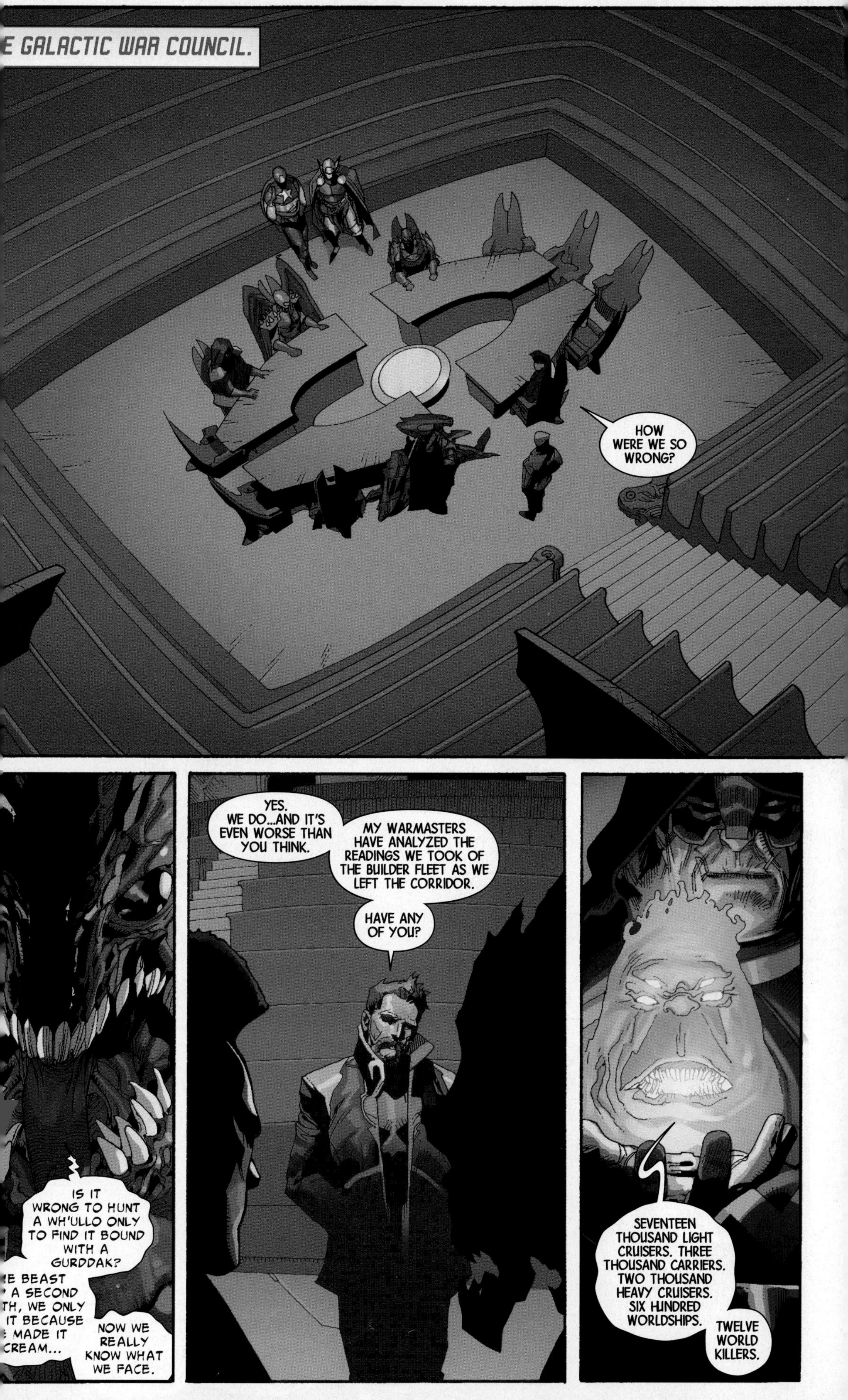
E GALACTIC WAR COUNCIL.
HOW WERE WE SO WRONG?
IS IT WRONG TO HUNT A WH'ULLO ONLY TO FIND IT BOUND WITH A GURDDAK?
E BEAST A SECOND TH, WE ONLY IT BECAUSE MADE IT CREAM...
NOW WE REALLY KNOW WHAT WE FACE.
YES. WE DO...AND IT'S EVEN WORSE THAN YOU THINK.
MY WARMASTERS HAVE ANALYZED THE READINGS WE TOOK OF THE BUILDER FLEET AS WE LEFT THE CORRIDOR.
HAVE ANY OF YOU?
SEVENTEEN THOUSAND LIGHT CRUISERS. THREE THOUSAND CARRIERS. TWO THOUSAND HEAVY CRUISERS. SIX HUNDRED WORLDSHIPS.
TWELVE WORLD KILLERS.

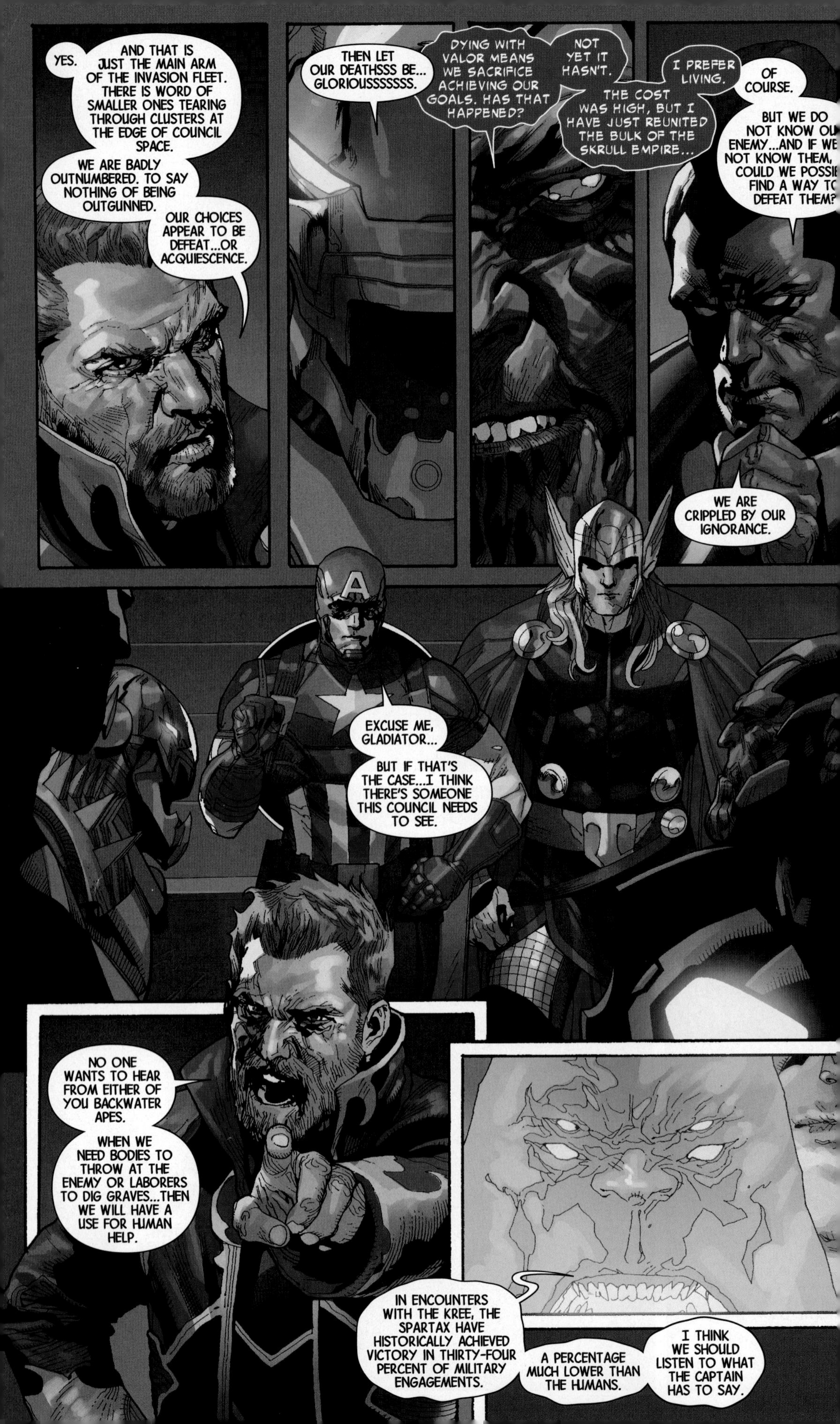
YES.
AND THAT IS JUST THE MAIN ARM OF THE INVASION FLEET. THERE IS WORD OF SMALLER ONES TEARING THROUGH CLUSTERS AT THE EDGE OF COUNCIL SPACE.
WE ARE BADLY OUTNUMBERED. TO SAY NOTHING OF BEING OUTGUNNED.
OUR CHOICES APPEAR TO BE DEFEAT...OR ACQUIESCENCE.
THEN LET OUR DEATHSSS BE... GLORIOUSSSSSSS.
DYING WITH VALOR MEANS WE SACRIFICE ACHIEVING OUR GOALS. HAS THAT HAPPENED?
NOT YET IT HASN'T.
THE COST WAS HIGH, BUT I HAVE JUST REUNITED THE BULK OF THE SKRULL EMPIRE...
I PREFER LIVING.
OF COURSE.
BUT WE DO NOT KNOW OU ENEMY...AND IF WE NOT KNOW THEM, COULD WE POSSI FIND A WAY TO DEFEAT THEM?
WE ARE CRIPPLED BY OUR IGNORANCE.
EXCUSE ME, GLADIATOR...
BUT IF THAT'S THE CASE...I THINK THERE'S SOMEONE THIS COUNCIL NEEDS TO SEE.
NO ONE WANTS TO HEAR FROM EITHER OF YOU BACKWATER APES.
WHEN WE NEED BODIES TO THROW AT THE ENEMY OR LABORERS TO DIG GRAVES...THEN WE WILL HAVE A USE FOR HUMAN HELP.
IN ENCOUNTERS WITH THE KREE, THE SPARTAX HAVE HISTORICALLY ACHIEVED VICTORY IN THIRTY-FOUR PERCENT OF MILITARY ENGAGEMENTS.
A PERCENTAGE MUCH LOWER THAN THE HUMANS.
I THINK WE SHOULD LISTEN TO WHAT THE CAPTAIN HAS TO SAY.

ALL THESE THINGS
WE'VE MADE

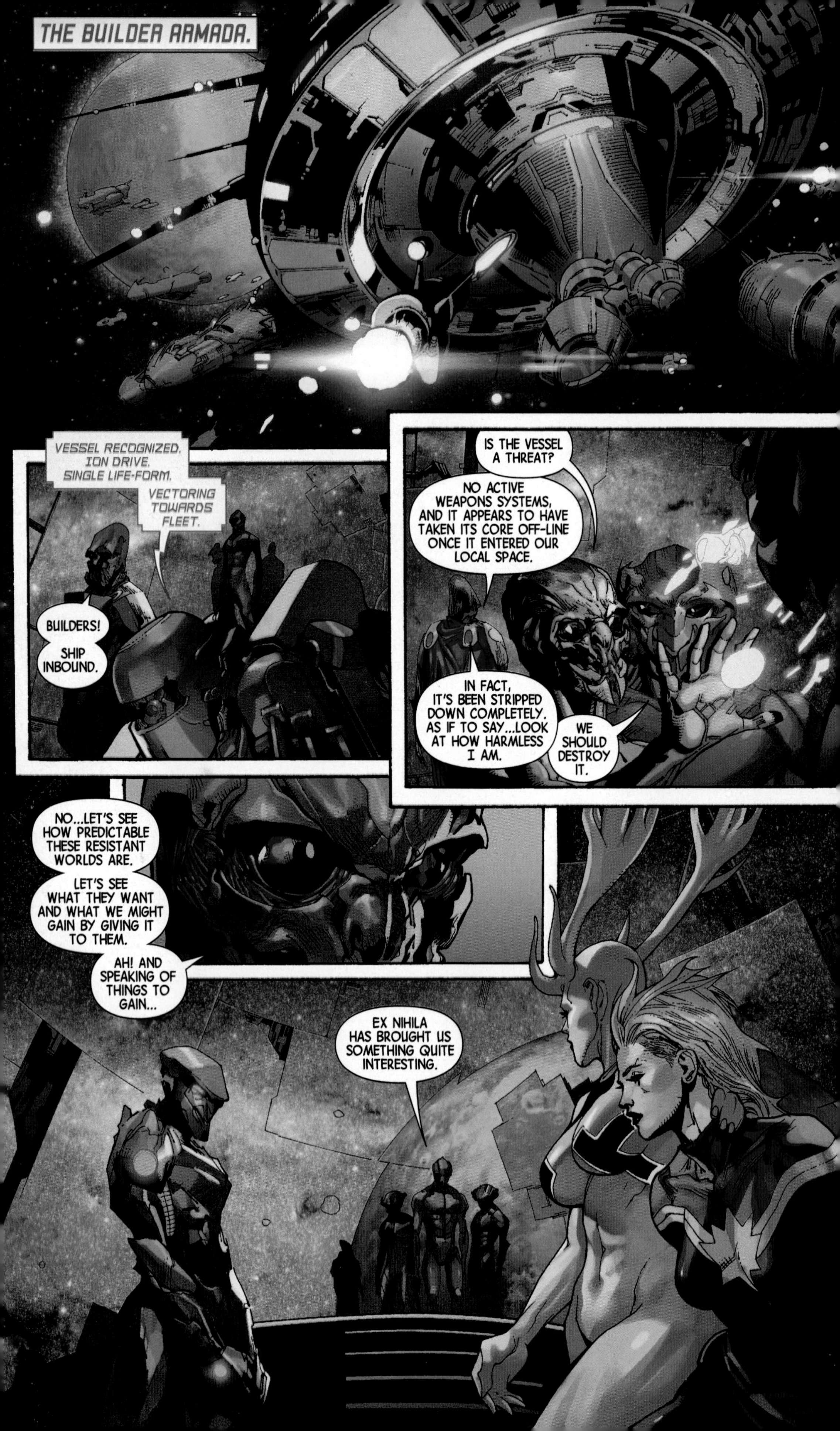
THE BUILDER ARMADA.
VESSEL RECOGNIZED. ION DRIVE. SINGLE LIFE-FORM.
VECTORING TOWARDS FLEET.
BUILDERS!
SHIP INBOUND.
IS THE VESSEL A THREAT?
NO ACTIVE WEAPONS SYSTEMS, AND IT APPEARS TO HAVE TAKEN ITS CORE OFF-LINE ONCE IT ENTERED OUR LOCAL SPACE.
IN FACT, IT'S BEEN STRIPPED DOWN COMPLETELY. AS IF TO SAY...LOOK AT HOW HARMLESS I AM.
WE SHOULD DESTROY IT.
NO...LET'S SEE HOW PREDICTABLE THESE RESISTANT WORLDS ARE.
LET'S SEE WHAT THEY WANT AND WHAT WE MIGHT GAIN BY GIVING IT TO THEM.
AH! AND SPEAKING OF THINGS TO GAIN...
EX NIHILA HAS BROUGHT US SOMETHING QUITE INTERESTING.

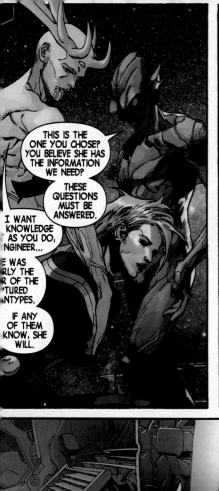

THIS IS THE ONE YOU CHOSE? YOU BELIEVE SHE HAS THE INFORMATION WE NEED?

THESE QUESTIONS MUST BE ANSWERED.

I WANT KNOWLEDGE AS YOU DO, ENGINEER...

E WAS RLY THE R OF THE TURED NTYPES.

IF ANY OF THEM KNOW, SHE WILL.

VERY WELL... LOOK HERE, HUMAN.

WE ARE NOT, BY OUR NATURE, DESTROYERS OF THINGS.

IN FACT, ALL THAT'S WORTH CONSIDERING IN THIS UNIVERSAL SPHERE WAS CULTIVATED BY US. IF NOT DIRECTLY BY OUR HANDS, THEN BY THE SYSTEMS WE CREATED TO DO THIS GOOD WORK.

ALL THAT THERE IS, FLOWING FROM OUR HANDS.

DO YOU UNDERSTAND?

WE MADE *THESE* TO DO OUR WORK.

HOW DID YOU COME TO POSSESS THEM?

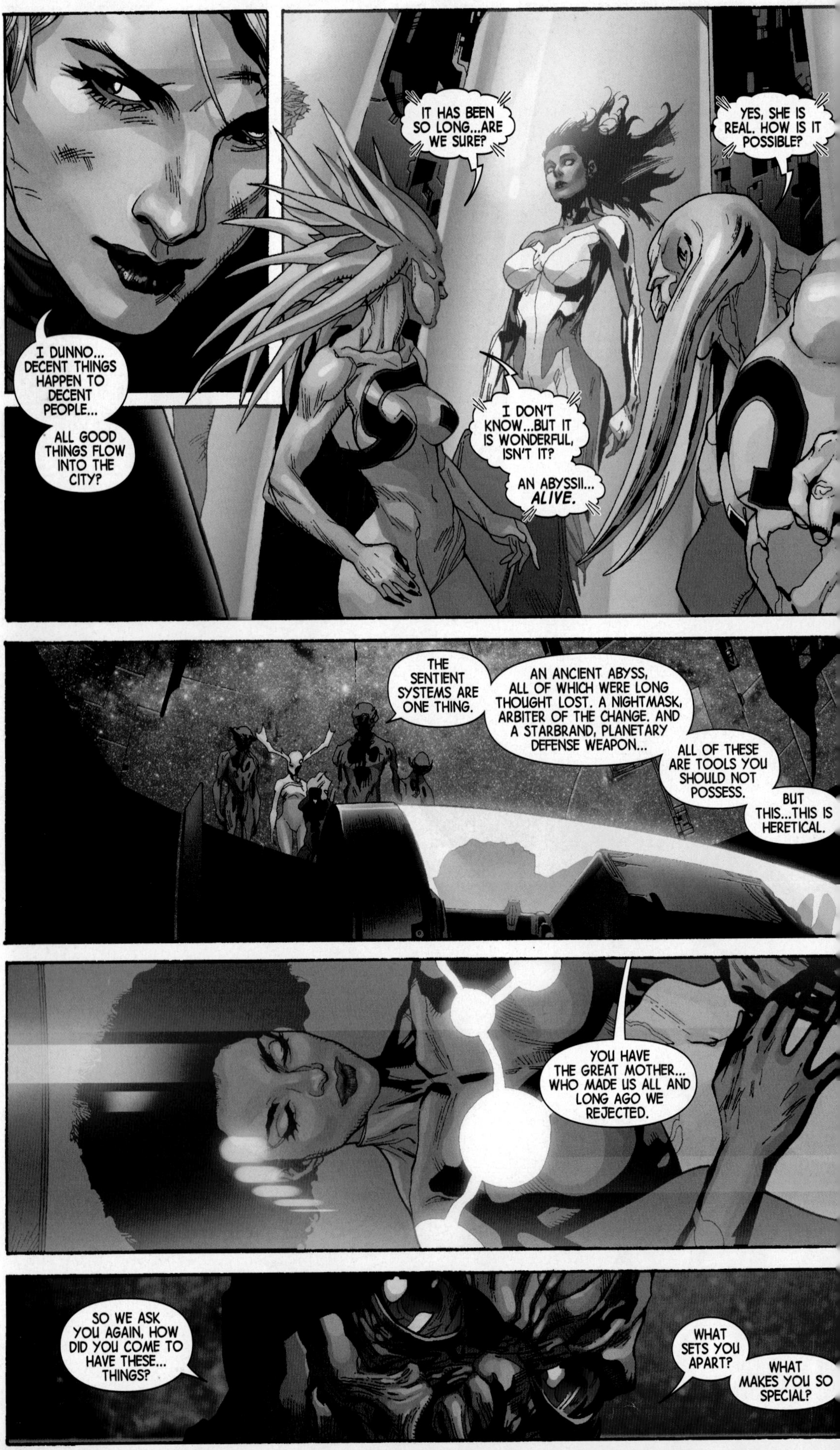
IT HAS BEEN SO LONG...ARE WE SURE?
YES, SHE IS REAL. HOW IS IT POSSIBLE?
I DUNNO... DECENT THINGS HAPPEN TO DECENT PEOPLE...
ALL GOOD THINGS FLOW INTO THE CITY?
I DON'T KNOW...BUT IT IS WONDERFUL, ISN'T IT?
AN ABYSSII... ALIVE.
THE SENTIENT SYSTEMS ARE ONE THING.
AN ANCIENT ABYSS, ALL OF WHICH WERE LONG THOUGHT LOST. A NIGHTMASK, ARBITER OF THE CHANGE. AND A STARBRAND, PLANETARY DEFENSE WEAPON...
ALL OF THESE ARE TOOLS YOU SHOULD NOT POSSESS.
BUT THIS...THIS IS HERETICAL.
YOU HAVE THE GREAT MOTHER... WHO MADE US ALL AND LONG AGO WE REJECTED.
SO WE ASK YOU AGAIN, HOW DID YOU COME TO HAVE THESE... THINGS?
WHAT SETS YOU APART?
WHAT MAKES YOU SO SPECIAL?

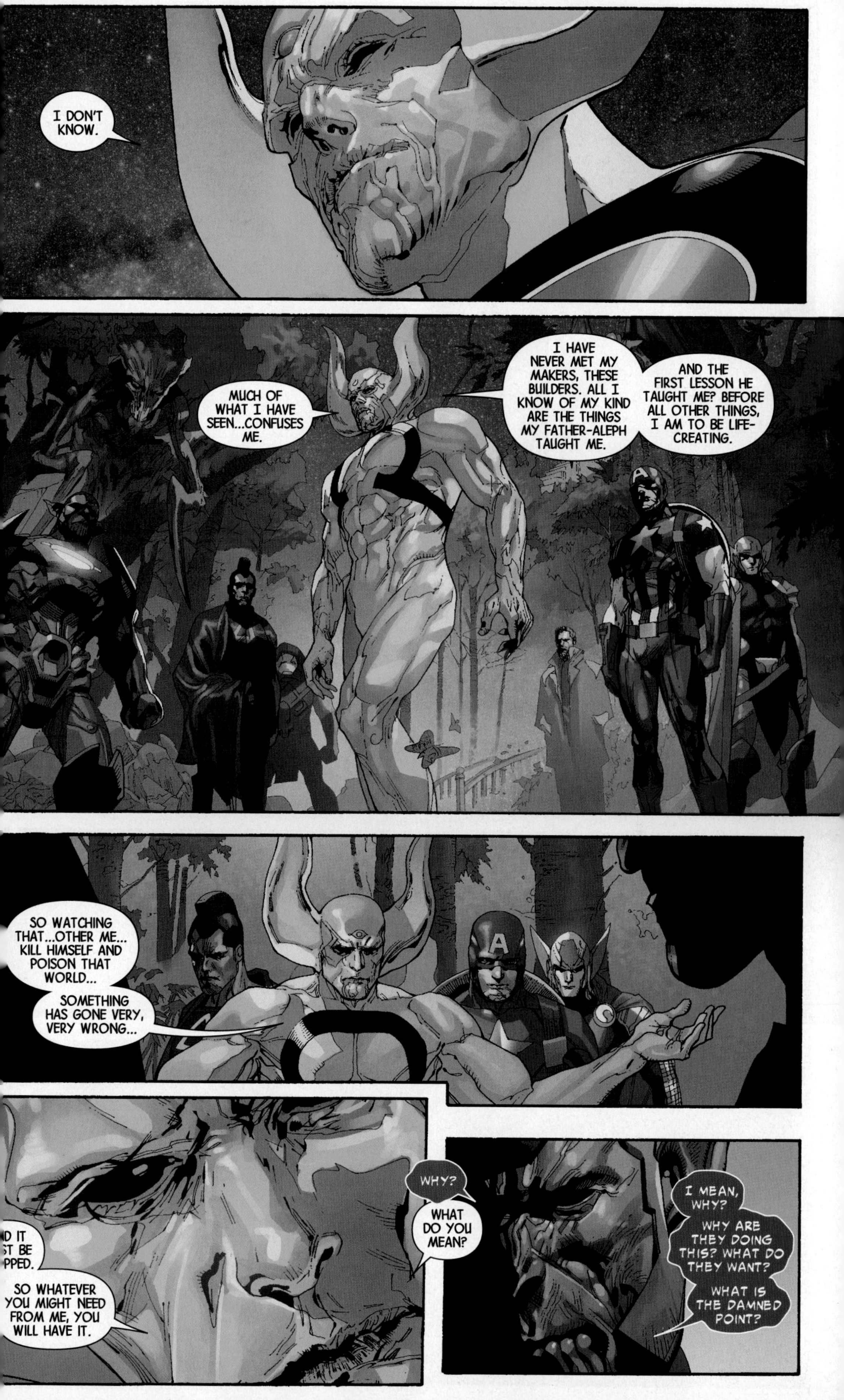

I DON'T KNOW.
MUCH OF WHAT I HAVE SEEN...CONFUSES ME.
I HAVE NEVER MET MY MAKERS, THESE BUILDERS. ALL I KNOW OF MY KIND ARE THE THINGS MY FATHER-ALEPH TAUGHT ME.
AND THE FIRST LESSON HE TAUGHT ME? BEFORE ALL OTHER THINGS, I AM TO BE LIFE-CREATING.
SO WATCHING THAT...OTHER ME... KILL HIMSELF AND POISON THAT WORLD...
SOMETHING HAS GONE VERY, VERY WRONG...
ND IT ST BE PPED.
SO WHATEVER YOU MIGHT NEED FROM ME, YOU WILL HAVE IT.
WHY?
WHAT DO YOU MEAN?
I MEAN, WHY?
WHY ARE THEY DOING THIS? WHAT DO THEY WANT?
WHAT IS THE DAMNED POINT?

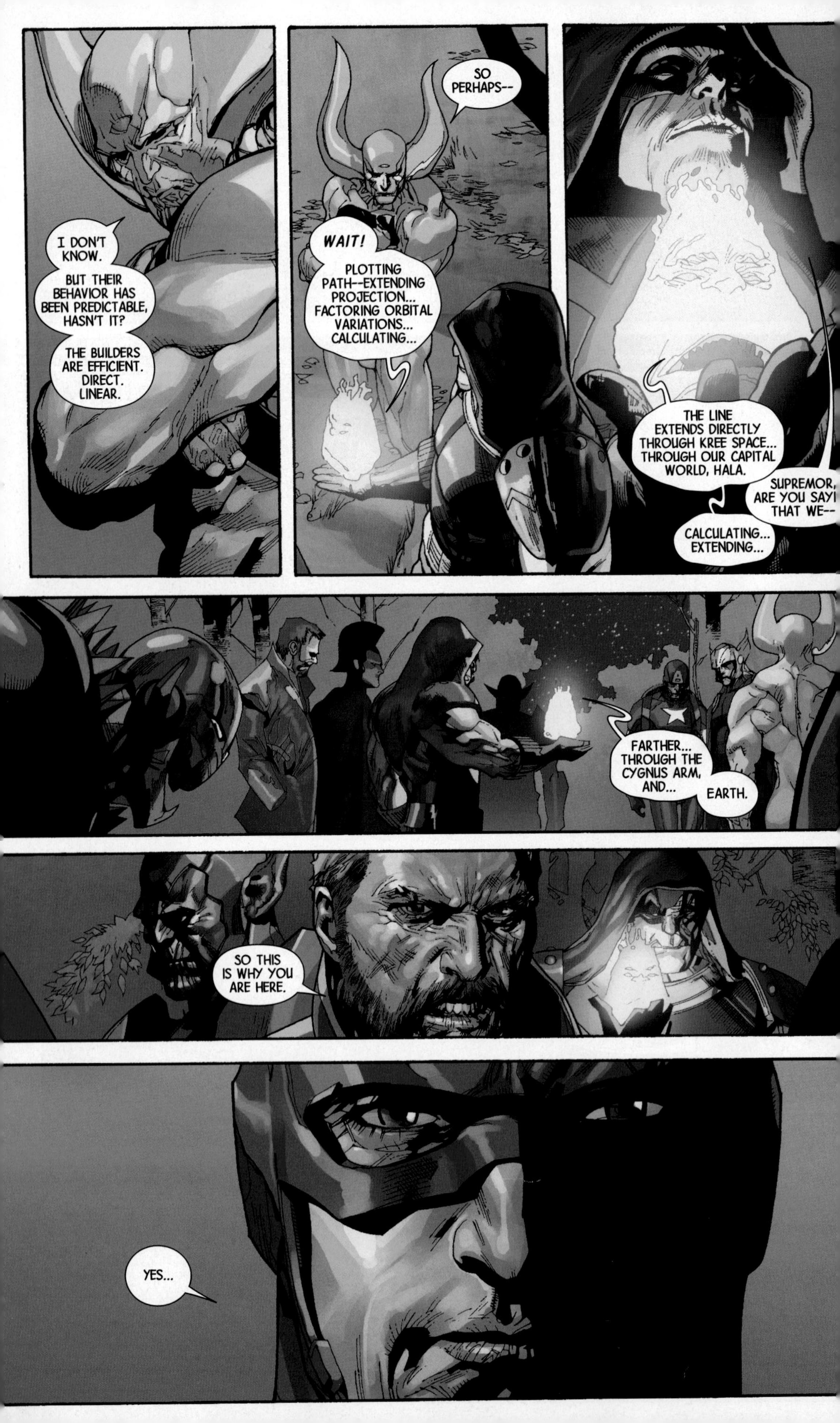
I DON'T KNOW.
BUT THEIR BEHAVIOR HAS BEEN PREDICTABLE, HASN'T IT?
THE BUILDERS ARE EFFICIENT. DIRECT. LINEAR.
SO PERHAPS--
WAIT!
PLOTTING PATH--EXTENDING PROJECTION... FACTORING ORBITAL VARIATIONS... CALCULATING...
THE LINE EXTENDS DIRECTLY THROUGH KREE SPACE... THROUGH OUR CAPITAL WORLD, HALA.
SUPREMOR, ARE YOU SAYI THAT WE--
CALCULATING... EXTENDING...
FARTHER... THROUGH THE CYGNUS ARM, AND...
EARTH.
SO THIS IS WHY YOU ARE HERE.
YES...

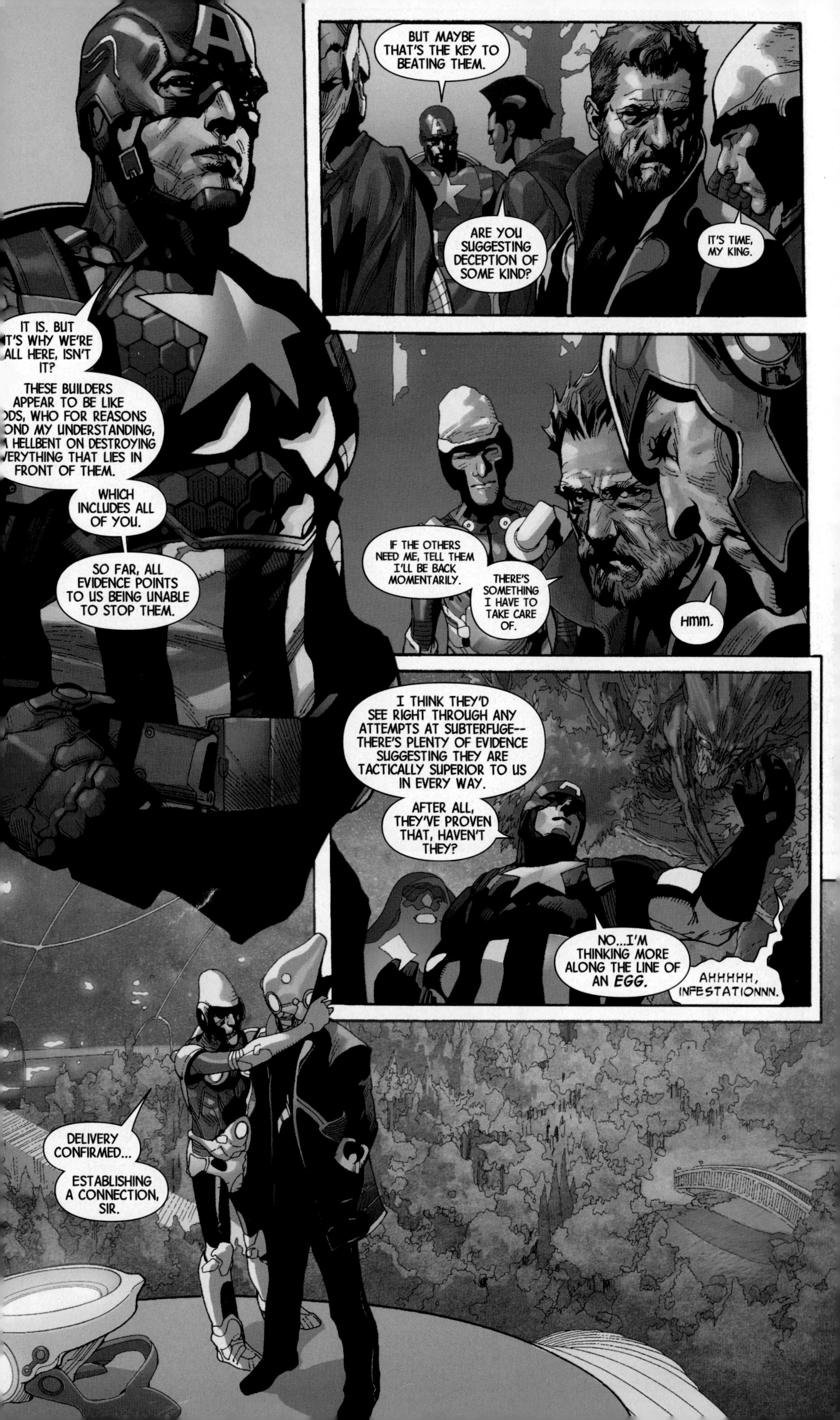
BUT MAYBE THAT'S THE KEY TO BEATING THEM.
ARE YOU SUGGESTING DECEPTION OF SOME KIND?
IT'S TIME, MY KING.
IT IS. BUT T'S WHY WE'RE ALL HERE, ISN'T IT?
THESE BUILDERS APPEAR TO BE LIKE ODS, WHO FOR REASONS OND MY UNDERSTANDING, HELLBENT ON DESTROYING VERYTHING THAT LIES IN FRONT OF THEM.
WHICH INCLUDES ALL OF YOU.
SO FAR, ALL EVIDENCE POINTS TO US BEING UNABLE TO STOP THEM.
IF THE OTHERS NEED ME, TELL THEM I'LL BE BACK MOMENTARILY.
THERE'S SOMETHING I HAVE TO TAKE CARE OF.
HMM.
I THINK THEY'D SEE RIGHT THROUGH ANY ATTEMPTS AT SUBTERFUGE-- THERE'S PLENTY OF EVIDENCE SUGGESTING THEY ARE TACTICALLY SUPERIOR TO US IN EVERY WAY.
AFTER ALL, THEY'VE PROVEN THAT, HAVEN'T THEY?
NO...I'M THINKING MORE ALONG THE LINE OF AN EGG.
AHHHHH, INFESTATIONNN.
DELIVERY CONFIRMED...
ESTABLISHING A CONNECTION, SIR.

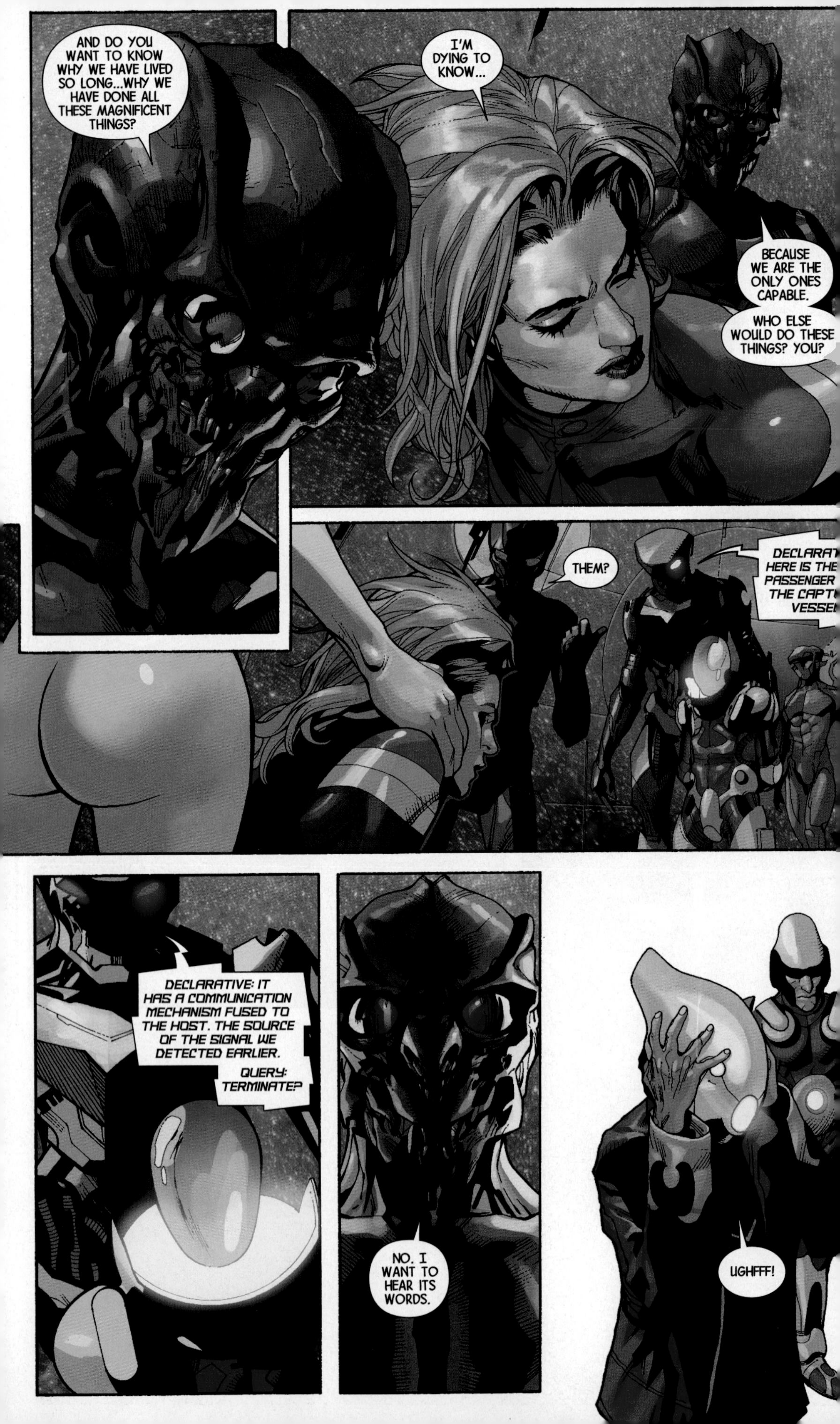
AND DO YOU WANT TO KNOW WHY WE HAVE LIVED SO LONG...WHY WE HAVE DONE ALL THESE MAGNIFICENT THINGS?
I'M DYING TO KNOW...
BECAUSE WE ARE THE ONLY ONES CAPABLE.
WHO ELSE WOULD DO THESE THINGS? YOU?
THEM?
DECLARAT HERE IS THE PASSENGER THE CAPT VESSE
DECLARATIVE: IT HAS A COMMUNICATION MECHANISM FUSED TO THE HOST. THE SOURCE OF THE SIGNAL WE DETECTED EARLIER.
QUERY: TERMINATE?
NO. I WANT TO HEAR ITS WORDS.
UGHFFF!

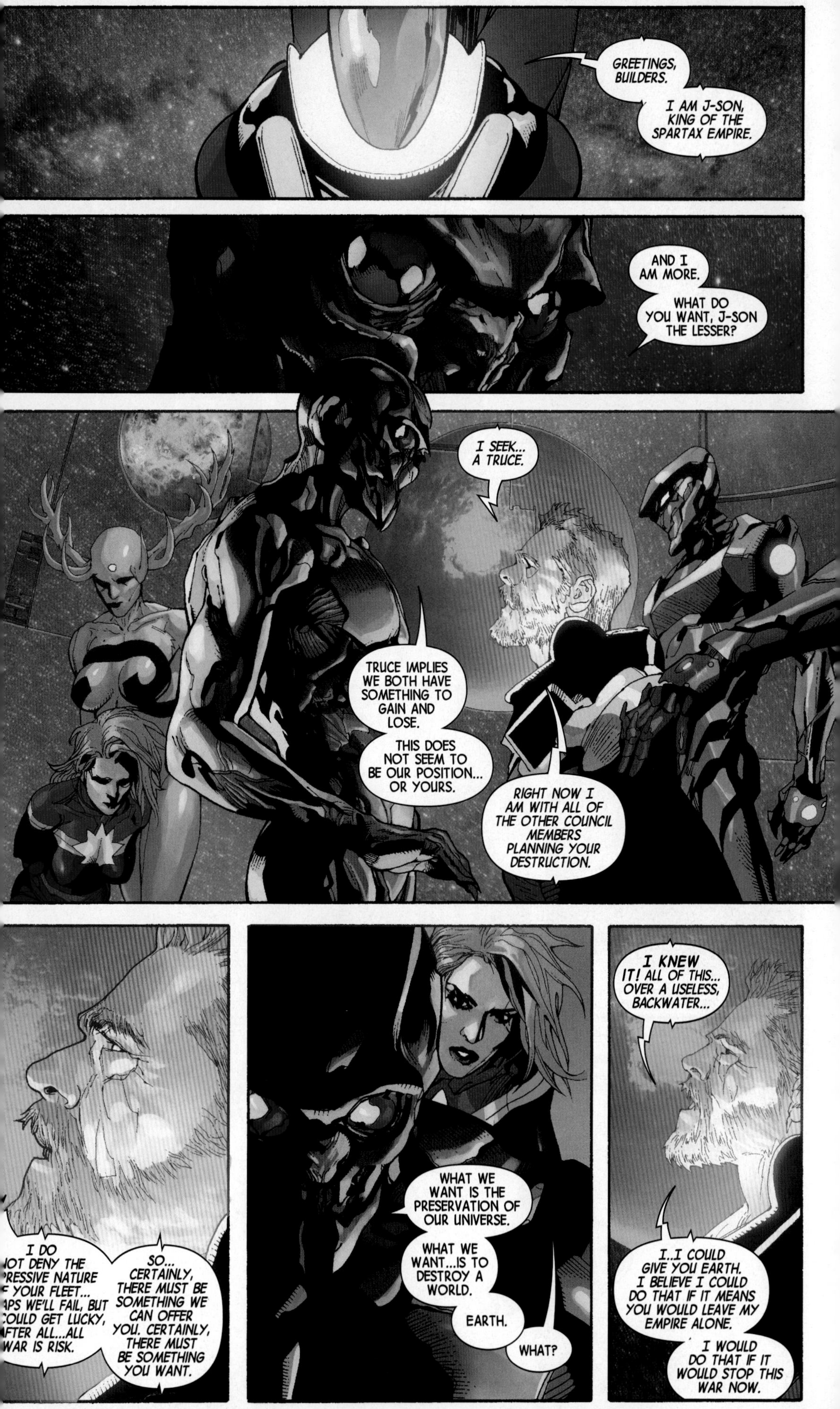
GREETINGS, BUILDERS.
I AM J-SON, KING OF THE SPARTAX EMPIRE.
AND I AM MORE.
WHAT DO YOU WANT, J-SON THE LESSER?
I SEEK... A TRUCE.
TRUCE IMPLIES WE BOTH HAVE SOMETHING TO GAIN AND LOSE.
THIS DOES NOT SEEM TO BE OUR POSITION... OR YOURS.
RIGHT NOW I AM WITH ALL OF THE OTHER COUNCIL MEMBERS PLANNING YOUR DESTRUCTION.
I DO NOT DENY THE PRESSIVE NATURE OF YOUR FLEET... APS WE'LL FAIL, BUT COULD GET LUCKY, AFTER ALL...ALL WAR IS RISK.
SO... CERTAINLY, THERE MUST BE SOMETHING WE CAN OFFER YOU. CERTAINLY, THERE MUST BE SOMETHING YOU WANT.
WHAT WE WANT IS THE PRESERVATION OF OUR UNIVERSE.
WHAT WE WANT...IS TO DESTROY A WORLD.
EARTH.
WHAT?
I KNEW IT! ALL OF THIS... OVER A USELESS, BACKWATER...
I..I COULD GIVE YOU EARTH. I BELIEVE I COULD DO THAT IF IT MEANS YOU WOULD LEAVE MY EMPIRE ALONE.
I WOULD DO THAT IF IT WOULD STOP THIS WAR NOW.

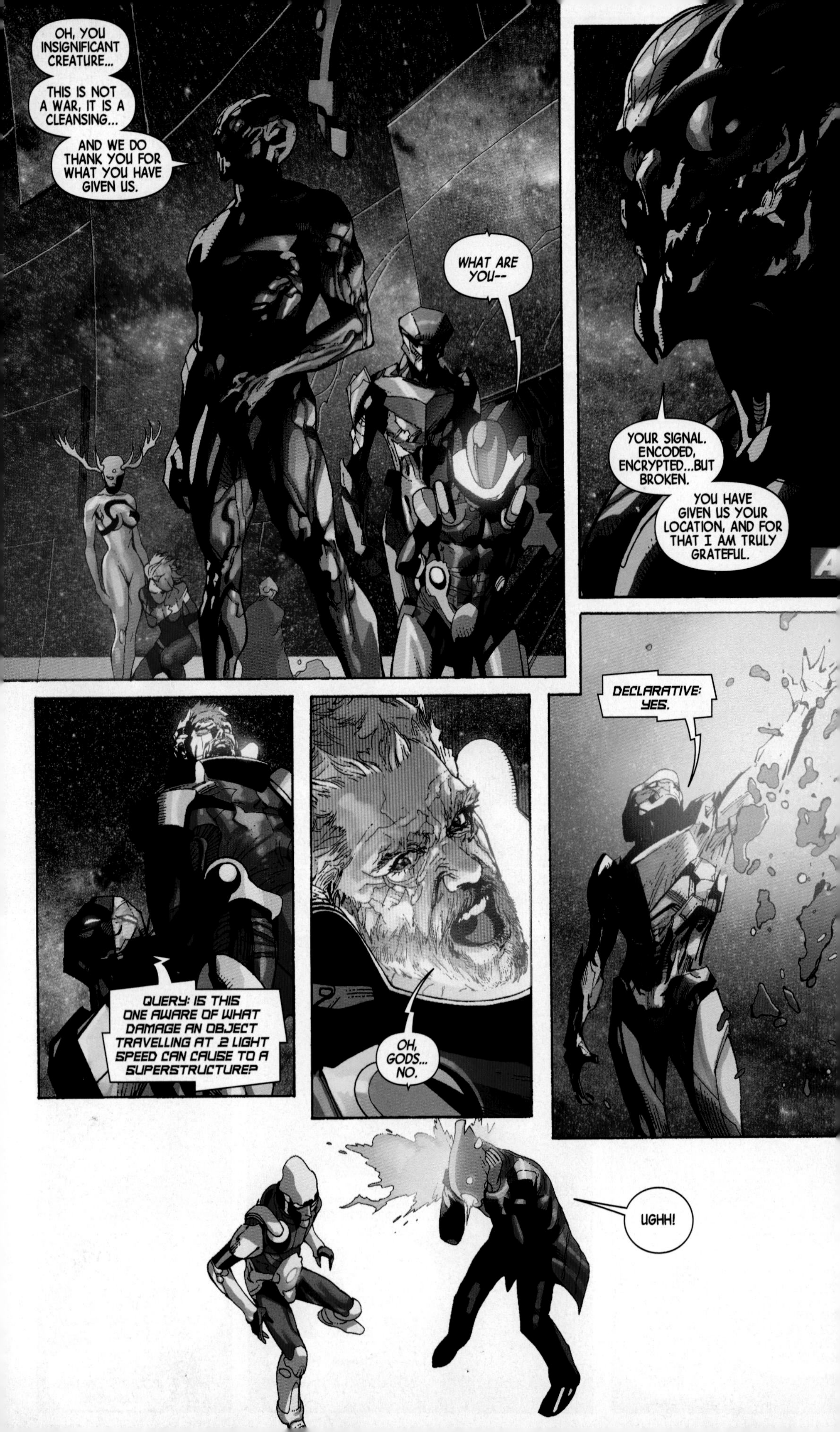
OH, YOU INSIGNIFICANT CREATURE...
THIS IS NOT A WAR, IT IS A CLEANSING...
AND WE DO THANK YOU FOR WHAT YOU HAVE GIVEN US.
WHAT ARE YOU--
YOUR SIGNAL. ENCODED, ENCRYPTED...BUT BROKEN.
YOU HAVE GIVEN US YOUR LOCATION, AND FOR THAT I AM TRULY GRATEFUL.
QUERY: IS THIS ONE AWARE OF WHAT DAMAGE AN OBJECT TRAVELLING AT .2 LIGHT SPEED CAN CAUSE TO A SUPERSTRUCTURE?
OH, GODS... NO.
DECLARATIVE: YES.
UGHH!

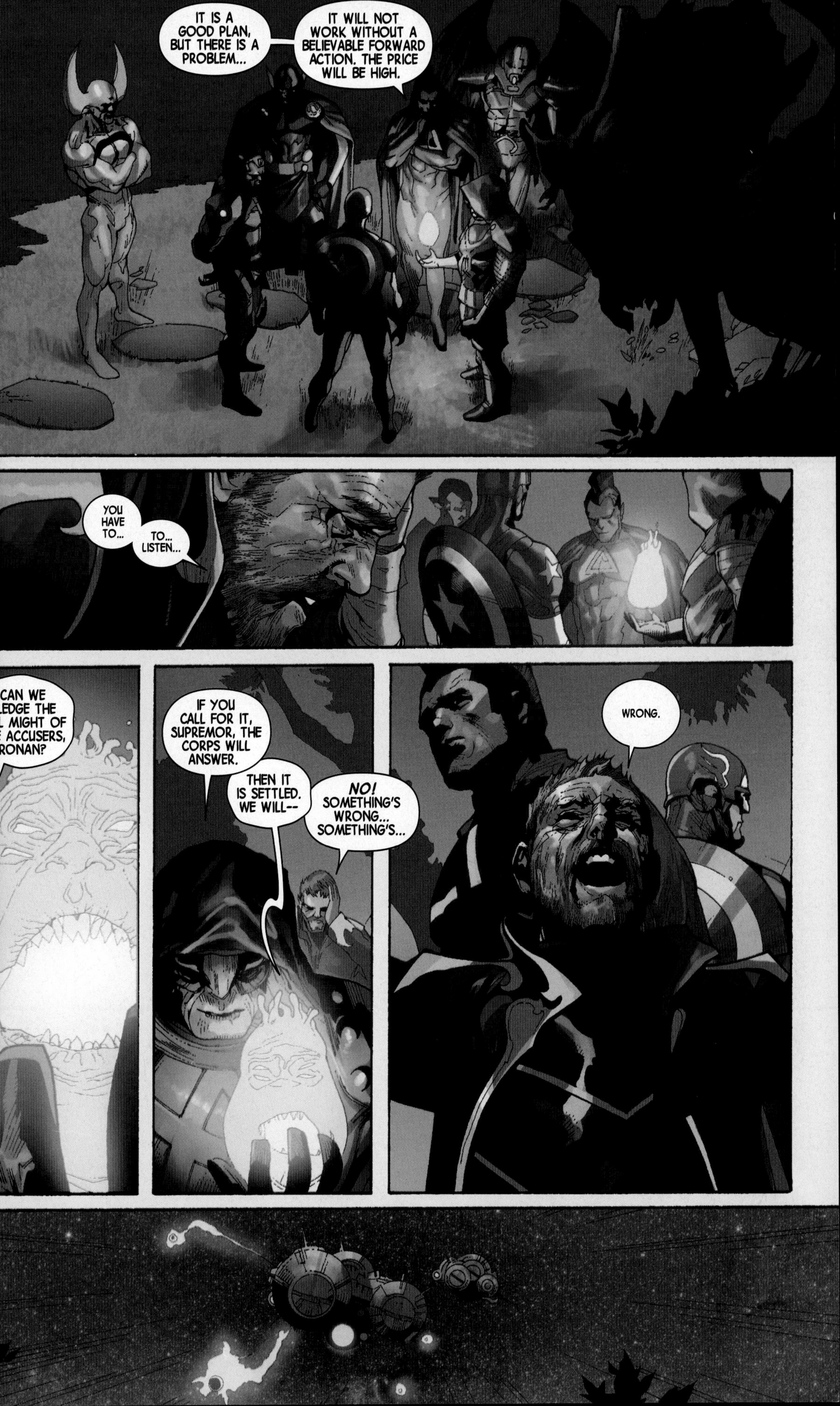
IT IS A GOOD PLAN, BUT THERE IS A PROBLEM...
IT WILL NOT WORK WITHOUT A BELIEVABLE FORWARD ACTION. THE PRICE WILL BE HIGH.
YOU HAVE TO...
TO... LISTEN...
CAN WE
LEDGE THE
L MIGHT OF
E ACCUSERS,
RONAN?
IF YOU CALL FOR IT, SUPREMOR, THE CORPS WILL ANSWER.
THEN IT IS SETTLED. WE WILL--
NO! SOMETHING'S WRONG... SOMETHING'S...
WRONG.

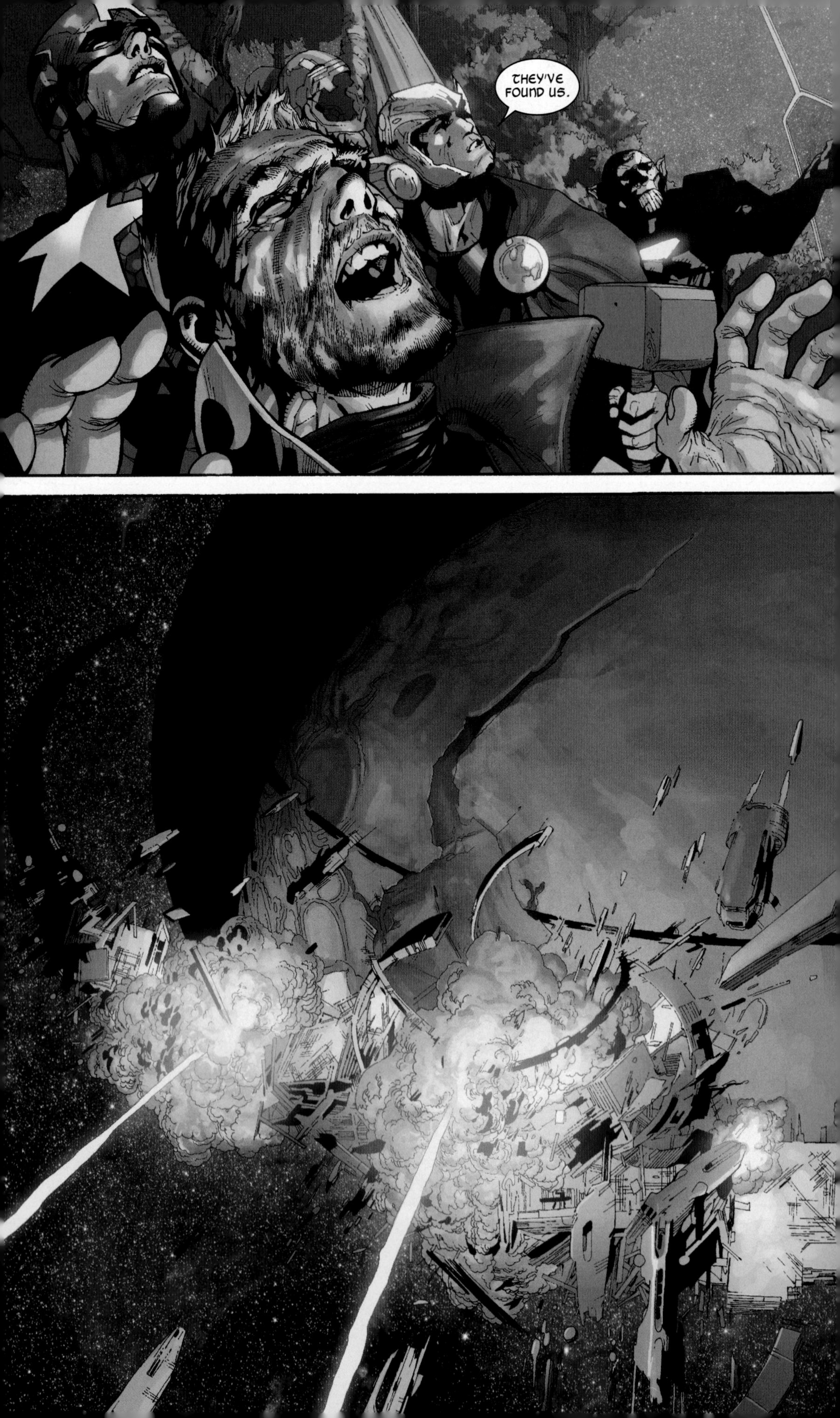
THEY'VE FOUND US.

"THE OFFER"

PREVIOUSLY IN INFINITY

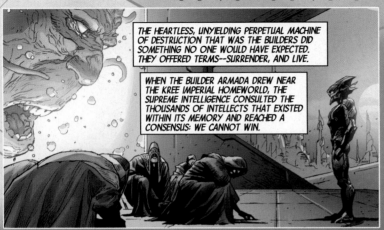

THE HEARTLESS, UNYIELDING PERPETUAL MACHINE OF DESTRUCTION THAT WAS THE BUILDERS DID SOMETHING NO ONE WOULD HAVE EXPECTED. THEY OFFERED TERMS--SURRENDER, AND LIVE.
WHEN THE BUILDER ARMADA DREW NEAR THE KREE IMPERIAL HOMEWORLD, THE SUPREME INTELLIGENCE CONSULTED THE THOUSANDS OF INTELLECTS THAT EXISTED WITHIN ITS MEMORY AND REACHED A CONSENSUS: WE CANNOT WIN.
IT HAS BEEN SO LONG...ARE WE SURE? HOW IS IT POSSIBLE?
I DON'T KNOW...BUT IT WONDERFUL, IS IT? AN ABYSS. ALIVE.
MUCH OF WHAT I HAVE SEEN...CONFUSES ME. I HAVE NEVER MET MY MAKERS, THESE BUILDERS. ALL I KNOW IS WHAT MY FATHER-ALEPH TAUGHT ME, FIRST AND FOREMOST BEING I WAS MADE TO BE LIFE-CREATING. SO WATCHING THAT...OTHER ME...KILL HIMSELF AND POISON THAT WORLD...
SOMETHING HAS GONE VERY, VERY WRONG...
AND IT MUST BE STOPPED.
POWER IS FAILING. WE NEED TO RETREAT. WE NEED TO--
NO. THERE IS NOWHERE LEFT TO RUN, SOLDIER.
WE WIN HERE NOW... OR WE LOSE IT ALL. GIVE THE ORDER...
FIRE EVERYTHING WE'VE GOT.
WE HAVE LOST EIGHT OF THE GREAT WEAPONS, BUILDERS--AND OUR COMMAND SHIP IS SHIELDLESS AND INCAPABLE OF ESCAPING. THE ROGUE PLANET KILLERS HAVE TURNED TO FIRING AT THE FLEET.
GIVE THE ORDER FOR THE BULK OF THE VESSELS TO LEAVE.
YOU MUST LEAVE AS WELL, CREATOR.
WE HAVE BEEN STUNG TODAY. IT IS AN INSULT I WILL NOT FORGET. SCUTTLE THE SHIP, THEN JOIN IN THE BATTLE. MAKE YOUR END MEAN SOMETHING, EX NIHILA.

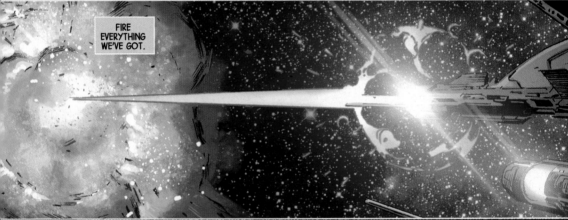

CAST

THE AVENGERS

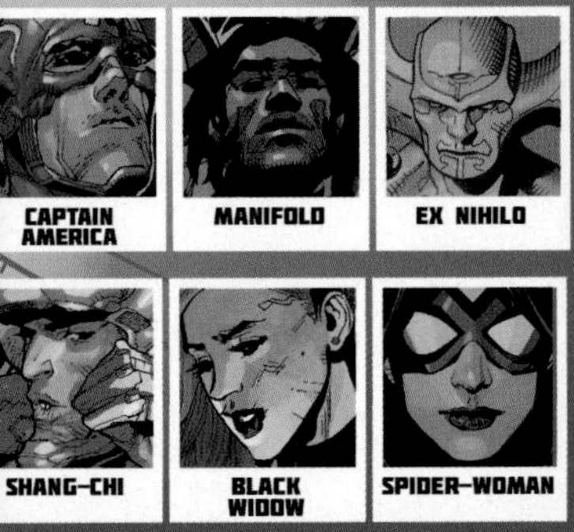
CAPTAIN AMERICA
MANIFOLD
EX NIHILO
SHANG-CHI
BLACK WIDOW
SPIDER-WOMAN

CAPTURED

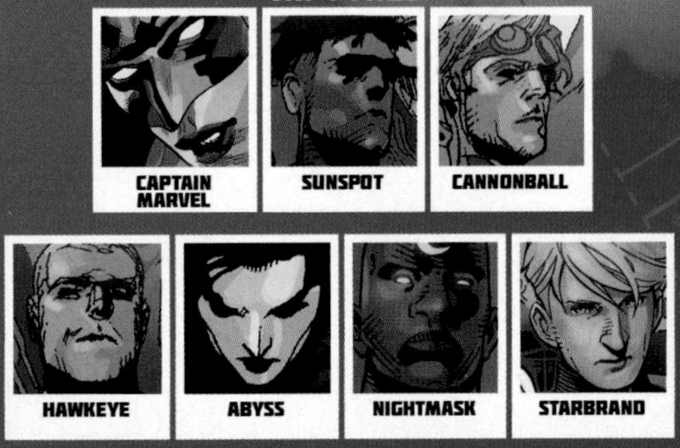
CAPTAIN MARVEL
SUNSPOT
CANNONBALL
HAWKEYE
ABYSS
NIGHTMASK
STARBRAND

THE BUILDERS

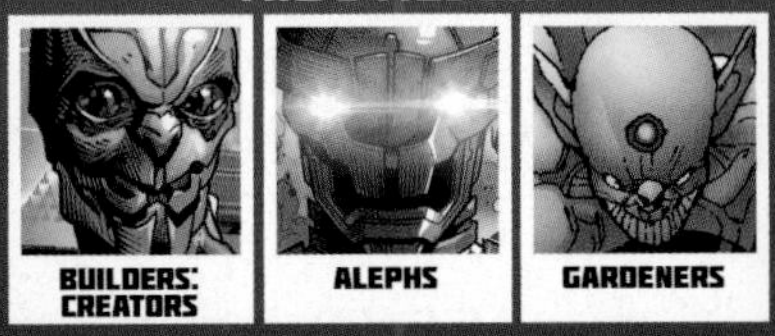
BUILDERS: CREATORS
ALEPHS
GARDENERS

THE GALACTIC COUNCIL

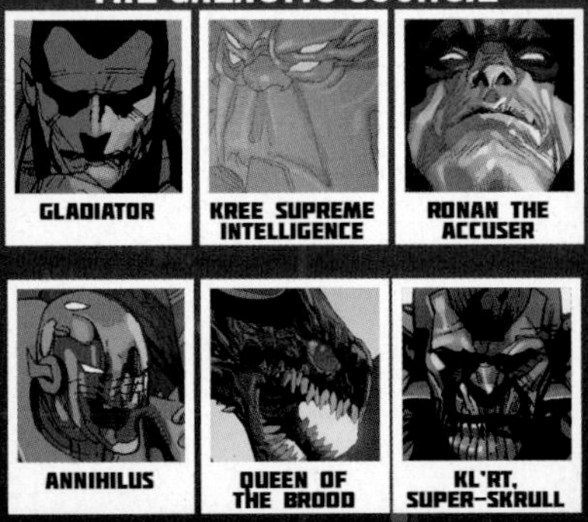
GLADIATOR
KREE SUPREME INTELLIGENCE
RONAN THE ACCUSER
ANNIHILUS
QUEEN OF THE BROOD
KL'RT, SUPER-SKRULL

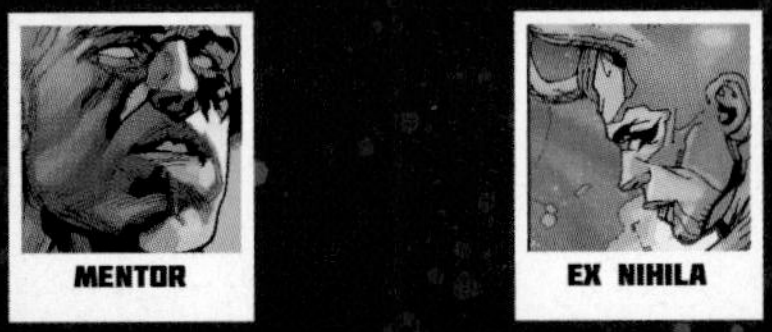
MENTOR
EX NIHILA

THE WORDS OF A GARDENER

◆

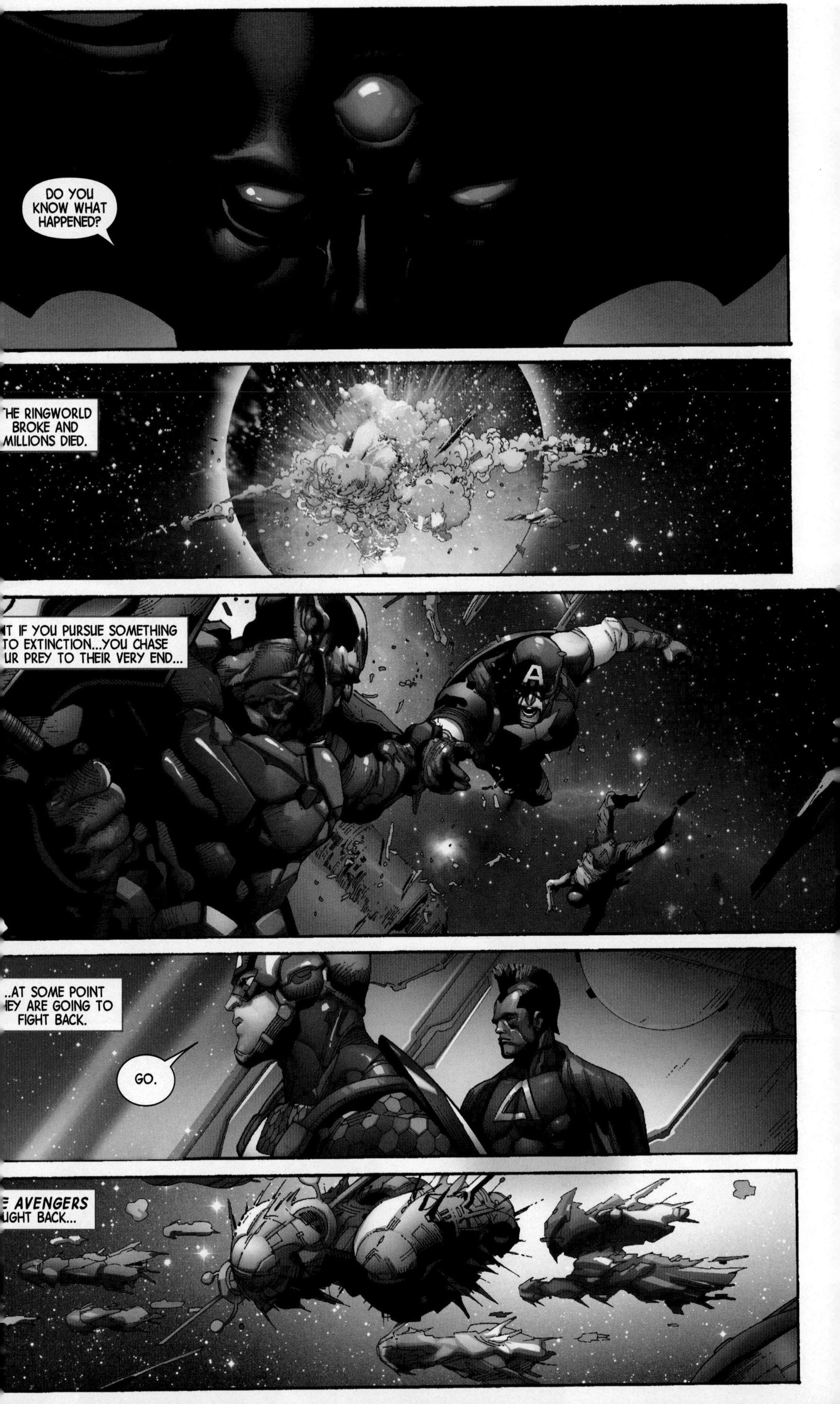
DO YOU KNOW WHAT HAPPENED?
'HE RINGWORLD BROKE AND MILLIONS DIED.
IT IF YOU PURSUE SOMETHING TO EXTINCTION...YOU CHASE UR PREY TO THEIR VERY END...
..AT SOME POINT IEY ARE GOING TO FIGHT BACK.
GO.
E AVENGERS UGHT BACK...

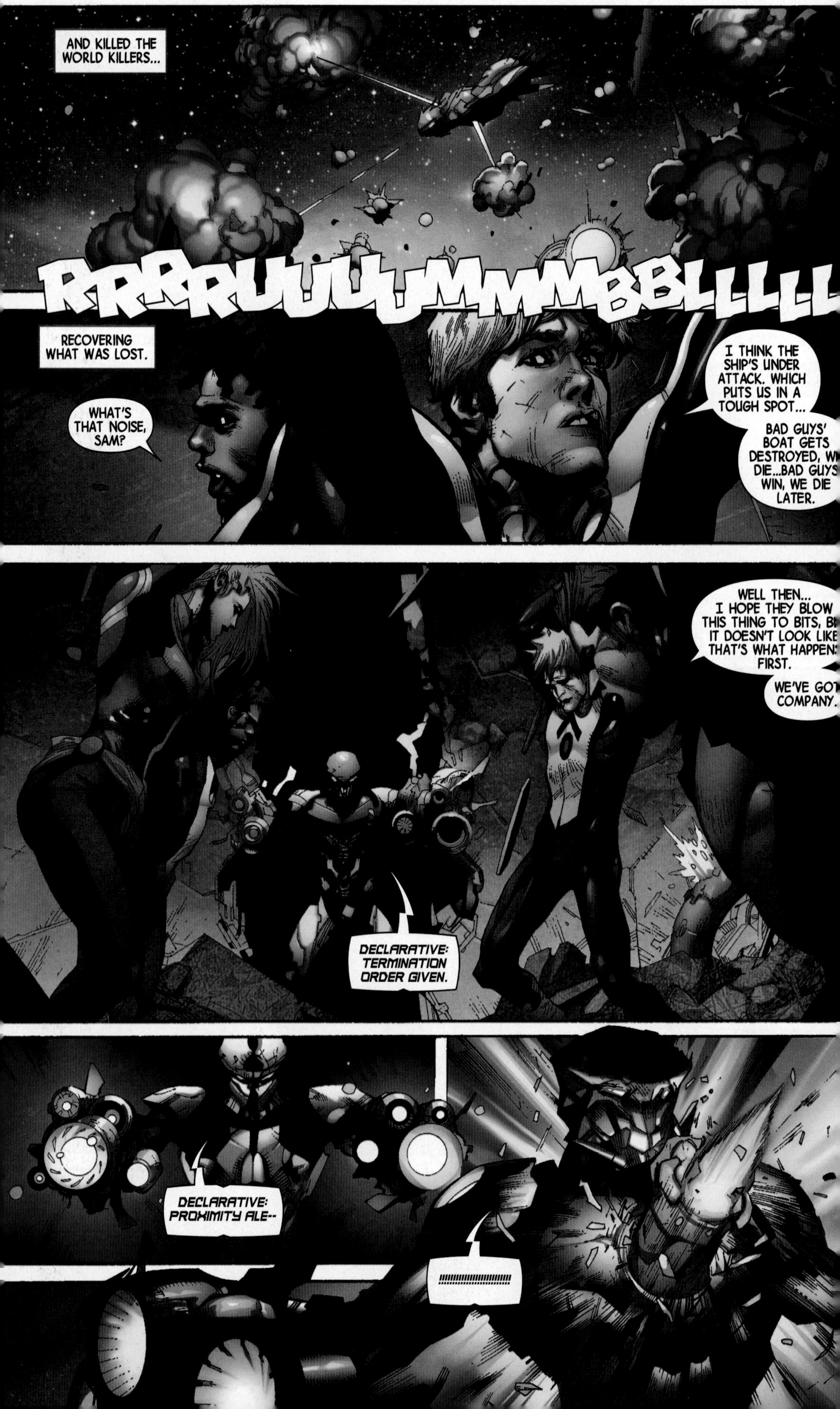
AND KILLED THE WORLD KILLERS...
RRRRUUUUMMMMBBLLLLL
RECOVERING WHAT WAS LOST.
WHAT'S THAT NOISE, SAM?
I THINK THE SHIP'S UNDER ATTACK. WHICH PUTS US IN A TOUGH SPOT...
BAD GUYS' BOAT GETS DESTROYED, WE DIE...BAD GUYS WIN, WE DIE LATER.
WELL THEN... I HOPE THEY BLOW THIS THING TO BITS, BUT IT DOESN'T LOOK LIKE THAT'S WHAT HAPPENS FIRST.
WE'VE GOT COMPANY.
DECLARATIVE: TERMINATION ORDER GIVEN.
DECLARATIVE: PROXIMITY ALE--

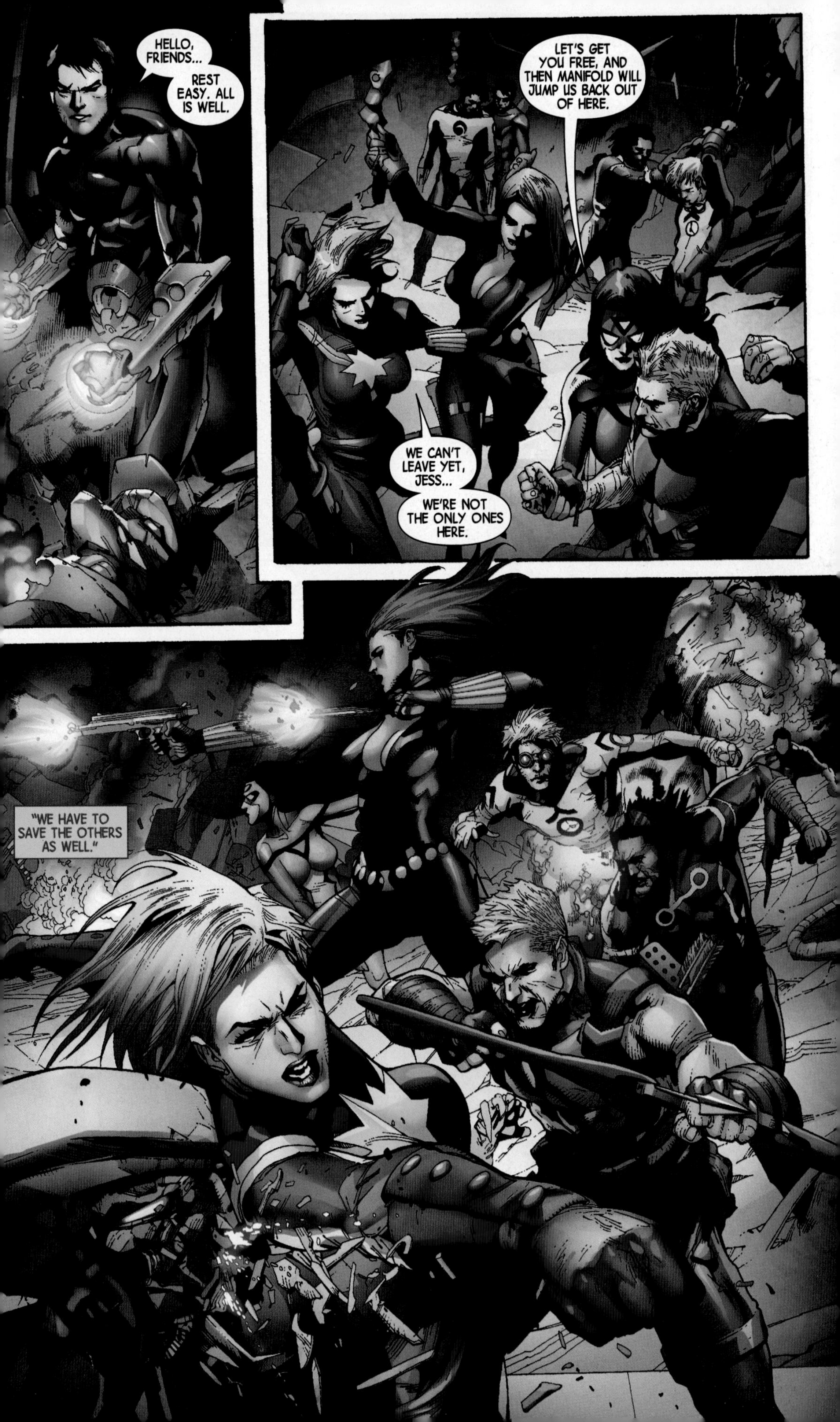
HELLO, FRIENDS...
REST EASY. ALL IS WELL.
LET'S GET YOU FREE, AND THEN MANIFOLD WILL JUMP US BACK OUT OF HERE.
WE CAN'T LEAVE YET, JESS...
WE'RE NOT THE ONLY ONES HERE.
"WE HAVE TO SAVE THE OTHERS AS WELL."

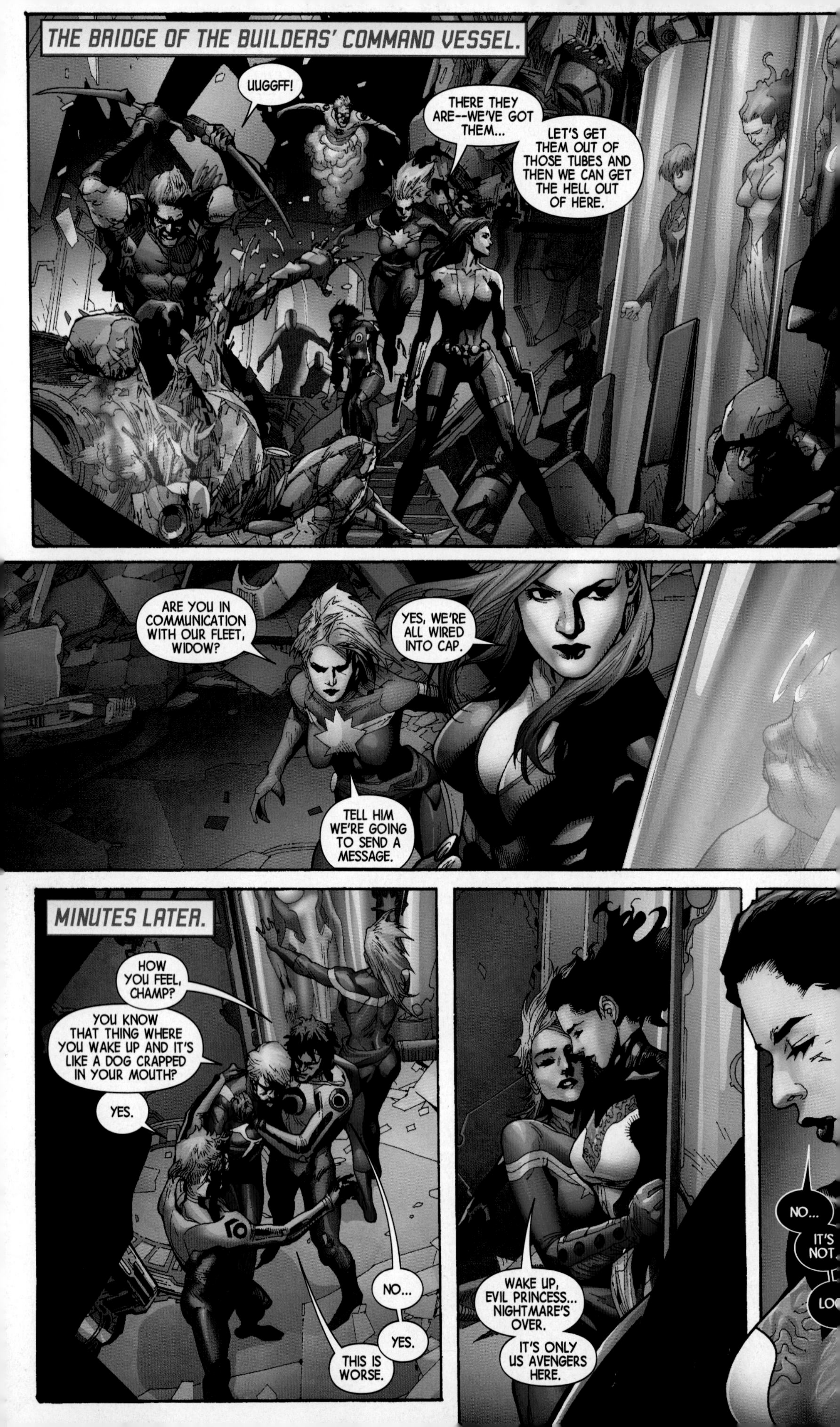
THE BRIDGE OF THE BUILDERS' COMMAND VESSEL.
UUGGFF!
THERE THEY ARE--WE'VE GOT THEM...
LET'S GET THEM OUT OF THOSE TUBES AND THEN WE CAN GET THE HELL OUT OF HERE.
ARE YOU IN COMMUNICATION WITH OUR FLEET, WIDOW?
YES, WE'RE ALL WIRED INTO CAP.
TELL HIM WE'RE GOING TO SEND A MESSAGE.
MINUTES LATER.
HOW YOU FEEL, CHAMP?
YOU KNOW THAT THING WHERE YOU WAKE UP AND IT'S LIKE A DOG CRAPPED IN YOUR MOUTH?
YES.
NO...
YES.
THIS IS WORSE.
WAKE UP, EVIL PRINCESS... NIGHTMARE'S OVER.
IT'S ONLY US AVENGERS HERE.
NO...
IT'S NOT.

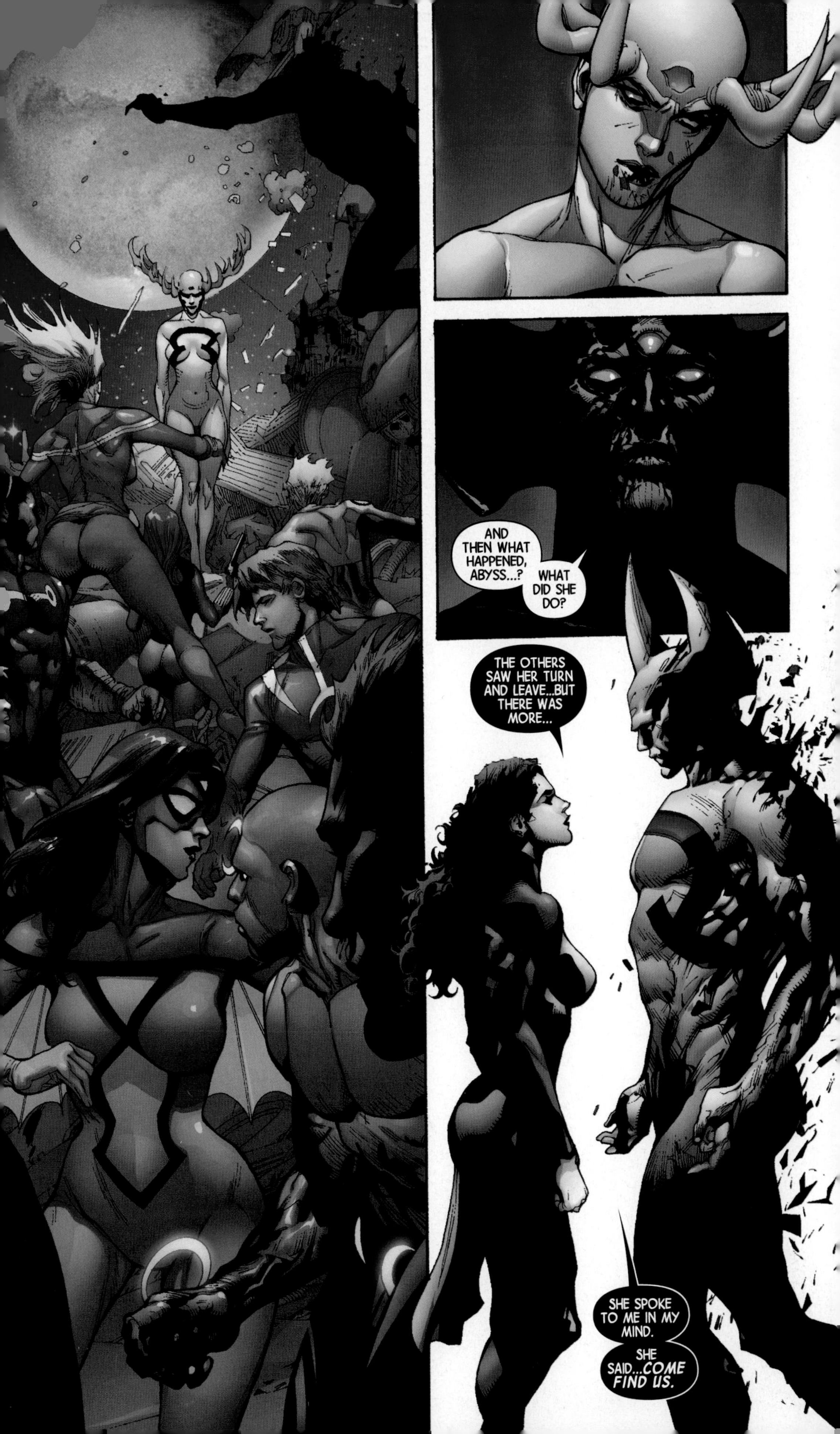
AND THEN WHAT HAPPENED, ABYSS...?
WHAT DID SHE DO?
THE OTHERS SAW HER TURN AND LEAVE...BUT THERE WAS MORE...
SHE SPOKE TO ME IN MY MIND.
SHE SAID...*COME FIND US.*

THE EDGE OF
ANNIHILATION

◆

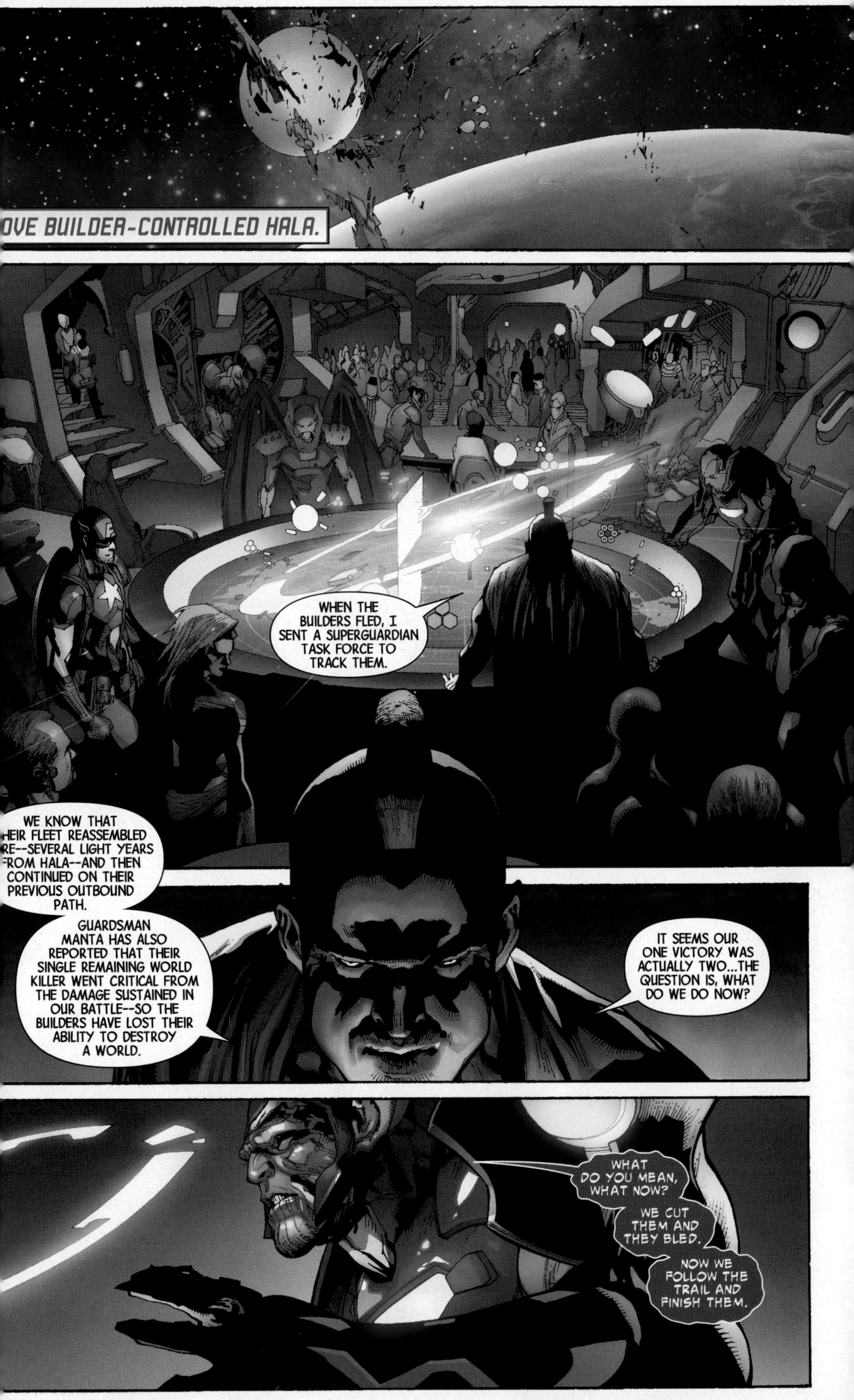
OVE BUILDER-CONTROLLED HALA.
WHEN THE BUILDERS FLED, I SENT A SUPERGUARDIAN TASK FORCE TO TRACK THEM.
WE KNOW THAT HEIR FLEET REASSEMBLED RE--SEVERAL LIGHT YEARS FROM HALA--AND THEN CONTINUED ON THEIR PREVIOUS OUTBOUND PATH.
GUARDSMAN MANTA HAS ALSO REPORTED THAT THEIR SINGLE REMAINING WORLD KILLER WENT CRITICAL FROM THE DAMAGE SUSTAINED IN OUR BATTLE--SO THE BUILDERS HAVE LOST THEIR ABILITY TO DESTROY A WORLD.
IT SEEMS OUR ONE VICTORY WAS ACTUALLY TWO...THE QUESTION IS, WHAT DO WE DO NOW?
WHAT DO YOU MEAN, WHAT NOW?
WE CUT THEM AND THEY BLED.
NOW WE FOLLOW THE TRAIL AND FINISH THEM.

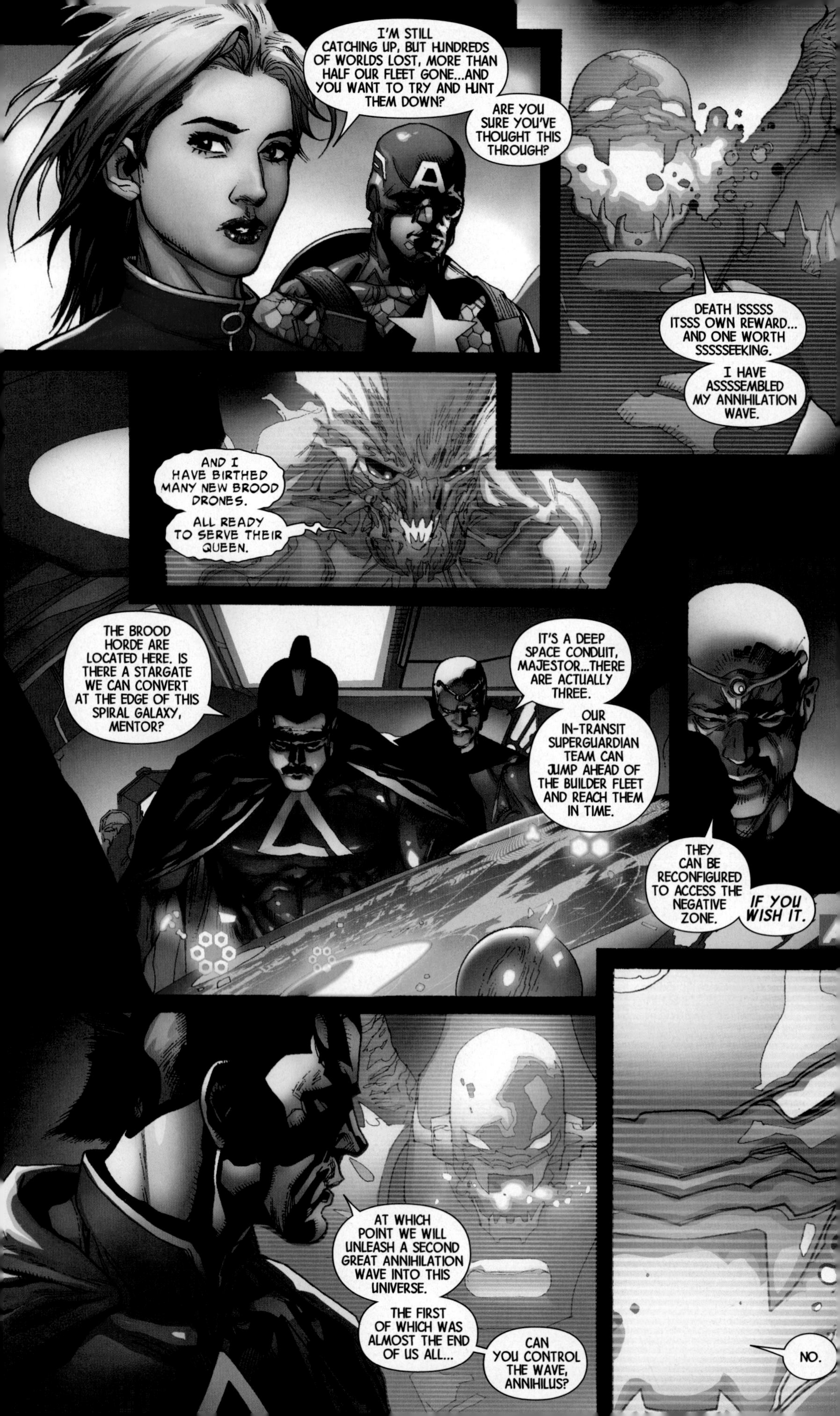
I'M STILL CATCHING UP, BUT HUNDREDS OF WORLDS LOST, MORE THAN HALF OUR FLEET GONE...AND YOU WANT TO TRY AND HUNT THEM DOWN?
ARE YOU SURE YOU'VE THOUGHT THIS THROUGH?
DEATH ISSSSS ITSSS OWN REWARD... AND ONE WORTH SSSSSEEKING.
I HAVE ASSSSEMBLED MY ANNIHILATION WAVE.
AND I HAVE BIRTHED MANY NEW BROOD DRONES.
ALL READY TO SERVE THEIR QUEEN.
THE BROOD HORDE ARE LOCATED HERE. IS THERE A STARGATE WE CAN CONVERT AT THE EDGE OF THIS SPIRAL GALAXY, MENTOR?
IT'S A DEEP SPACE CONDUIT, MAJESTOR...THERE ARE ACTUALLY THREE.
OUR IN-TRANSIT SUPERGUARDIAN TEAM CAN JUMP AHEAD OF THE BUILDER FLEET AND REACH THEM IN TIME.
THEY CAN BE RECONFIGURED TO ACCESS THE NEGATIVE ZONE.
IF YOU WISH IT.
AT WHICH POINT WE WILL UNLEASH A SECOND GREAT ANNIHILATION WAVE INTO THIS UNIVERSE.
THE FIRST OF WHICH WAS ALMOST THE END OF US ALL...
CAN YOU CONTROL THE WAVE, ANNIHILUS?
NO.

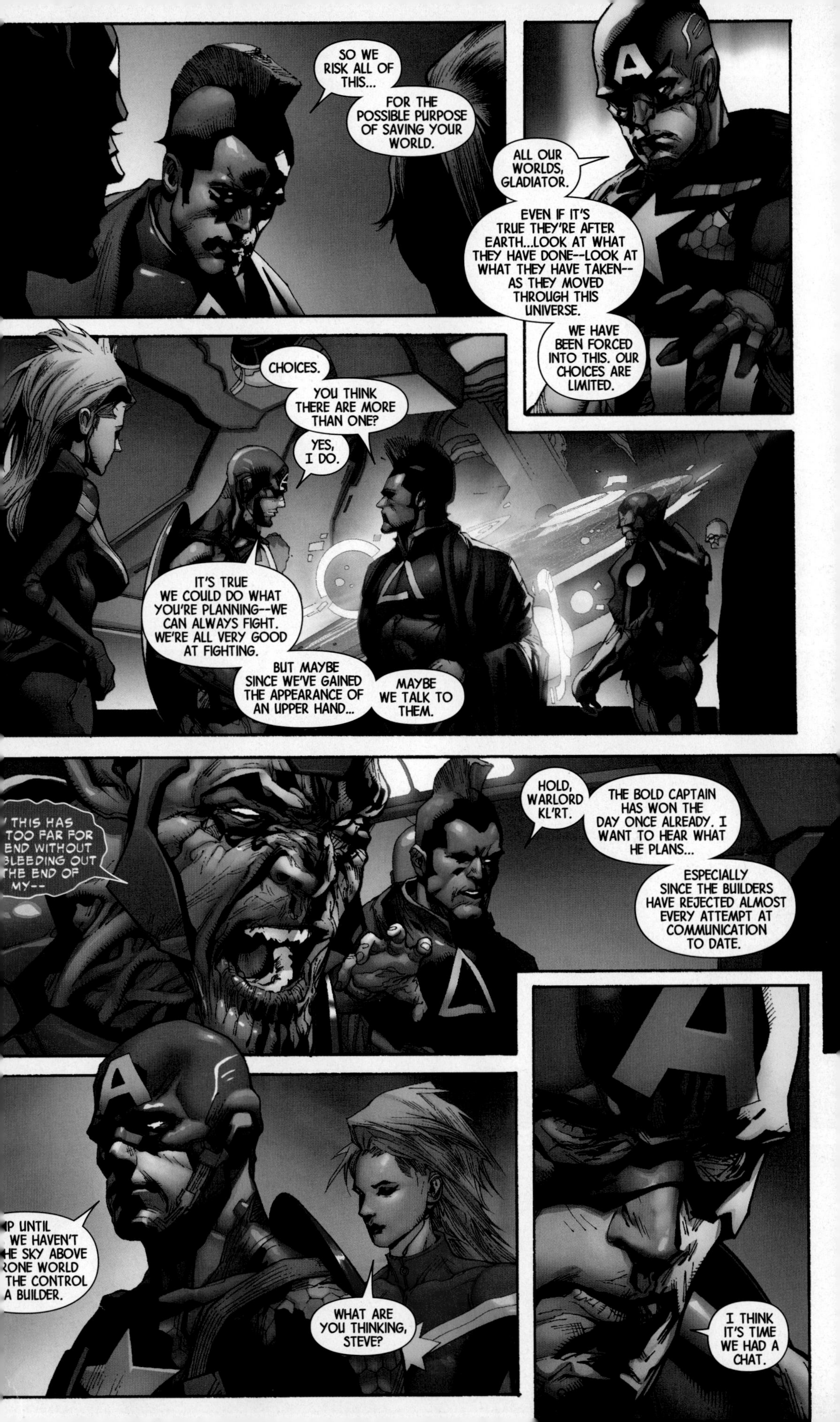

SO WE RISK ALL OF THIS...
FOR THE POSSIBLE PURPOSE OF SAVING YOUR WORLD.
ALL OUR WORLDS, GLADIATOR.
EVEN IF IT'S TRUE THEY'RE AFTER EARTH...LOOK AT WHAT THEY HAVE DONE--LOOK AT WHAT THEY HAVE TAKEN--AS THEY MOVED THROUGH THIS UNIVERSE.
WE HAVE BEEN FORCED INTO THIS. OUR CHOICES ARE LIMITED.
CHOICES.
YOU THINK THERE ARE MORE THAN ONE?
YES, I DO.
IT'S TRUE WE COULD DO WHAT YOU'RE PLANNING--WE CAN ALWAYS FIGHT. WE'RE ALL VERY GOOD AT FIGHTING.
BUT MAYBE SINCE WE'VE GAINED THE APPEARANCE OF AN UPPER HAND...
MAYBE WE TALK TO THEM.
THIS HAS TOO FAR FOR END WITHOUT BLEEDING OUT THE END OF MY--
HOLD, WARLORD KL'RT.
THE BOLD CAPTAIN HAS WON THE DAY ONCE ALREADY. I WANT TO HEAR WHAT HE PLANS...
ESPECIALLY SINCE THE BUILDERS HAVE REJECTED ALMOST EVERY ATTEMPT AT COMMUNICATION TO DATE.
P UNTIL WE HAVEN'T HE SKY ABOVE RONE WORLD THE CONTROL A BUILDER.
WHAT ARE YOU THINKING, STEVE?
I THINK IT'S TIME WE HAD A CHAT.

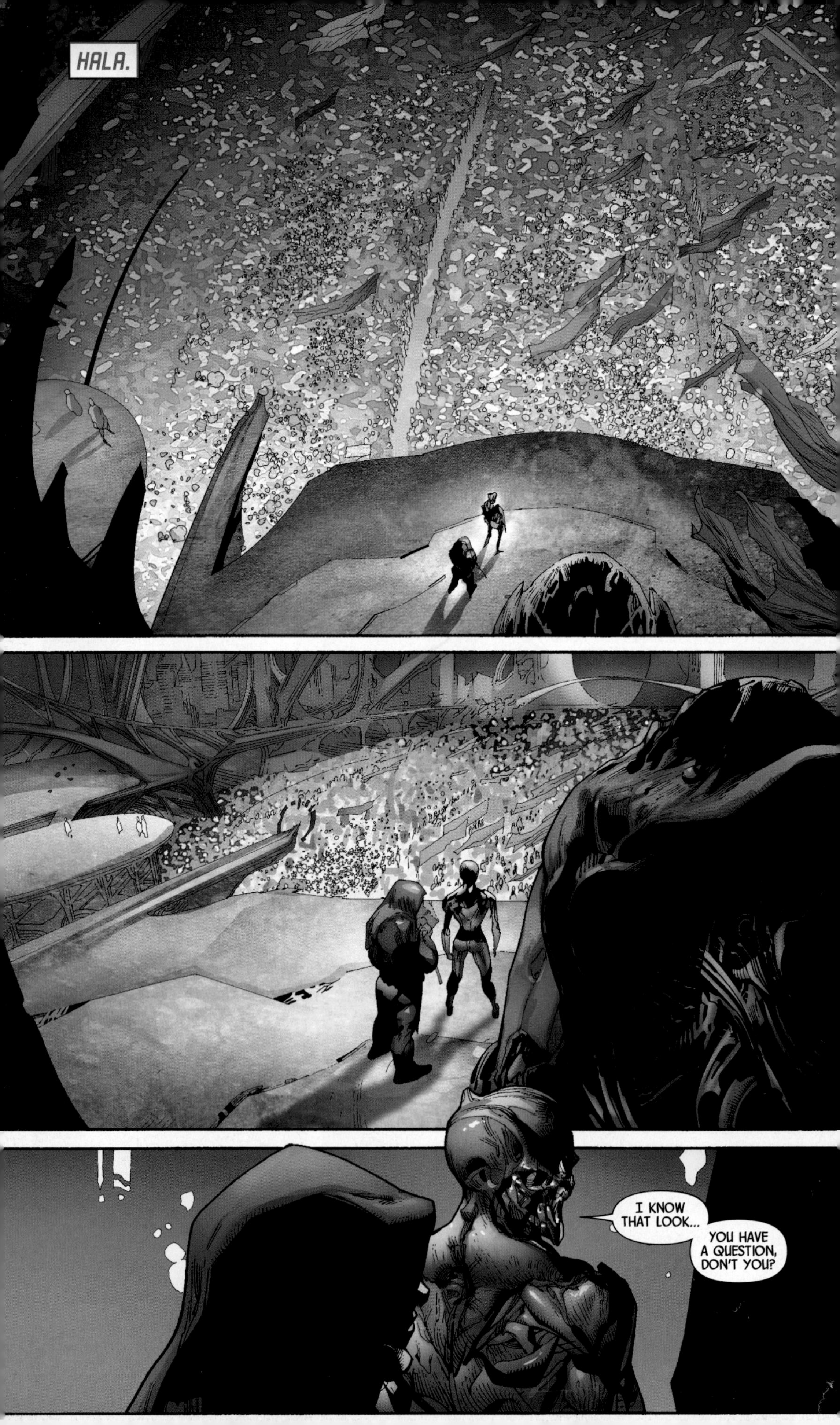
HALA.
I KNOW THAT LOOK...
YOU HAVE A QUESTION, DON'T YOU?

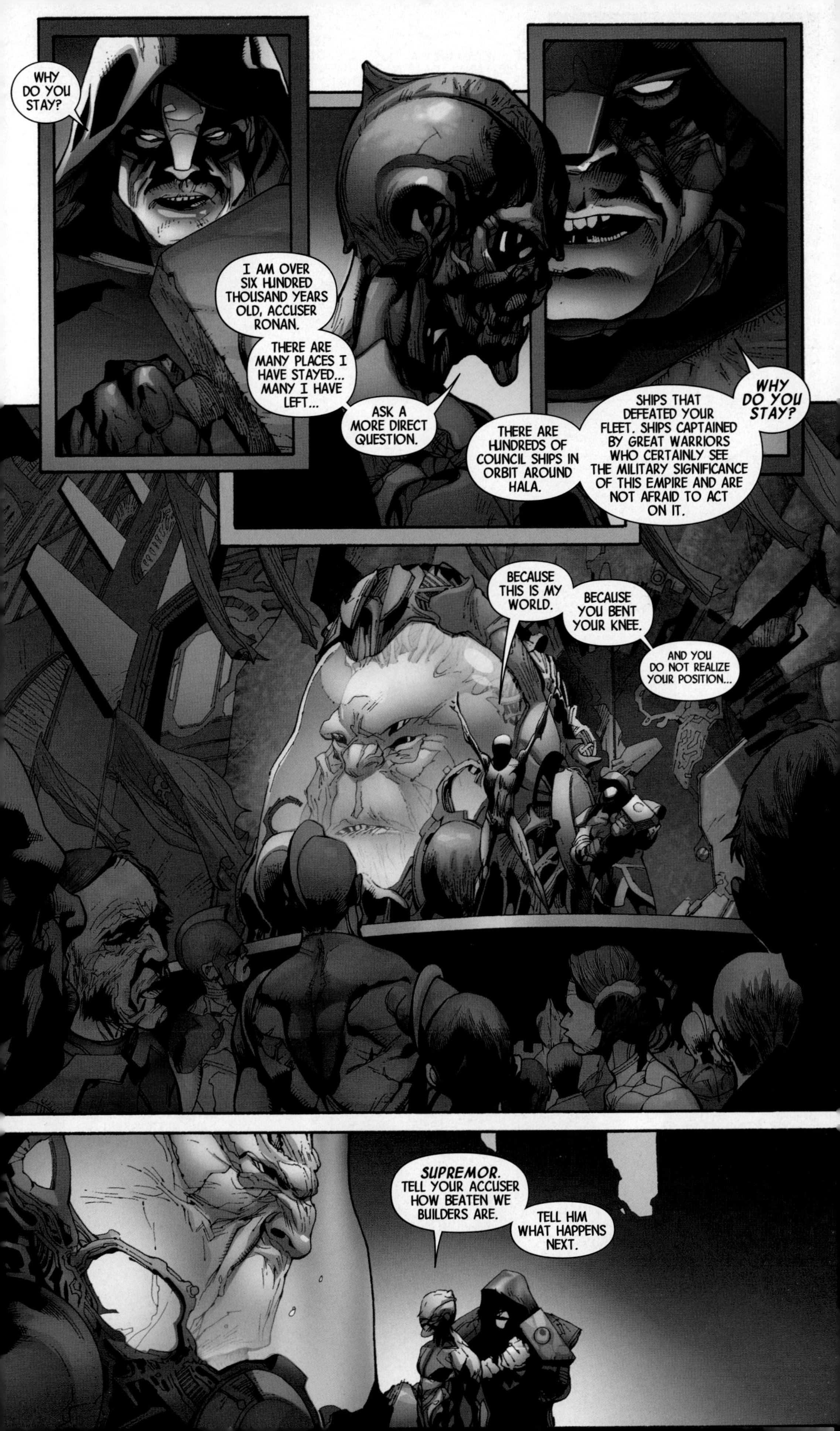
WHY DO YOU STAY?
I AM OVER SIX HUNDRED THOUSAND YEARS OLD, ACCUSER RONAN.
THERE ARE MANY PLACES I HAVE STAYED... MANY I HAVE LEFT...
ASK A MORE DIRECT QUESTION.
THERE ARE HUNDREDS OF COUNCIL SHIPS IN ORBIT AROUND HALA.
SHIPS THAT DEFEATED YOUR FLEET. SHIPS CAPTAINED BY GREAT WARRIORS WHO CERTAINLY SEE THE MILITARY SIGNIFICANCE OF THIS EMPIRE AND ARE NOT AFRAID TO ACT ON IT.
WHY DO YOU STAY?
BECAUSE THIS IS MY WORLD.
BECAUSE YOU BENT YOUR KNEE.
AND YOU DO NOT REALIZE YOUR POSITION...
SUPREMOR. TELL YOUR ACCUSER HOW BEATEN WE BUILDERS ARE.
TELL HIM WHAT HAPPENS NEXT.

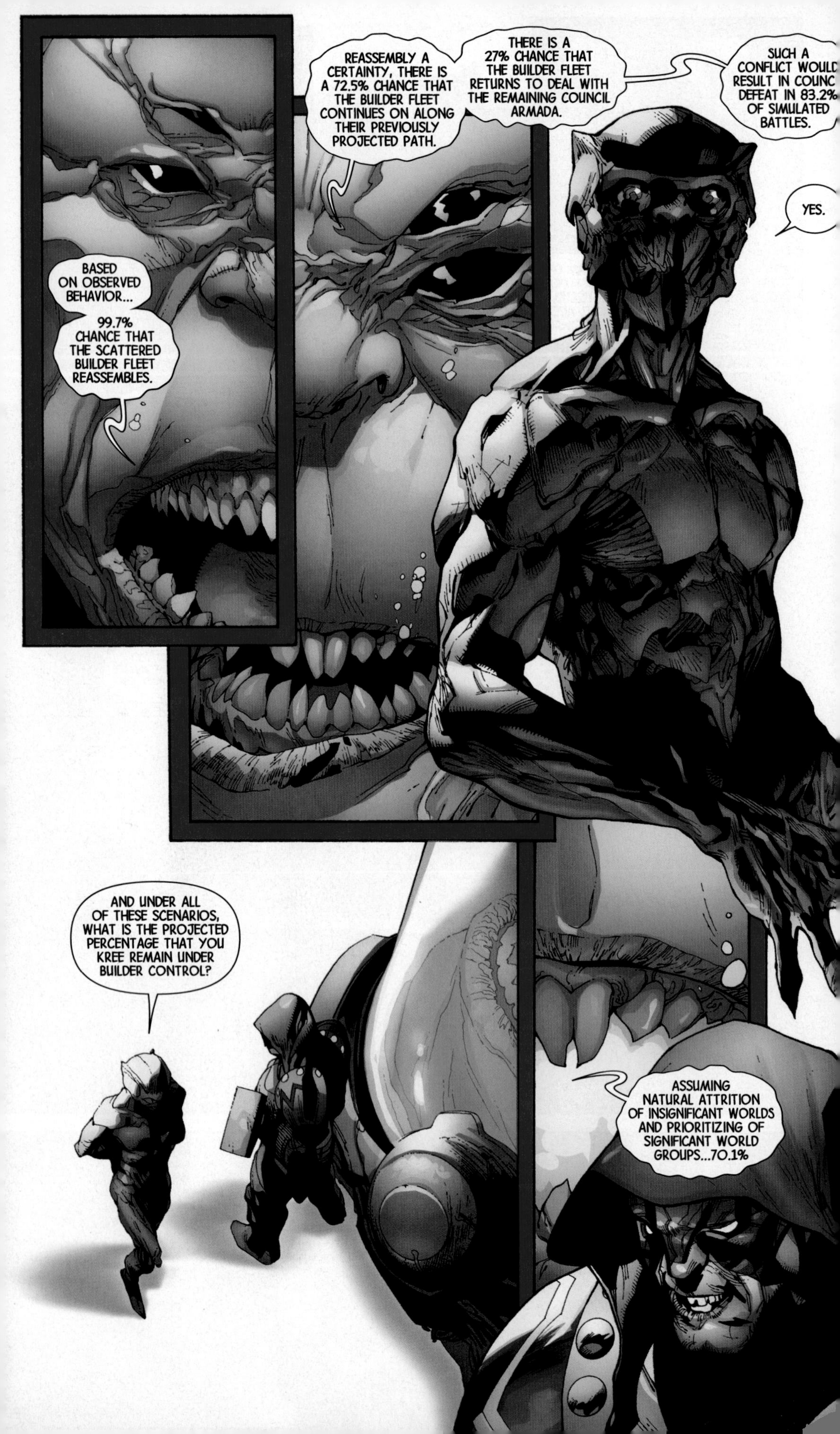
BASED ON OBSERVED BEHAVIOR...
99.7% CHANCE THAT THE SCATTERED BUILDER FLEET REASSEMBLES.
REASSEMBLY A CERTAINTY, THERE IS A 72.5% CHANCE THAT THE BUILDER FLEET CONTINUES ON ALONG THEIR PREVIOUSLY PROJECTED PATH.
THERE IS A 27% CHANCE THAT THE BUILDER FLEET RETURNS TO DEAL WITH THE REMAINING COUNCIL ARMADA.
SUCH A CONFLICT WOULD RESULT IN COUNC DEFEAT IN 83.2% OF SIMULATED BATTLES.
YES.
AND UNDER ALL OF THESE SCENARIOS, WHAT IS THE PROJECTED PERCENTAGE THAT YOU KREE REMAIN UNDER BUILDER CONTROL?
ASSUMING NATURAL ATTRITION OF INSIGNIFICANT WORLDS AND PRIORITIZING OF SIGNIFICANT WORLD GROUPS...70.1%

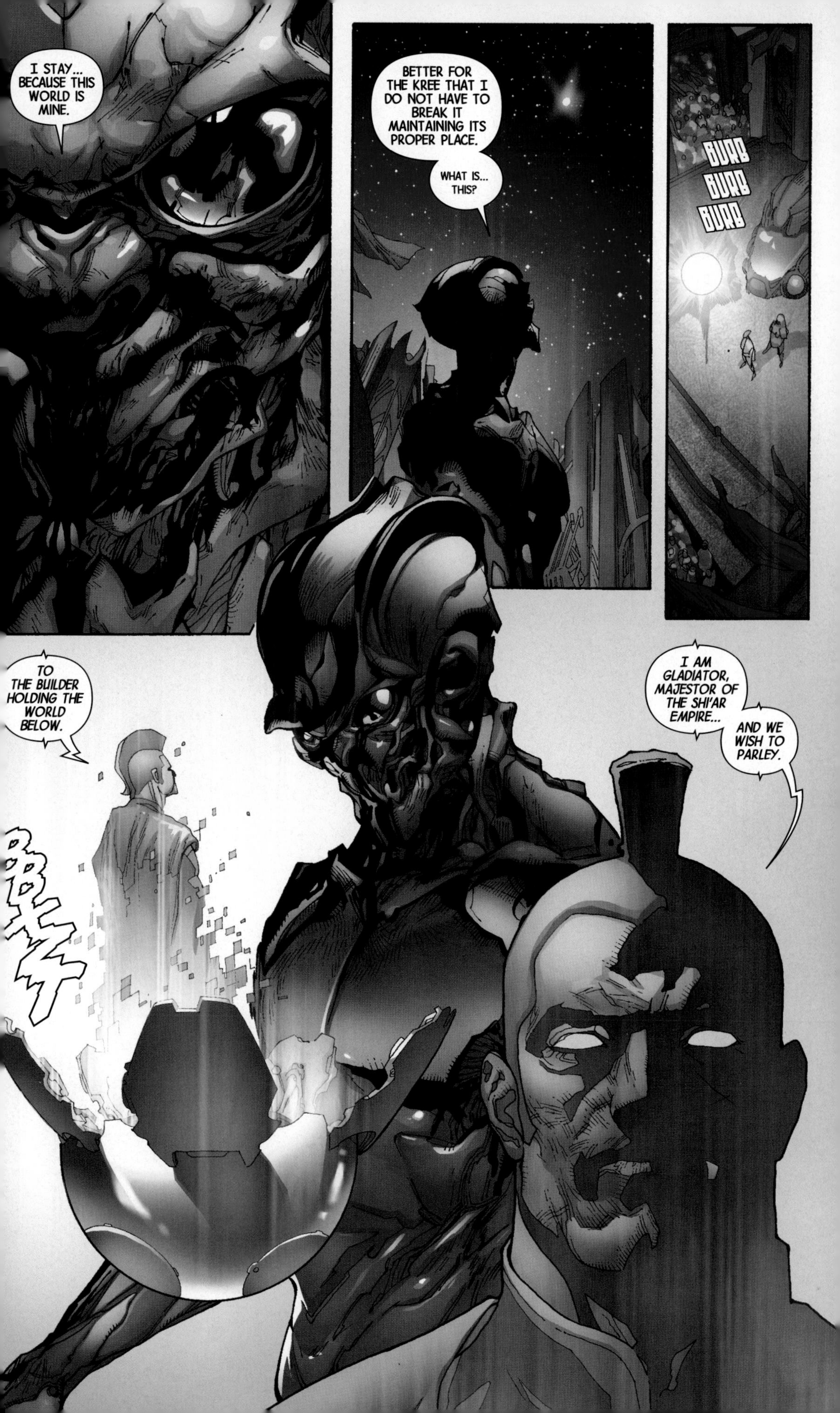
I STAY... BECAUSE THIS WORLD IS MINE.
BETTER FOR THE KREE THAT I DO NOT HAVE TO BREAK IT MAINTAINING ITS PROPER PLACE.
WHAT IS... THIS?
BURB BURB BURB
TO THE BUILDER HOLDING THE WORLD BELOW.
BBZZT
I AM GLADIATOR, MAJESTOR OF THE SHI'AR EMPIRE...
AND WE WISH TO PARLEY.

WITHOUT JUDGES
WE ARE LOST

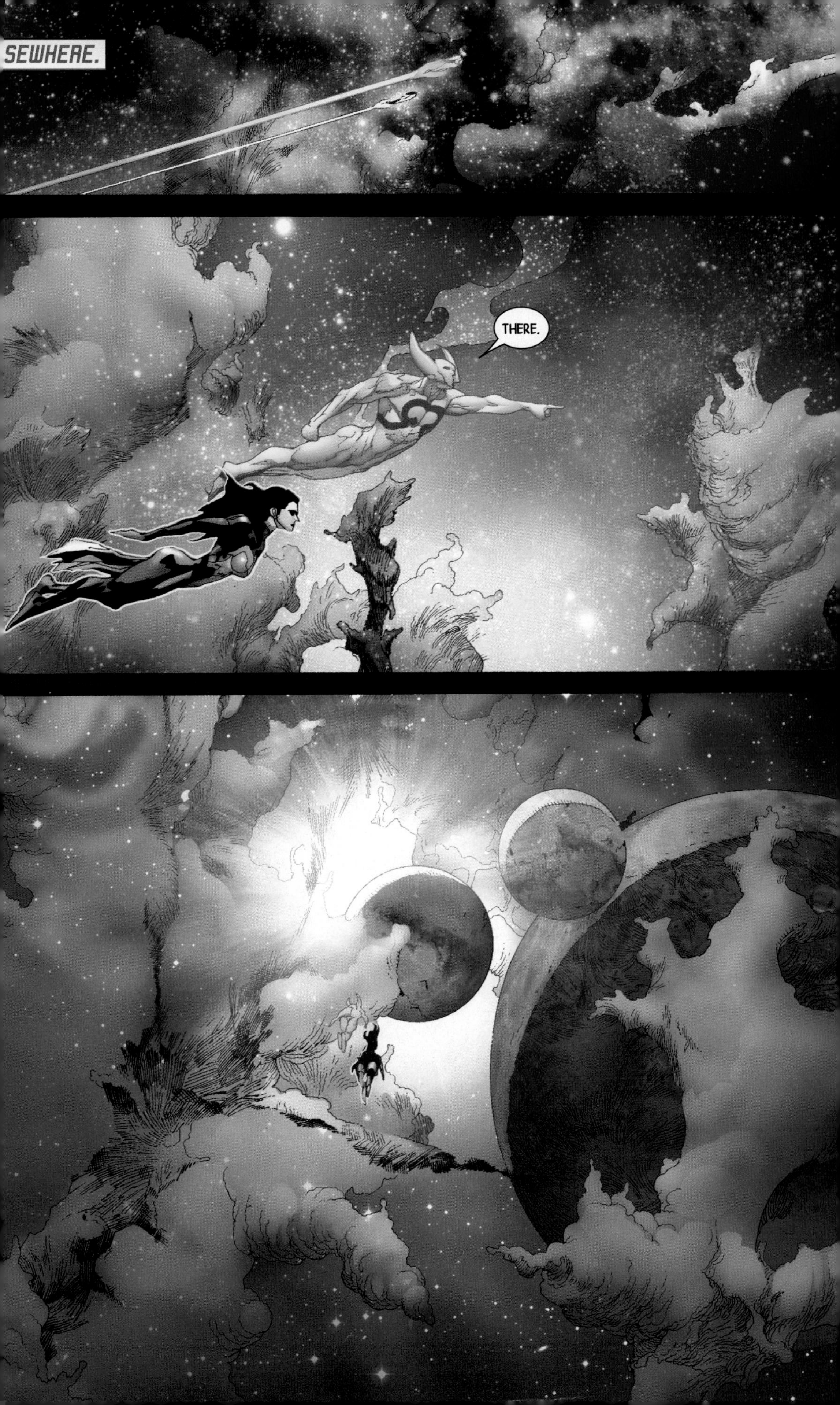
SEWHERE.
THERE.

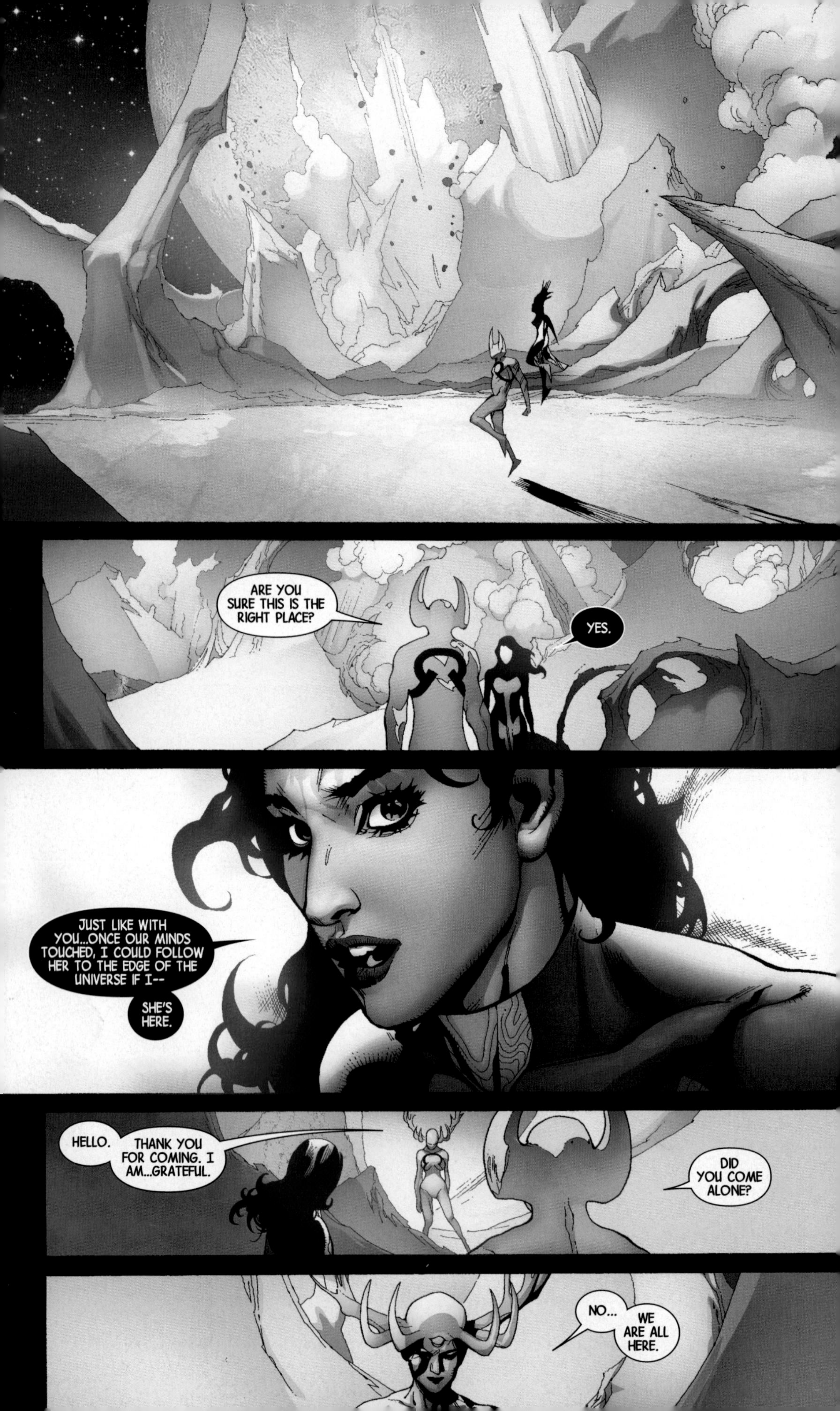
ARE YOU SURE THIS IS THE RIGHT PLACE?
YES.
JUST LIKE WITH YOU...ONCE OUR MINDS TOUCHED, I COULD FOLLOW HER TO THE EDGE OF THE UNIVERSE IF I--
SHE'S HERE.
HELLO.
THANK YOU FOR COMING. I AM...GRATEFUL.
DID YOU COME ALONE?
NO...
WE ARE ALL HERE.

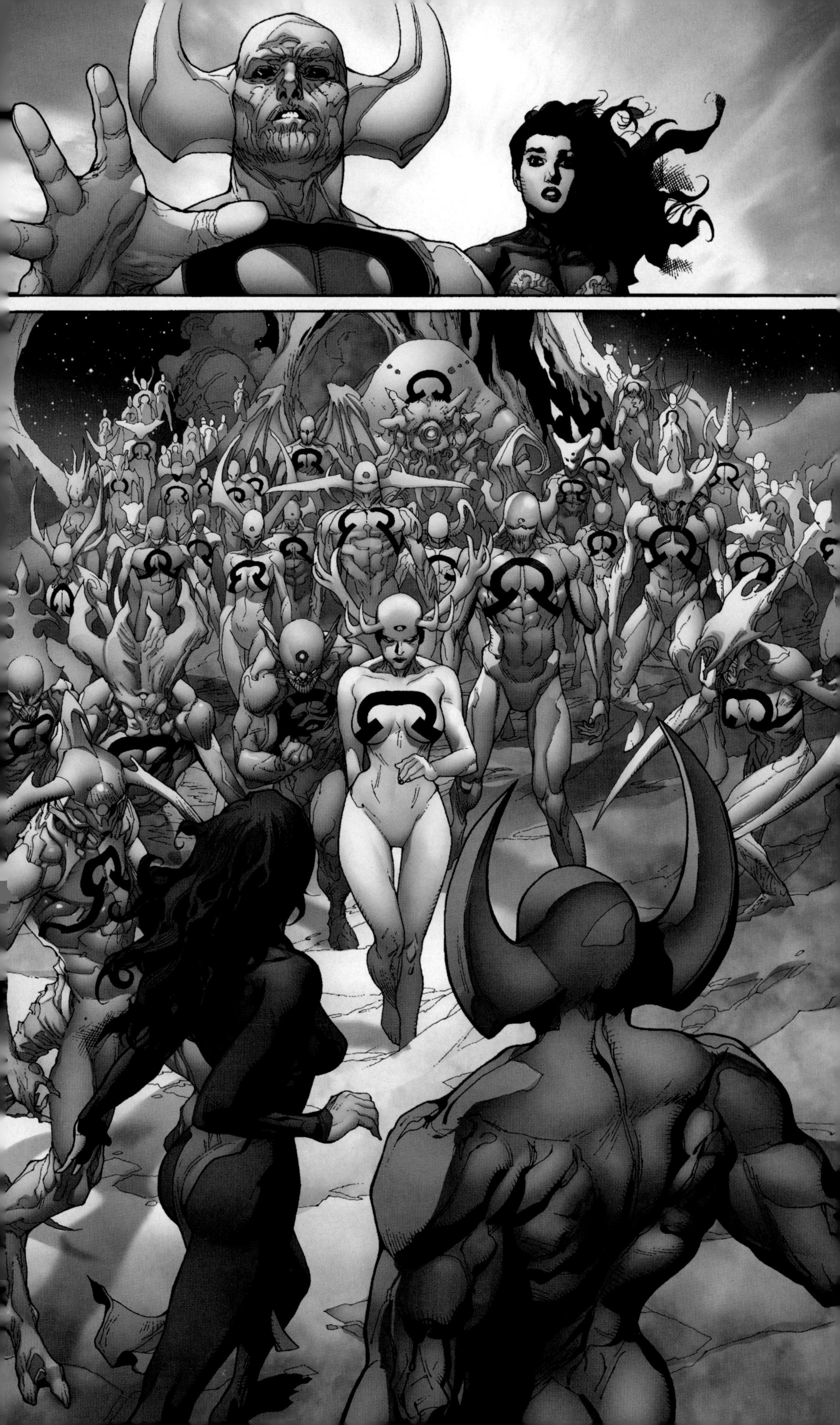

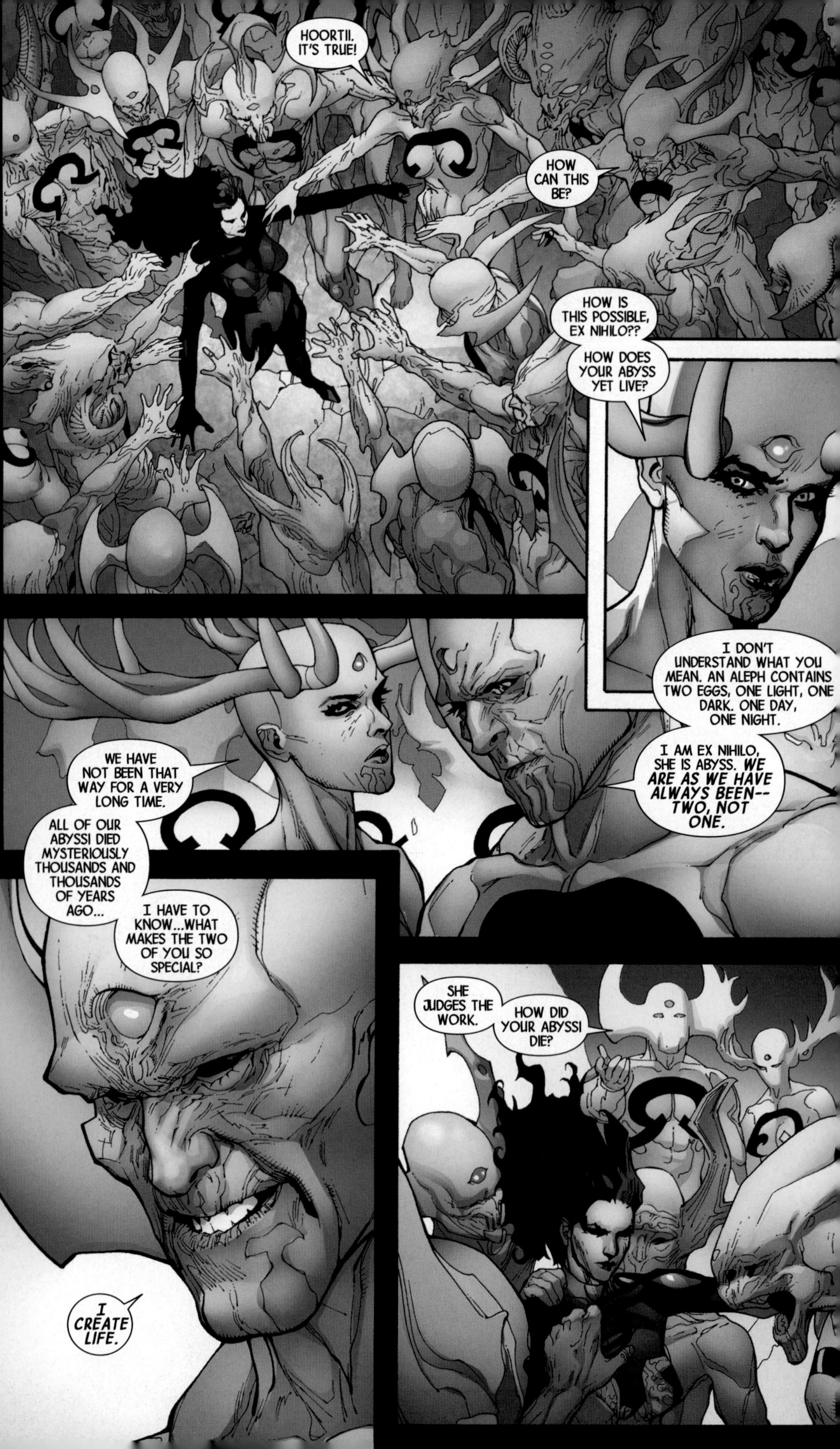
HOORTII. IT'S TRUE!
HOW CAN THIS BE?
HOW IS THIS POSSIBLE, EX NIHILO??
HOW DOES YOUR ABYSS YET LIVE?
I DON'T UNDERSTAND WHAT YOU MEAN. AN ALEPH CONTAINS TWO EGGS, ONE LIGHT, ONE DARK. ONE DAY, ONE NIGHT.
I AM EX NIHILO, SHE IS ABYSS. WE ARE AS WE HAVE ALWAYS BEEN-- TWO, NOT ONE.
WE HAVE NOT BEEN THAT WAY FOR A VERY LONG TIME.
ALL OF OUR ABYSSI DIED MYSTERIOUSLY THOUSANDS AND THOUSANDS OF YEARS AGO...
I HAVE TO KNOW...WHAT MAKES THE TWO OF YOU SO SPECIAL?
I CREATE LIFE.
SHE JUDGES THE WORK.
HOW DID YOUR ABYSSI DIE?

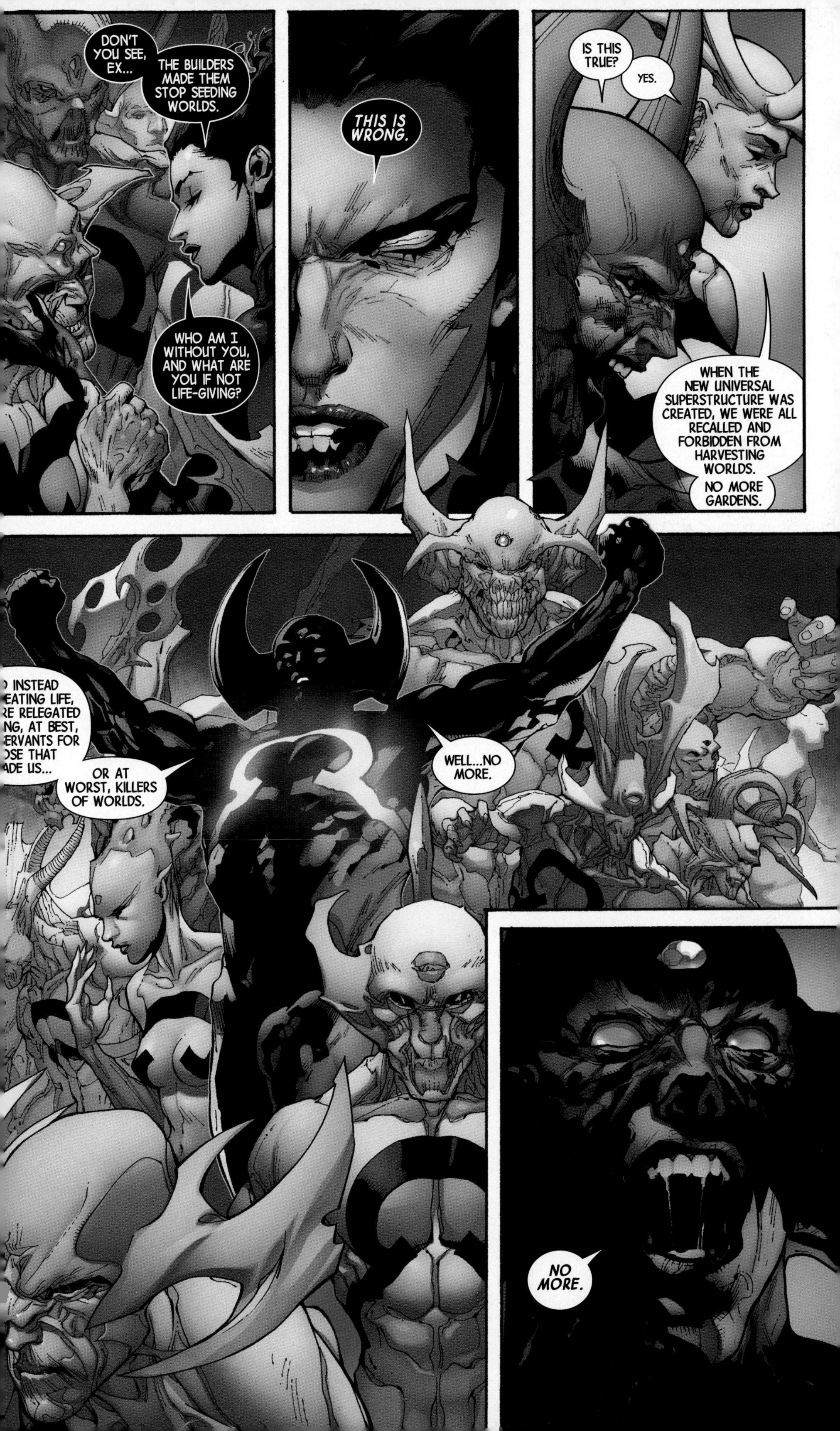

DON'T YOU SEE, EX...
THE BUILDERS MADE THEM STOP SEEDING WORLDS.
WHO AM I WITHOUT YOU, AND WHAT ARE YOU IF NOT LIFE-GIVING?
THIS IS WRONG.
IS THIS TRUE?
YES.
WHEN THE NEW UNIVERSAL SUPERSTRUCTURE WAS CREATED, WE WERE ALL RECALLED AND FORBIDDEN FROM HARVESTING WORLDS.
NO MORE GARDENS.
OR AT WORST, KILLERS OF WORLDS.
WELL...NO MORE.
NO MORE.

ONE MAN KNEELS

◆

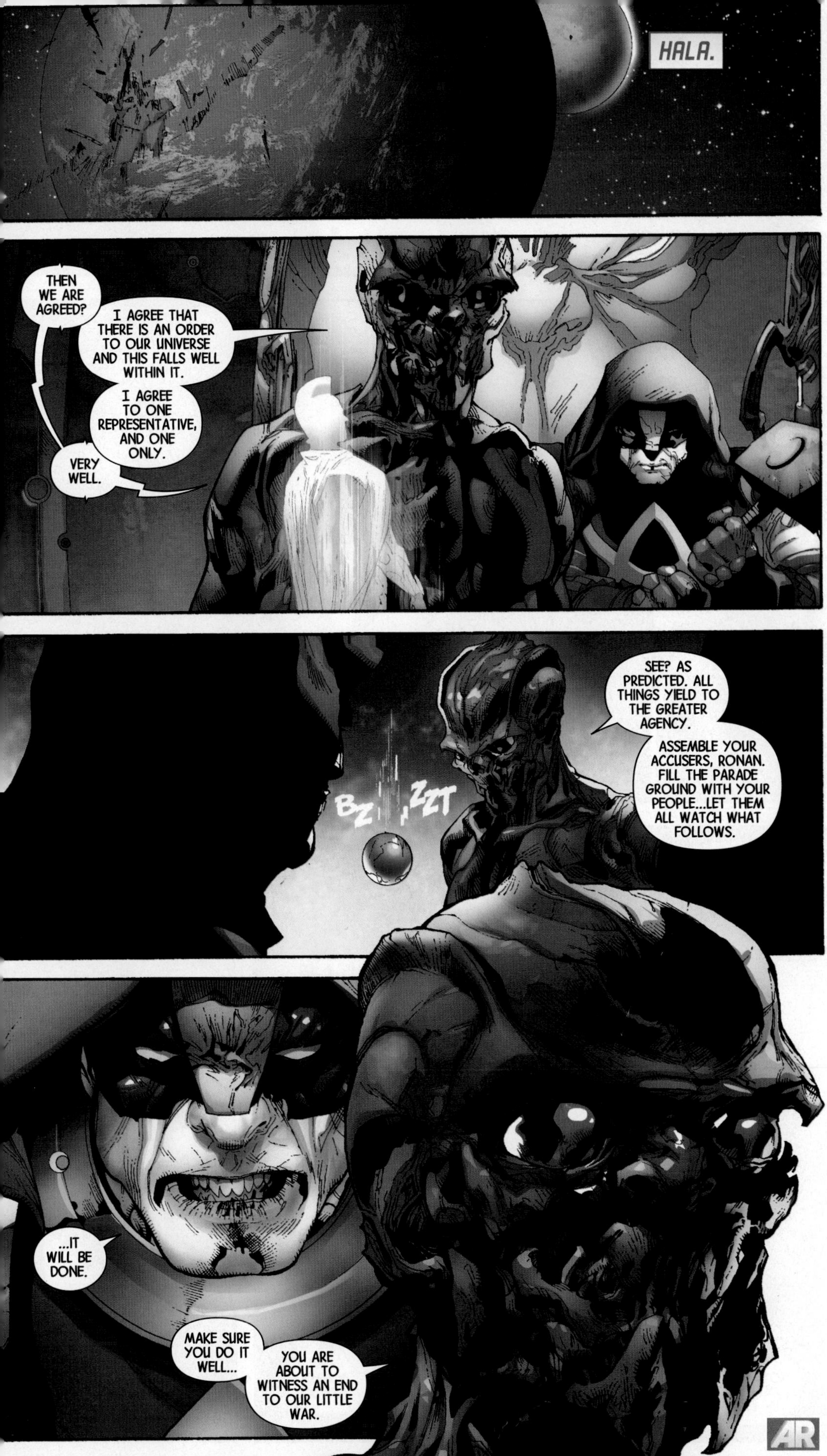
HALA.
THEN WE ARE AGREED?
I AGREE THAT THERE IS AN ORDER TO OUR UNIVERSE AND THIS FALLS WELL WITHIN IT.
I AGREE TO ONE REPRESENTATIVE, AND ONE ONLY.
VERY WELL.
SEE? AS PREDICTED. ALL THINGS YIELD TO THE GREATER AGENCY.
ASSEMBLE YOUR ACCUSERS, RONAN. FILL THE PARADE GROUND WITH YOUR PEOPLE...LET THEM ALL WATCH WHAT FOLLOWS.
BZZZZT
...IT WILL BE DONE.
MAKE SURE YOU DO IT WELL...
YOU ARE ABOUT TO WITNESS AN END TO OUR LITTLE WAR.
AR

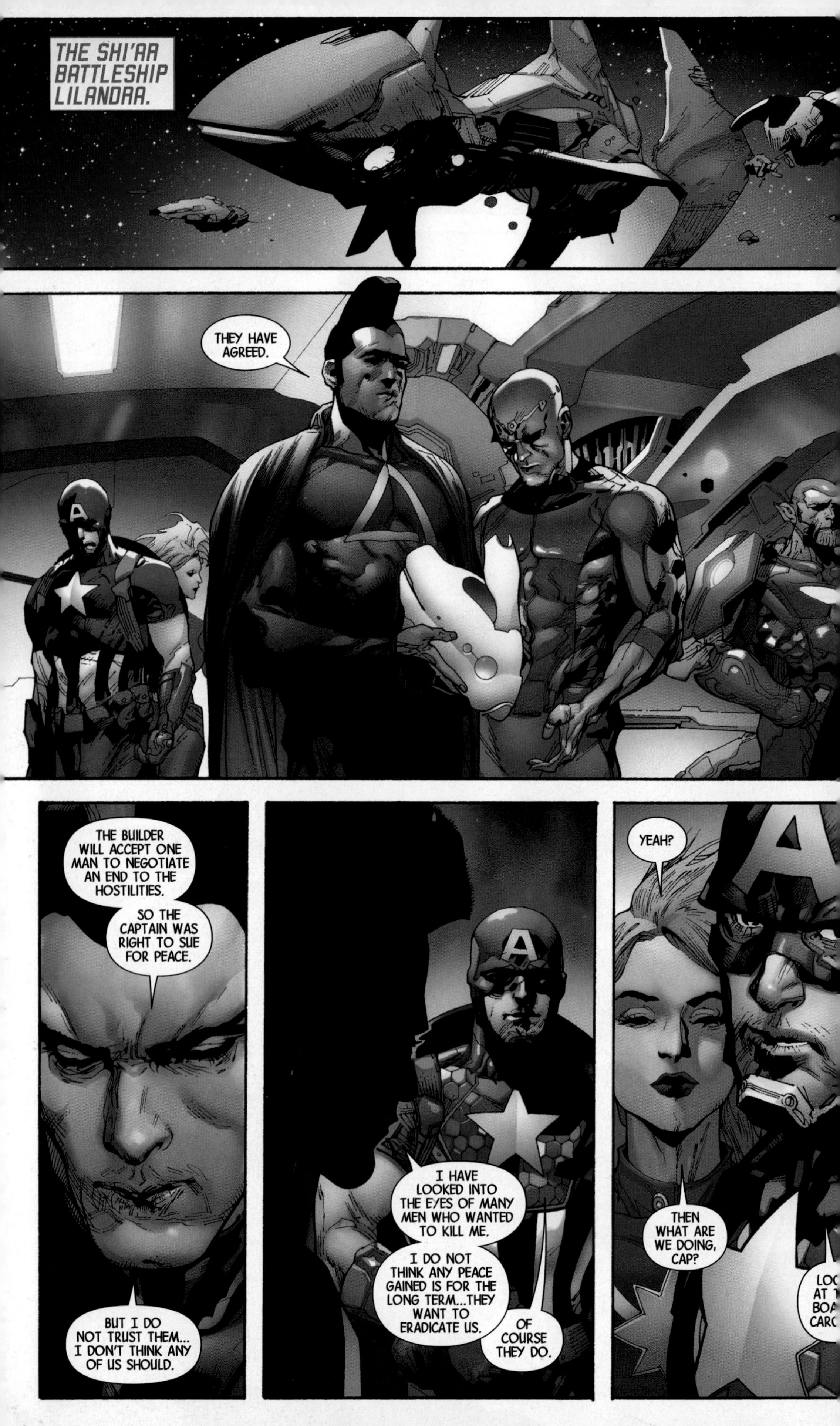
THE SHI'AR BATTLESHIP LILANDRA.
THEY HAVE AGREED.
THE BUILDER WILL ACCEPT ONE MAN TO NEGOTIATE AN END TO THE HOSTILITIES.
SO THE CAPTAIN WAS RIGHT TO SUE FOR PEACE.
BUT I DO NOT TRUST THEM... I DON'T THINK ANY OF US SHOULD.
I HAVE LOOKED INTO THE EYES OF MANY MEN WHO WANTED TO KILL ME.
I DO NOT THINK ANY PEACE GAINED IS FOR THE LONG TERM...THEY WANT TO ERADICATE US.
OF COURSE THEY DO.
YEAH?
THEN WHAT ARE WE DOING, CAP?

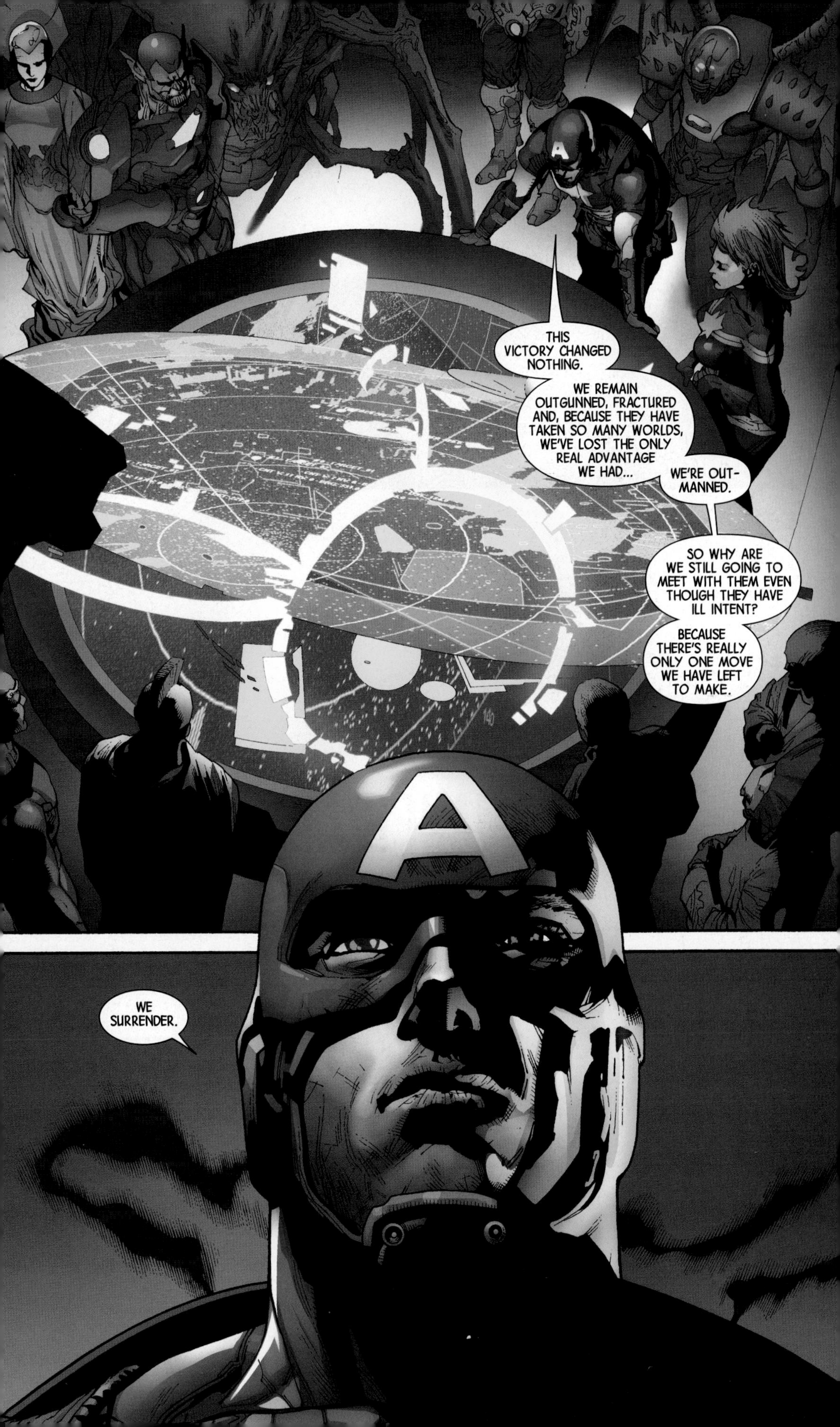

THIS VICTORY CHANGED NOTHING.
WE REMAIN OUTGUNNED, FRACTURED AND, BECAUSE THEY HAVE TAKEN SO MANY WORLDS, WE'VE LOST THE ONLY REAL ADVANTAGE WE HAD...
WE'RE OUT-MANNED.
SO WHY ARE WE STILL GOING TO MEET WITH THEM EVEN THOUGH THEY HAVE ILL INTENT?
BECAUSE THERE'S REALLY ONLY ONE MOVE WE HAVE LEFT TO MAKE.
WE SURRENDER.

"EMANCIPATION"

PREVIOUSLY IN
INFINITY

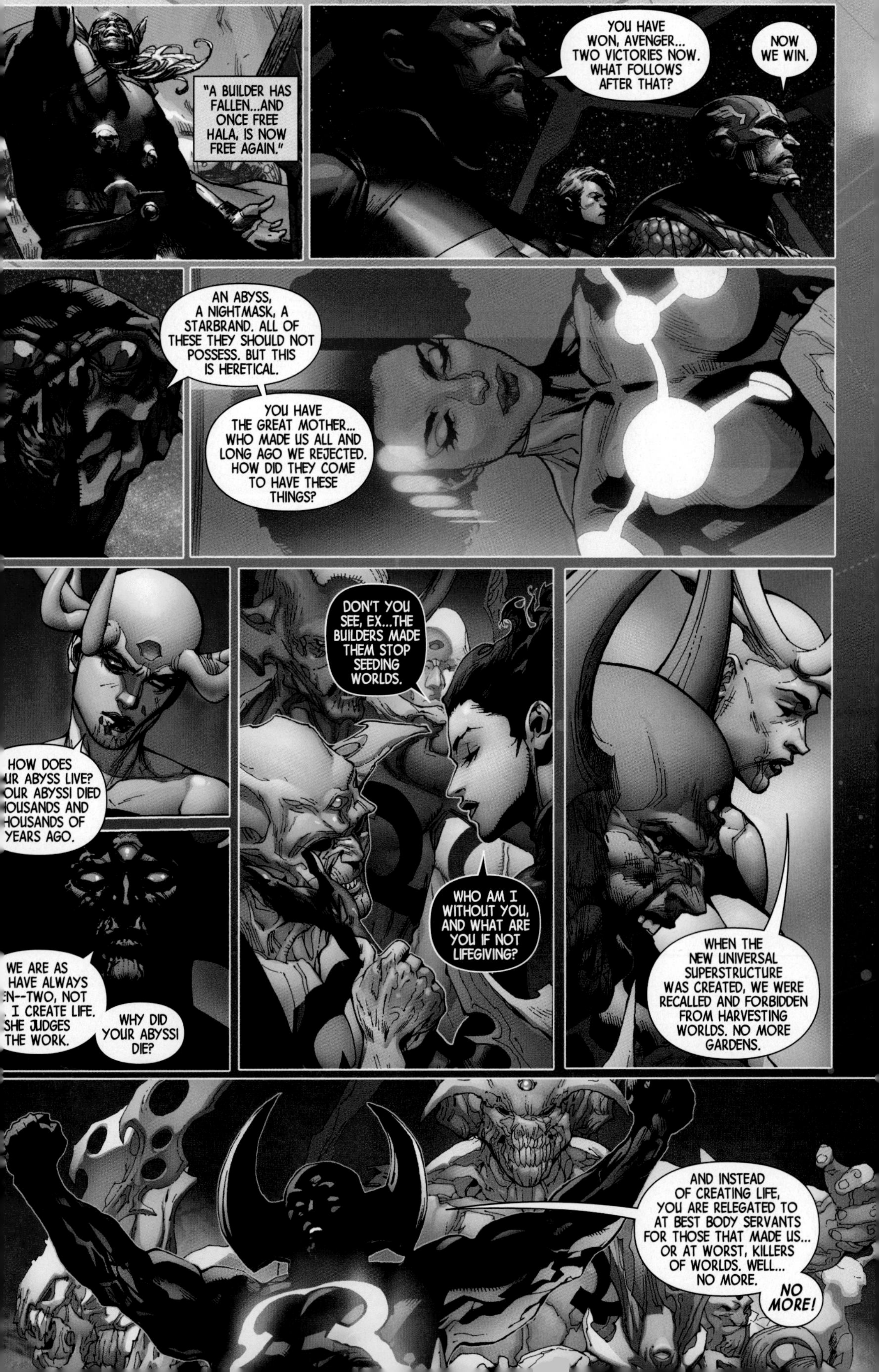
"A BUILDER HAS FALLEN...AND ONCE FREE HALA, IS NOW FREE AGAIN."
YOU HAVE WON, AVENGER... TWO VICTORIES NOW. WHAT FOLLOWS AFTER THAT?
NOW WE WIN.
AN ABYSS, A NIGHTMASK, A STARBRAND. ALL OF THESE THEY SHOULD NOT POSSESS. BUT THIS IS HERETICAL.
YOU HAVE THE GREAT MOTHER... WHO MADE US ALL AND LONG AGO WE REJECTED. HOW DID THEY COME TO HAVE THESE THINGS?
HOW DOES UR ABYSS LIVE? OUR ABYSSI DIED HOUSANDS AND HOUSANDS OF YEARS AGO.
WE ARE AS HAVE ALWAYS EN--TWO, NOT I CREATE LIFE. SHE JUDGES THE WORK.
WHY DID YOUR ABYSSI DIE?
DON'T YOU SEE, EX...THE BUILDERS MADE THEM STOP SEEDING WORLDS.
WHO AM I WITHOUT YOU, AND WHAT ARE YOU IF NOT LIFEGIVING?
WHEN THE NEW UNIVERSAL SUPERSTRUCTURE WAS CREATED, WE WERE RECALLED AND FORBIDDEN FROM HARVESTING WORLDS. NO MORE GARDENS.
AND INSTEAD OF CREATING LIFE, YOU ARE RELEGATED TO AT BEST BODY SERVANTS FOR THOSE THAT MADE US... OR AT WORST, KILLERS OF WORLDS. WELL... NO MORE.
NO MORE!

CAST

THE AVENGERS

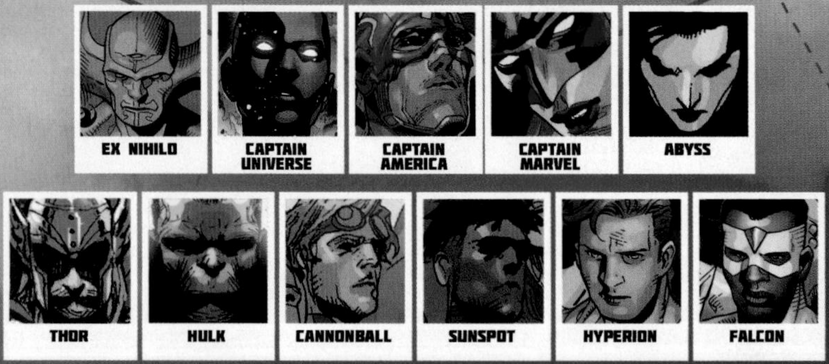

EX NIHILO · CAPTAIN UNIVERSE · CAPTAIN AMERICA · CAPTAIN MARVEL · ABYSS

THOR · HULK · CANNONBALL · SUNSPOT · HYPERION · FALCON

THE BUILDERS

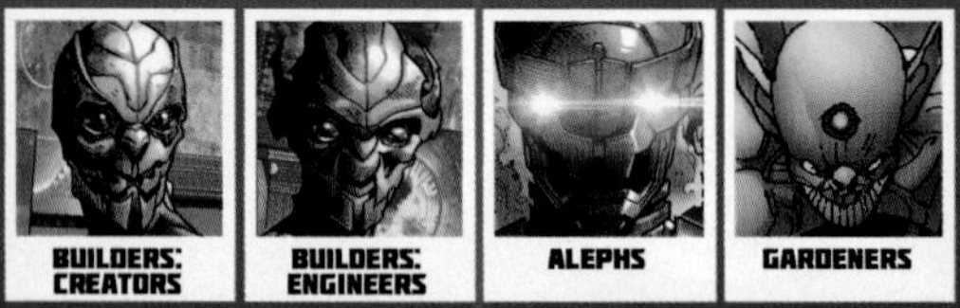

BUILDERS: CREATORS · BUILDERS: ENGINEERS · ALEPHS · GARDENERS

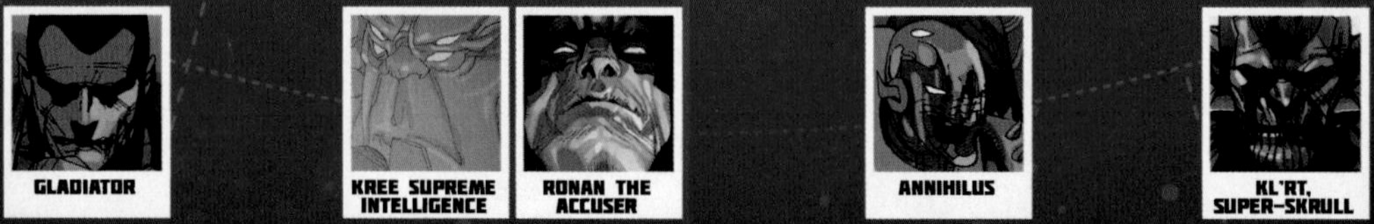

GLADIATOR · KREE SUPREME INTELLIGENCE · RONAN THE ACCUSER · ANNIHILUS · KL'RT, SUPER-SKRULL

SHI'AR IMPERIAL GUARD

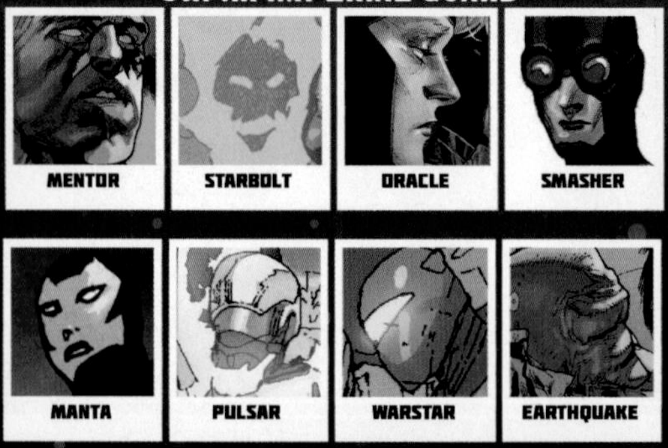

MENTOR · STARBOLT · ORACLE · SMASHER

MANTA · PULSAR · WARSTAR · EARTHQUAKE

SPACEKNIGHTS

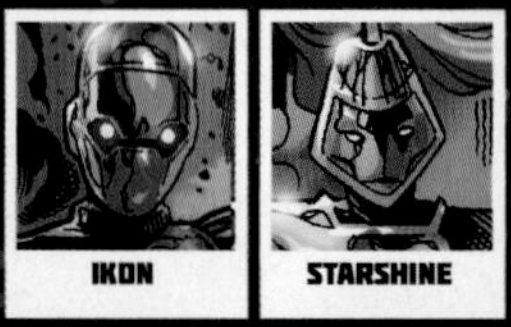

IKON · STARSHINE

THE PROMISE OF
THE UNIVERSE

◆

THE SHI'AR BATTLESHIP LILANDRA.

CAPTAIN UNIVERSE SHOULD HAVE RECOVERED BY NOW.

SHE HASN'T, BECAUSE SOMETHING'S WRONG.

YES. SOMETHING'S WRONG.

THAT'S VERY ASTUTE OF YOU, EX NIHILO.

WHAT GAVE IT AWAY...

THE UNIVERSE-SPANNING WAR, PERHAPS?

ALL OF THAT... IS THE EXTERNAL EVIDENCE OF A LARGER, UNDERLYING PROBLEM.

LADY, I'VE GOT ALL THE PROBLEMS I CAN HANDLE RIGHT NOW--NO ROOM FOR ANY MORE.

BUT WHAT IF THE MOTHER COULD SOLVE ALL YOUR PROBLEMS?

I'LL BELIEVE IT WHEN I SEE IT.

THE QUESTION IS, WHEN YOU SEE IT...WILL YOU BELIEVE?

WHEN WAS THE LAST TIME YOU SAW A MIRACLE, CAPTAIN?

THE SECOND WAVE

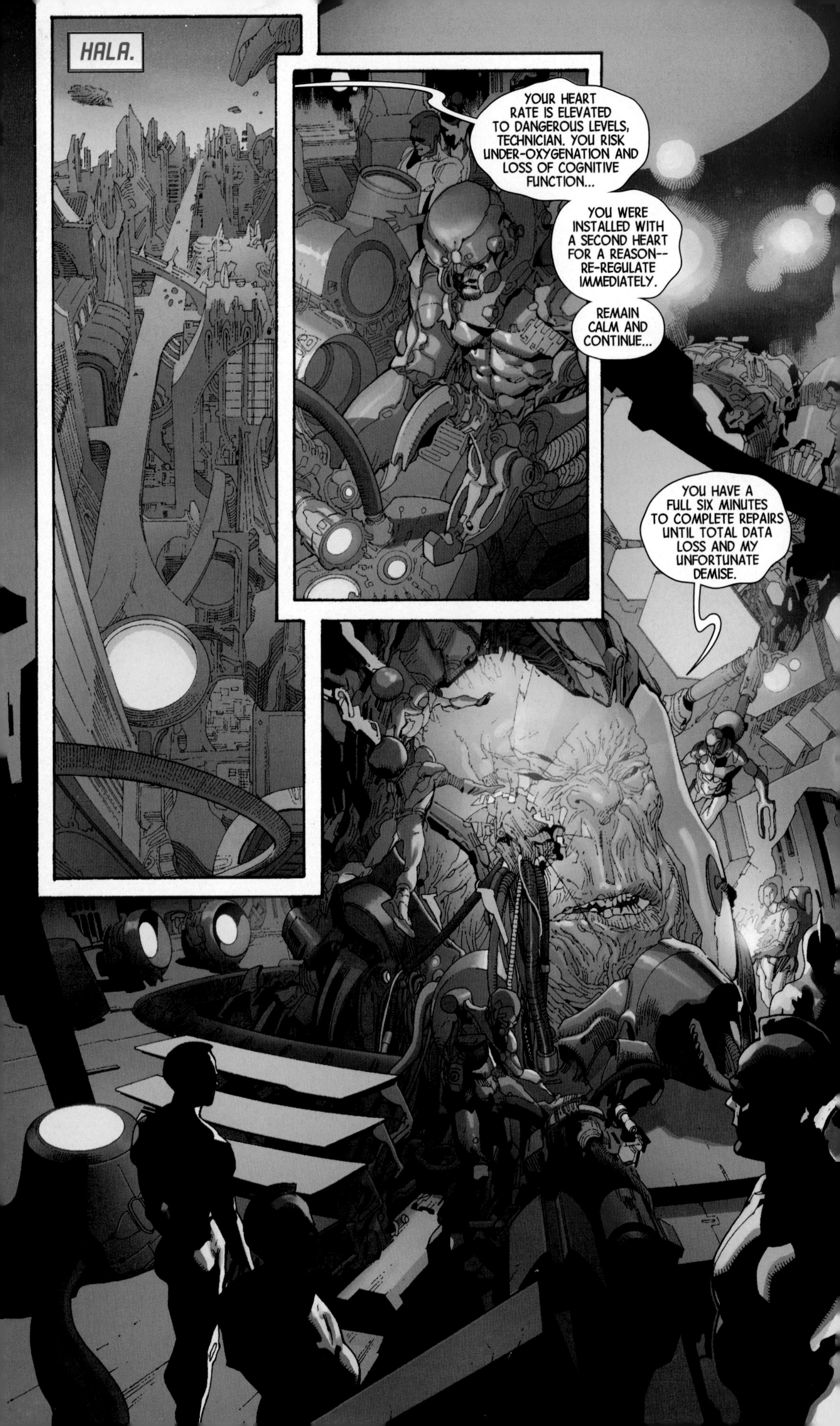
HALA.
YOUR HEART RATE IS ELEVATED TO DANGEROUS LEVELS, TECHNICIAN. YOU RISK UNDER-OXYGENATION AND LOSS OF COGNITIVE FUNCTION...
YOU WERE INSTALLED WITH A SECOND HEART FOR A REASON-- RE-REGULATE IMMEDIATELY.
REMAIN CALM AND CONTINUE...
YOU HAVE A FULL SIX MINUTES TO COMPLETE REPAIRS UNTIL TOTAL DATA LOSS AND MY UNFORTUNATE DEMISE.

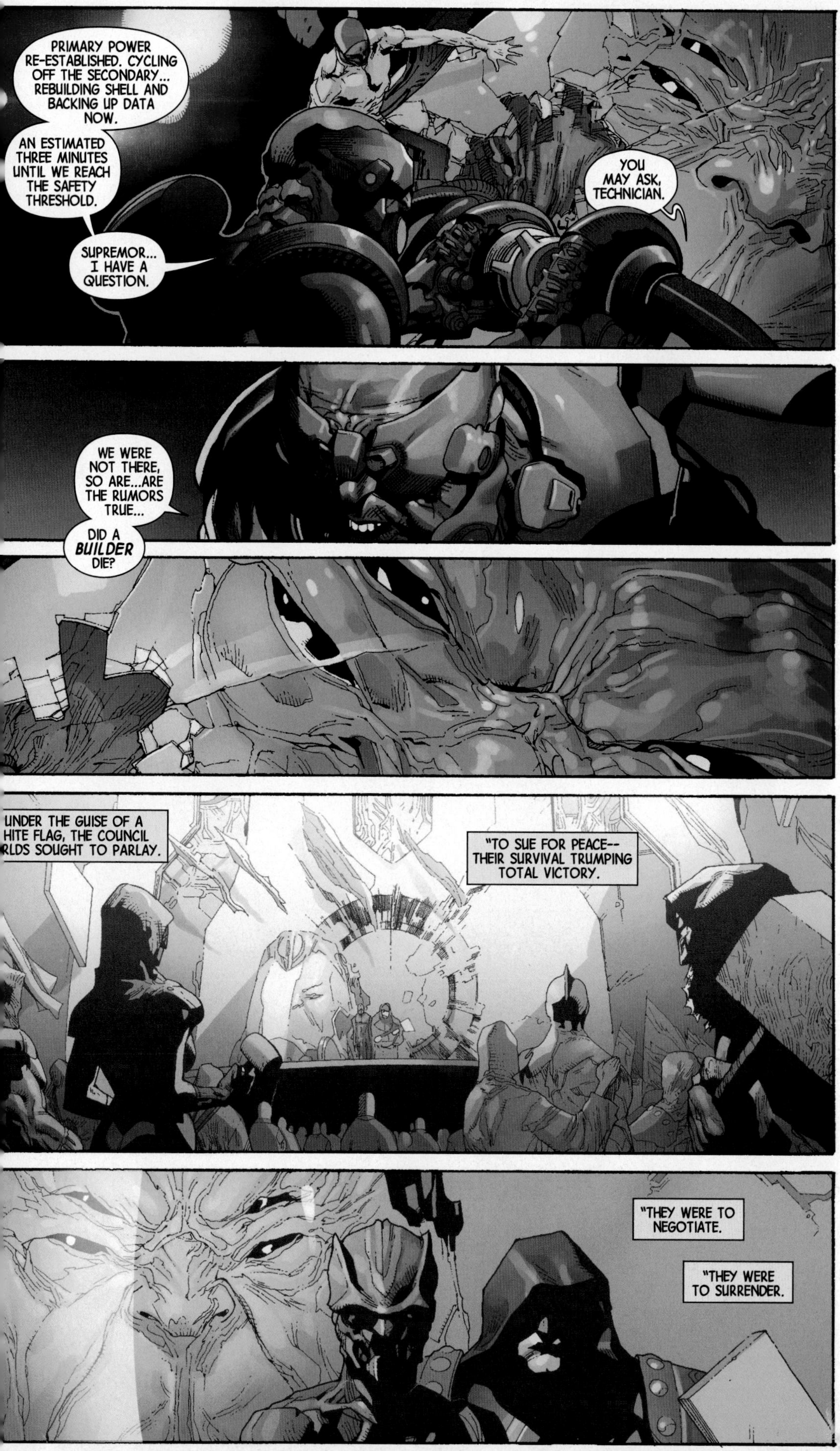
PRIMARY POWER RE-ESTABLISHED. CYCLING OFF THE SECONDARY... REBUILDING SHELL AND BACKING UP DATA NOW.
AN ESTIMATED THREE MINUTES UNTIL WE REACH THE SAFETY THRESHOLD.
SUPREMOR... I HAVE A QUESTION.
YOU MAY ASK, TECHNICIAN.
WE WERE NOT THERE, SO ARE...ARE THE RUMORS TRUE...
DID A BUILDER DIE?
UNDER THE GUISE OF A HITE FLAG, THE COUNCIL RLDS SOUGHT TO PARLAY.
"TO SUE FOR PEACE-- THEIR SURVIVAL TRUMPING TOTAL VICTORY.
"THEY WERE TO NEGOTIATE.
"THEY WERE TO SURRENDER.

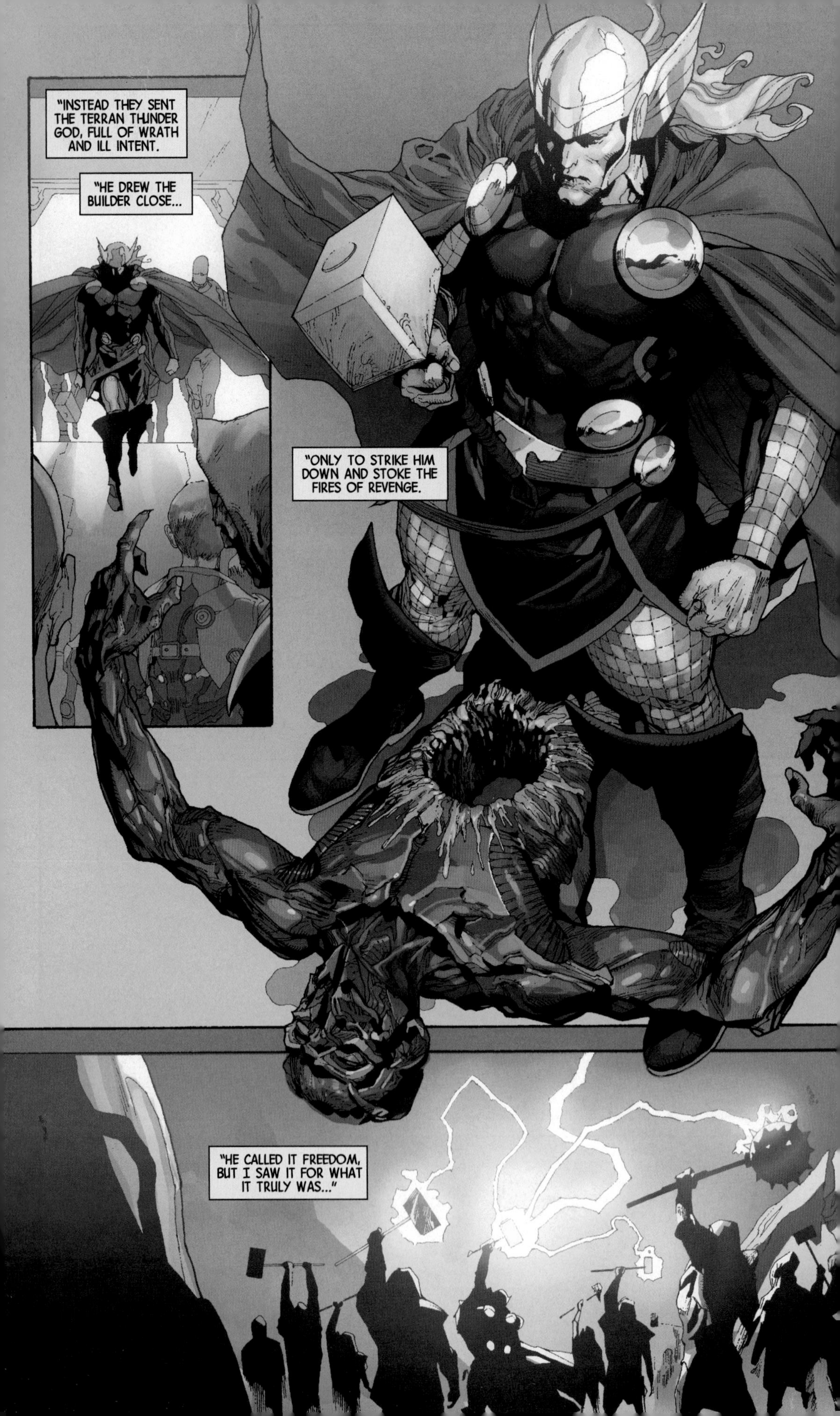
"INSTEAD THEY SENT THE TERRAN THUNDER GOD, FULL OF WRATH AND ILL INTENT.
"HE DREW THE BUILDER CLOSE...
"ONLY TO STRIKE HIM DOWN AND STOKE THE FIRES OF REVENGE.
"HE CALLED IT FREEDOM, BUT I SAW IT FOR WHAT IT TRULY WAS..."

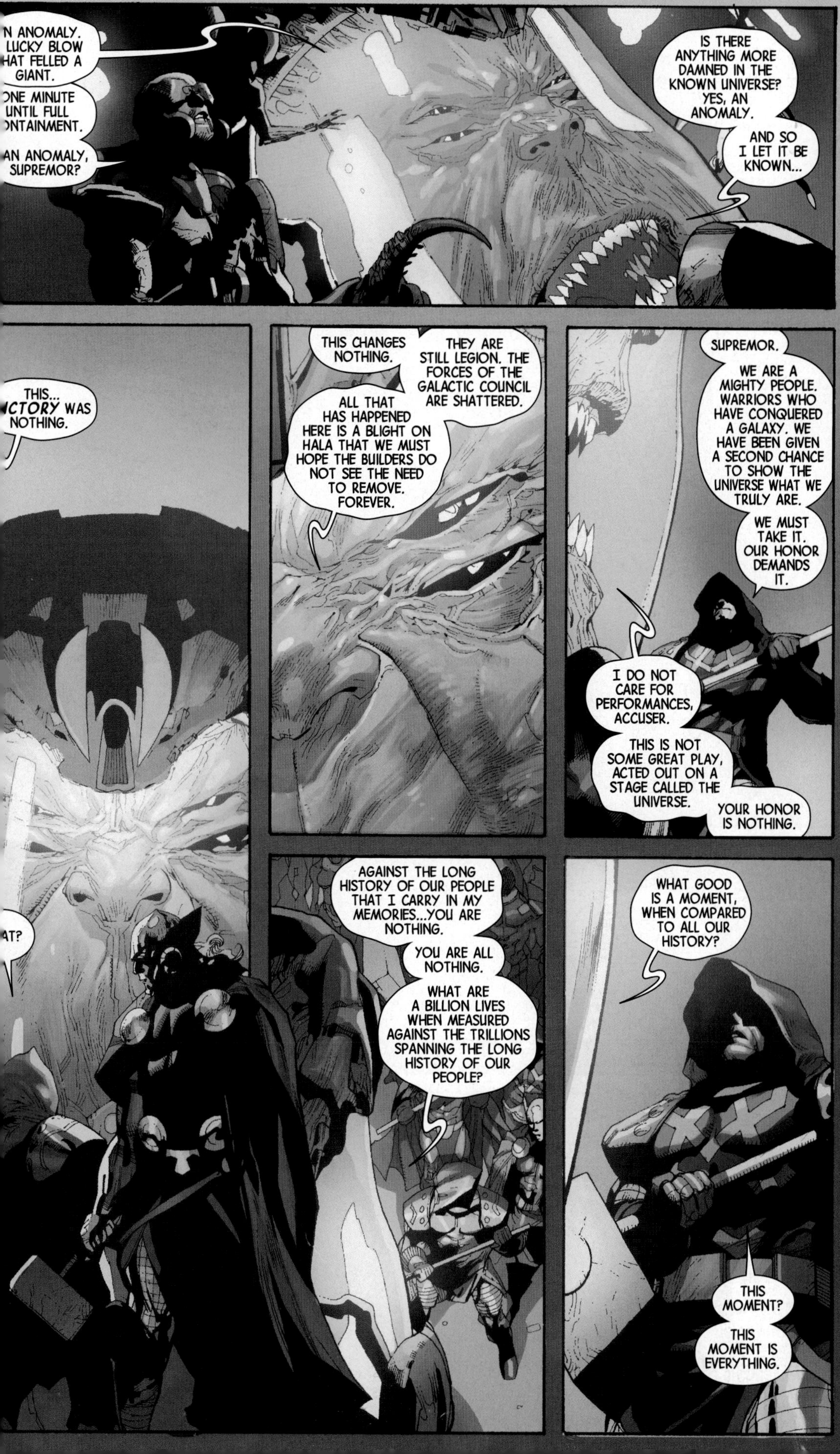

N ANOMALY. LUCKY BLOW HAT FELLED A GIANT.
ONE MINUTE UNTIL FULL ONTAINMENT.
AN ANOMALY, SUPREMOR?
IS THERE ANYTHING MORE DAMNED IN THE KNOWN UNIVERSE? YES, AN ANOMALY.
AND SO I LET IT BE KNOWN...
THIS... *CTORY* WAS NOTHING.
THIS CHANGES NOTHING.
THEY ARE STILL LEGION. THE FORCES OF THE GALACTIC COUNCIL ARE SHATTERED.
ALL THAT HAS HAPPENED HERE IS A BLIGHT ON HALA THAT WE MUST HOPE THE BUILDERS DO NOT SEE THE NEED TO REMOVE. FOREVER.
SUPREMOR.
WE ARE A MIGHTY PEOPLE. WARRIORS WHO HAVE CONQUERED A GALAXY. WE HAVE BEEN GIVEN A SECOND CHANCE TO SHOW THE UNIVERSE WHAT WE TRULY ARE.
WE MUST TAKE IT. OUR HONOR DEMANDS IT.
I DO NOT CARE FOR PERFORMANCES, ACCUSER.
THIS IS NOT SOME GREAT PLAY, ACTED OUT ON A STAGE CALLED THE UNIVERSE.
YOUR HONOR IS NOTHING.
AT?
AGAINST THE LONG HISTORY OF OUR PEOPLE THAT I CARRY IN MY MEMORIES...YOU ARE NOTHING.
YOU ARE ALL NOTHING.
WHAT ARE A BILLION LIVES WHEN MEASURED AGAINST THE TRILLIONS SPANNING THE LONG HISTORY OF OUR PEOPLE?
WHAT GOOD IS A MOMENT, WHEN COMPARED TO ALL OUR HISTORY?
THIS MOMENT?
THIS MOMENT IS EVERYTHING.

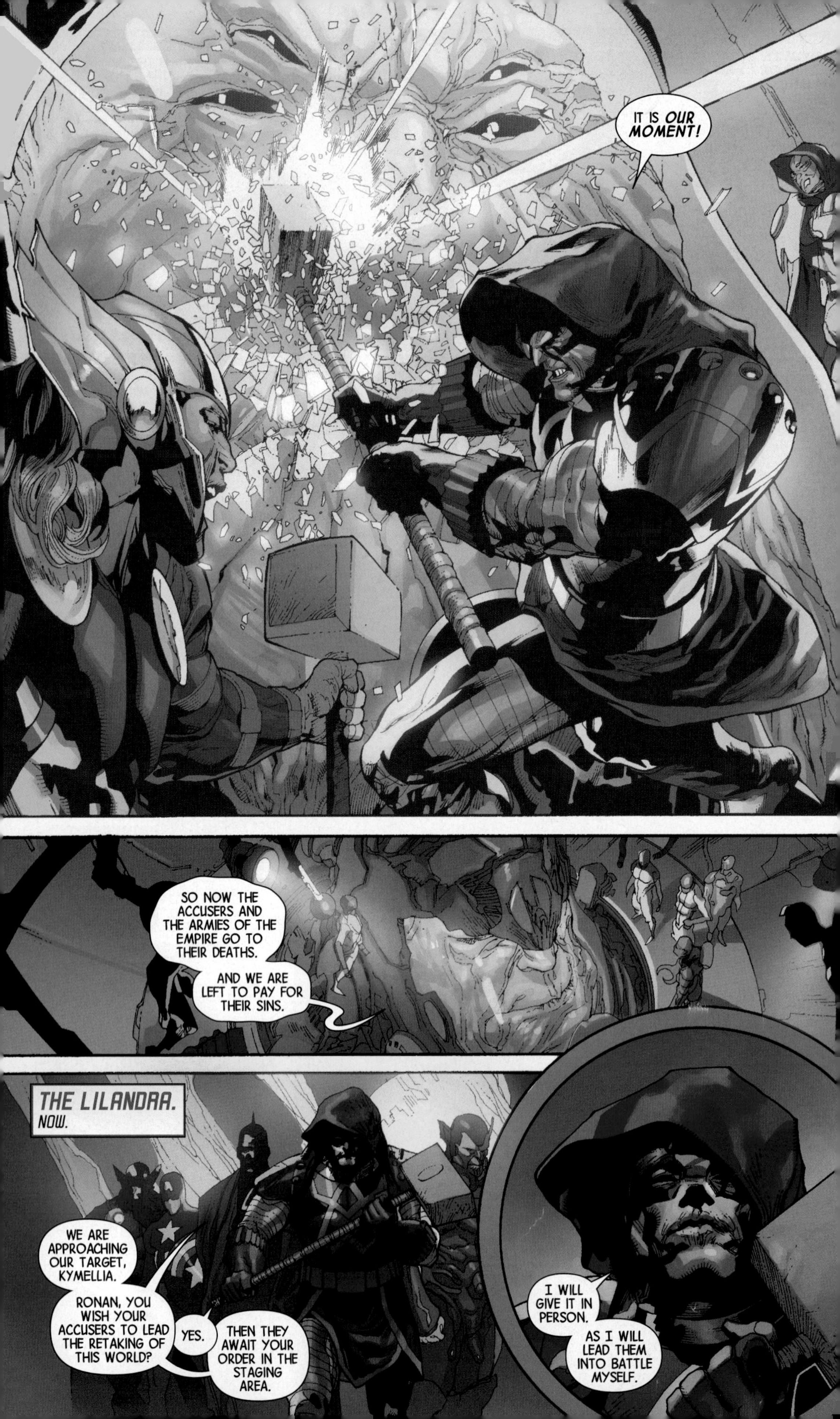
IT IS OUR MOMENT!
SO NOW THE ACCUSERS AND THE ARMIES OF THE EMPIRE GO TO THEIR DEATHS.
AND WE ARE LEFT TO PAY FOR THEIR SINS.
THE LILANDRA. NOW.
WE ARE APPROACHING OUR TARGET, KYMELLIA.
RONAN, YOU WISH YOUR ACCUSERS TO LEAD THE RETAKING OF THIS WORLD?
YES.
THEN THEY AWAIT YOUR ORDER IN THE STAGING AREA.
I WILL GIVE IT IN PERSON.
AS I WILL LEAD THEM INTO BATTLE MYSELF.

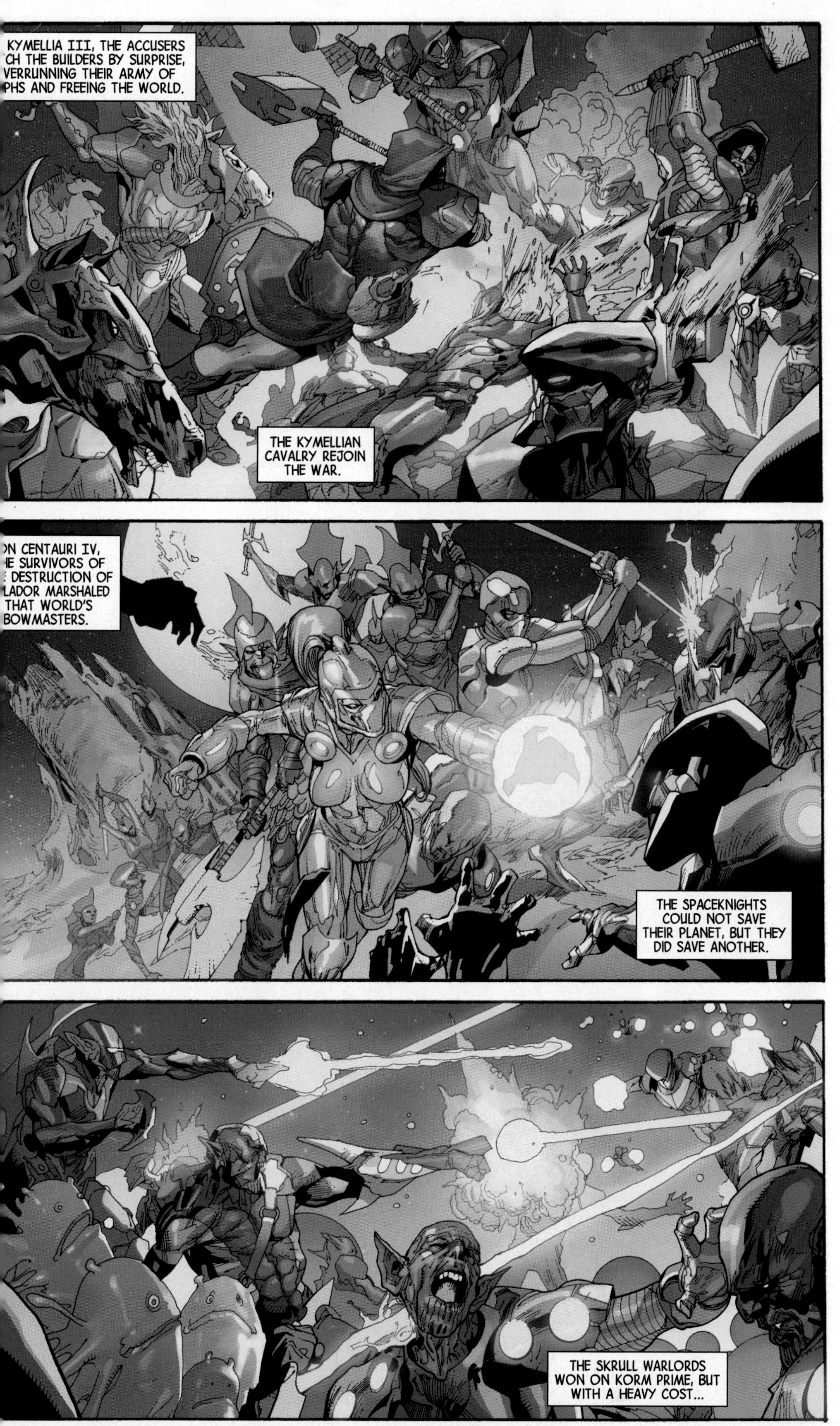
KYMELLIA III, THE ACCUSERS
CH THE BUILDERS BY SURPRISE,
VERRUNNING THEIR ARMY OF
PHS AND FREEING THE WORLD.
THE KYMELLIAN CAVALRY REJOIN THE WAR.
ON CENTAURI IV,
HE SURVIVORS OF
DESTRUCTION OF
LADOR MARSHALED
THAT WORLD'S
BOWMASTERS.
THE SPACEKNIGHTS COULD NOT SAVE THEIR PLANET, BUT THEY DID SAVE ANOTHER.
THE SKRULL WARLORDS WON ON KORM PRIME, BUT WITH A HEAVY COST...

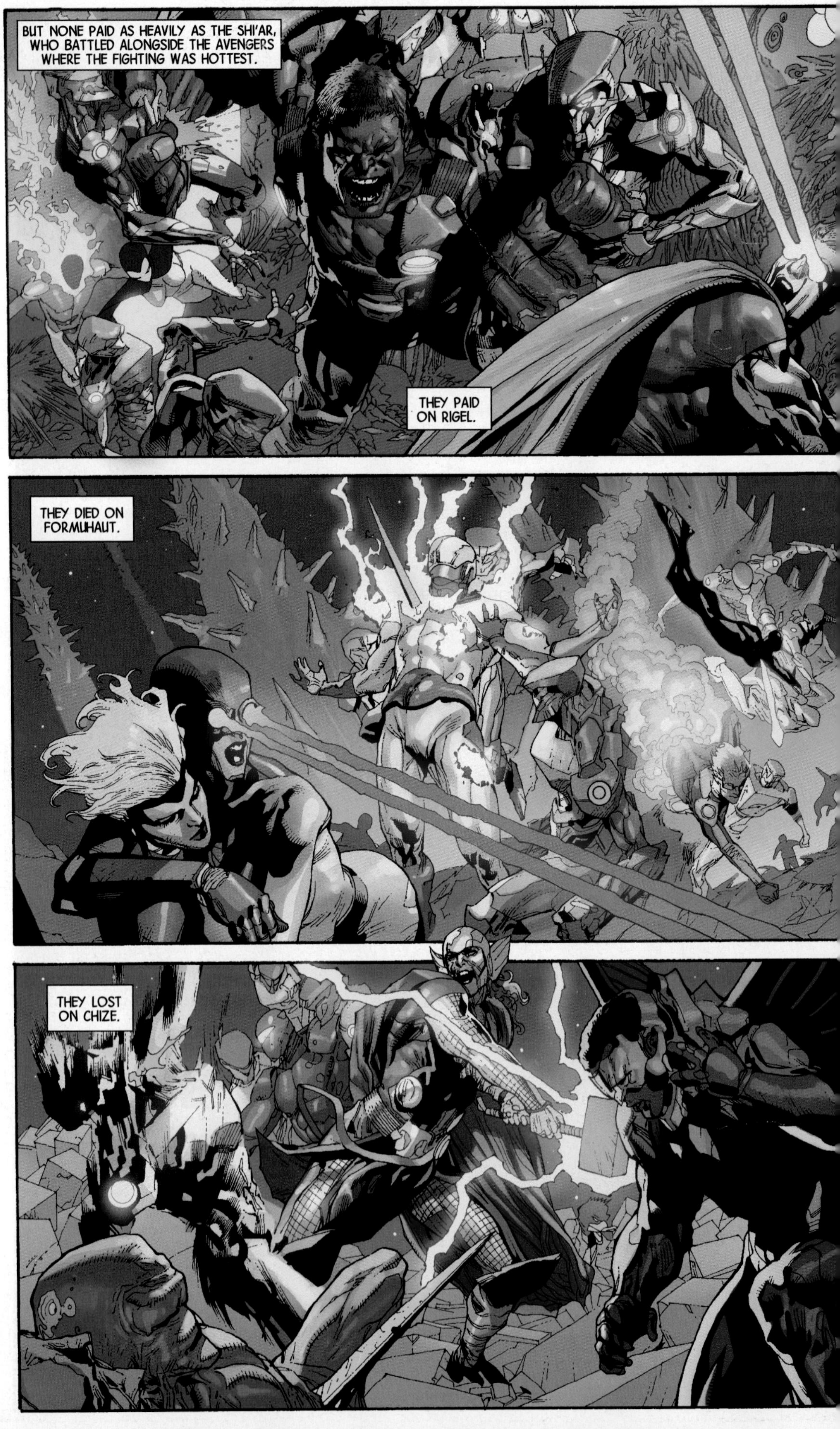
BUT NONE PAID AS HEAVILY AS THE SHI'AR, WHO BATTLED ALONGSIDE THE AVENGERS WHERE THE FIGHTING WAS HOTTEST.
THEY PAID ON RIGEL.
THEY DIED ON FORMUHAUT.
THEY LOST ON CHIZE.

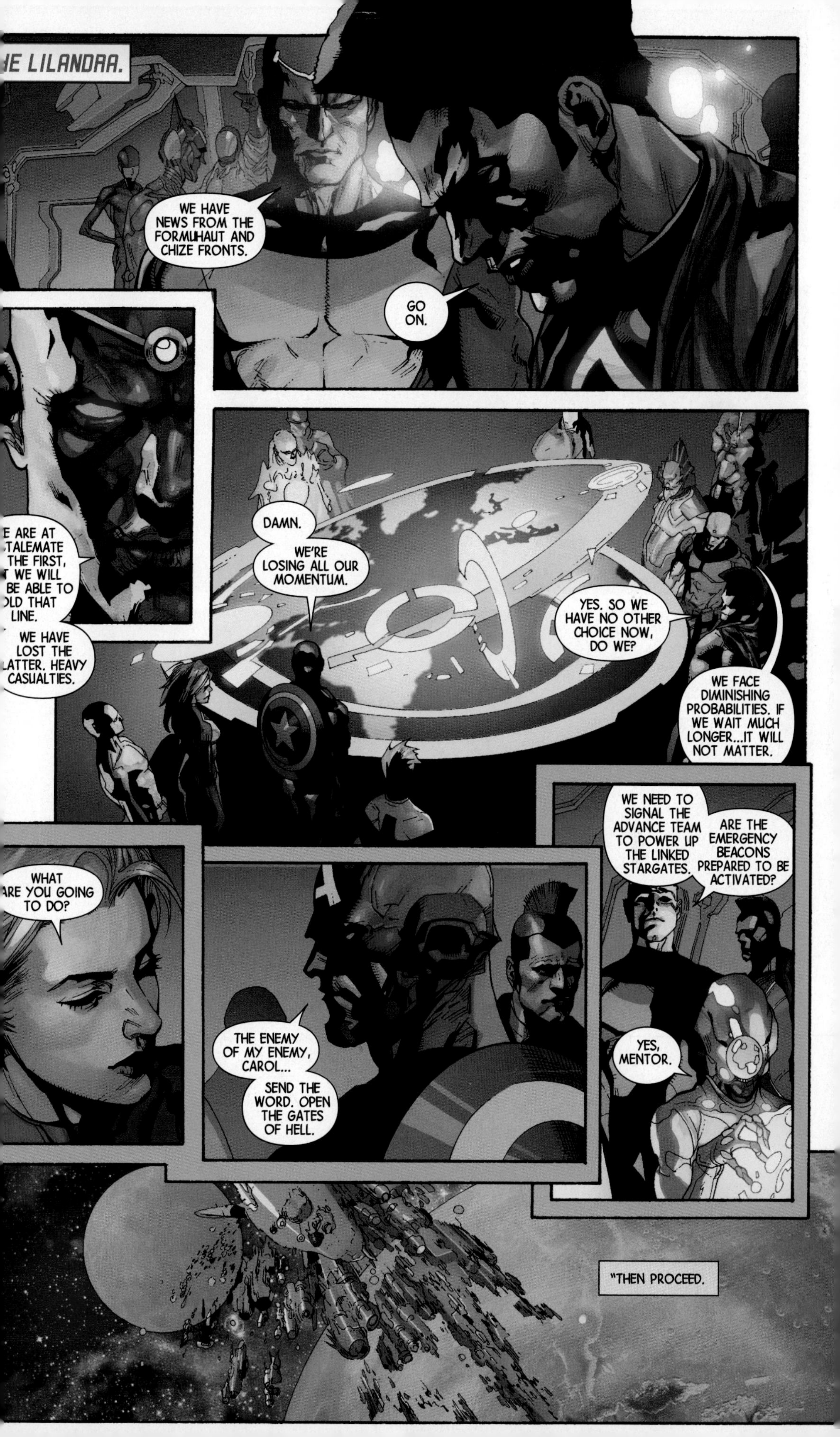

HE LILANDRA.
WE HAVE NEWS FROM THE FORMUHAUT AND CHIZE FRONTS.
GO ON.
E ARE AT TALEMATE THE FIRST, T WE WILL BE ABLE TO OLD THAT LINE.
WE HAVE LOST THE LATTER. HEAVY CASUALTIES.
DAMN.
WE'RE LOSING ALL OUR MOMENTUM.
YES. SO WE HAVE NO OTHER CHOICE NOW, DO WE?
WE FACE DIMINISHING PROBABILITIES. IF WE WAIT MUCH LONGER...IT WILL NOT MATTER.
WHAT ARE YOU GOING TO DO?
THE ENEMY OF MY ENEMY, CAROL...
SEND THE WORD. OPEN THE GATES OF HELL.
WE NEED TO SIGNAL THE ADVANCE TEAM TO POWER UP THE LINKED STARGATES.
ARE THE EMERGENCY BEACONS PREPARED TO BE ACTIVATED?
YES, MENTOR.
"THEN PROCEED.

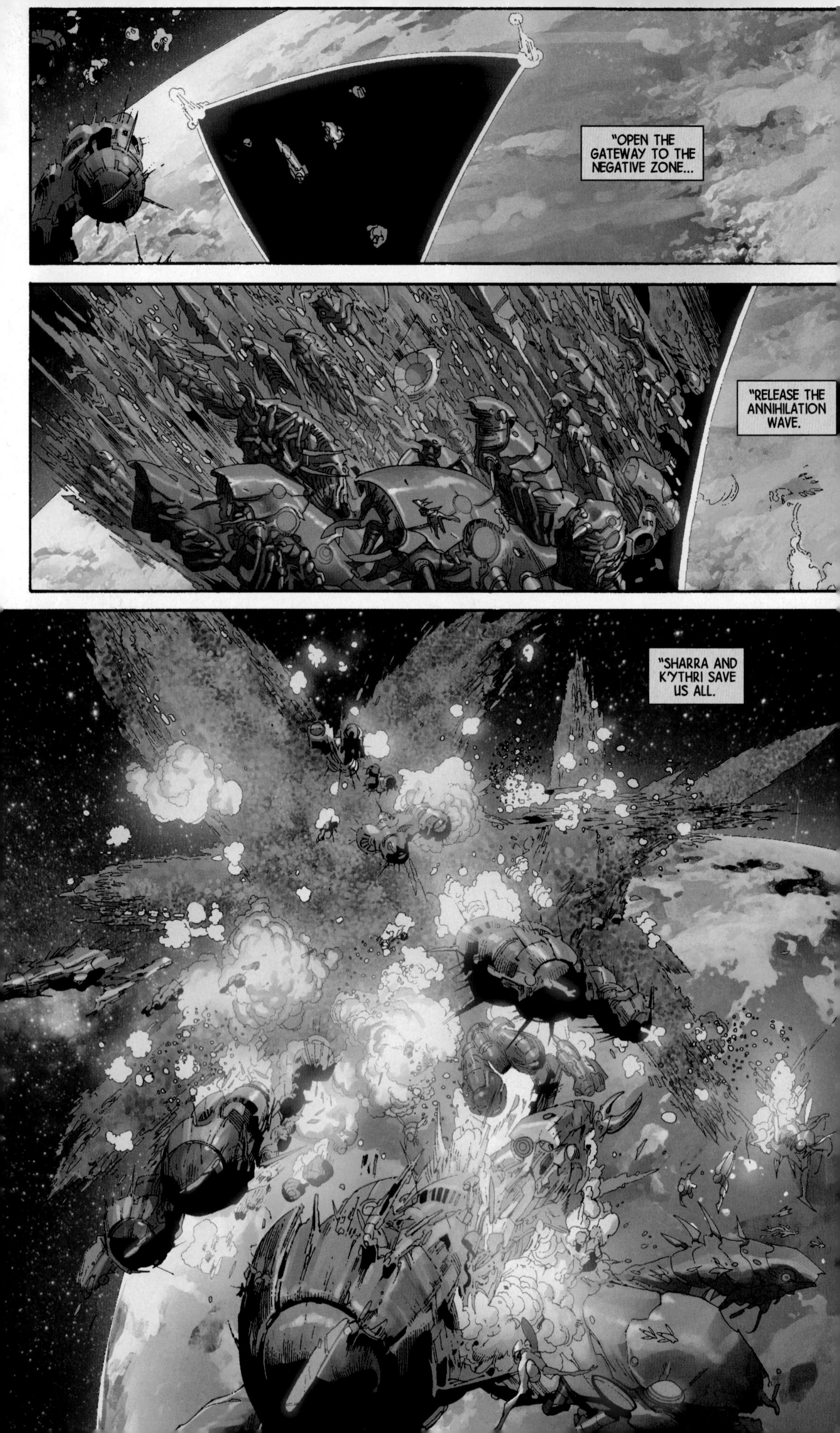
"OPEN THE GATEWAY TO THE NEGATIVE ZONE...
"RELEASE THE ANNIHILATION WAVE.
"SHARRA AND K'YTHRI SAVE US ALL.

"FOUR CYCLES AGO, THE ANNIHILATION WAVE RIPPED THROUGH THIS UNIVERSE. FROM THE DIMENSION CALLED THE NEGATIVE ZONE, ANNIHILUS CAME TO CONQUER.

"ONLY AFTER THE DEATH OF EMPIRES, THE DESTRUCTION OF WORLDS AND THE LOSS OF BILLIONS WAS HE DEFEATED.

"HOW DESPERATE HAVE WE BECOME THAT HE IS ONE OF OUR LAST HOPES?"

HHSSSSSSSSSS!

KILL ALL BUILDERSSSSSS!

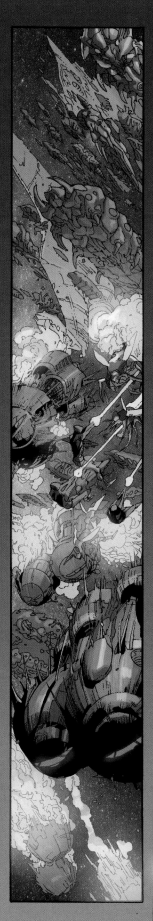

HIVE SWARM EMERGING FROM LOCALIZED WORMHOLE-- SECONDARY POINT... SOME PLACE THE REBELS REFER TO AS THE NEGATIVE ZONE.

A FAILED POCKET UNIVERSE RESTING INSIDE AN EXISTING ONE.

AH, LIKE A TUMOR.

AND HIVE MINDS...HOW SIMPLE.

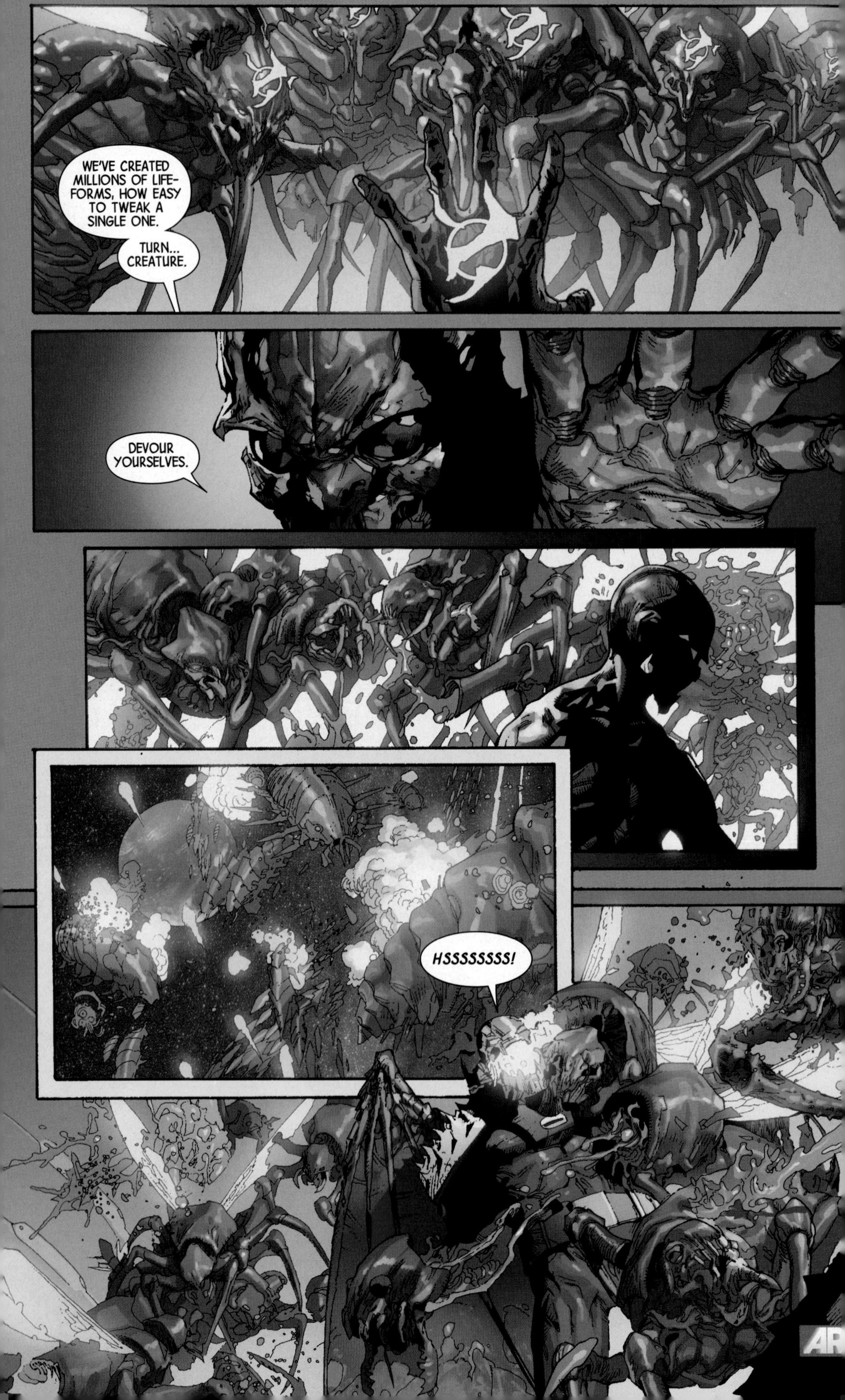
WE'VE CREATED MILLIONS OF LIFE-FORMS, HOW EASY TO TWEAK A SINGLE ONE.
TURN... CREATURE.
DEVOUR YOURSELVES.
HSSSSSSSS!

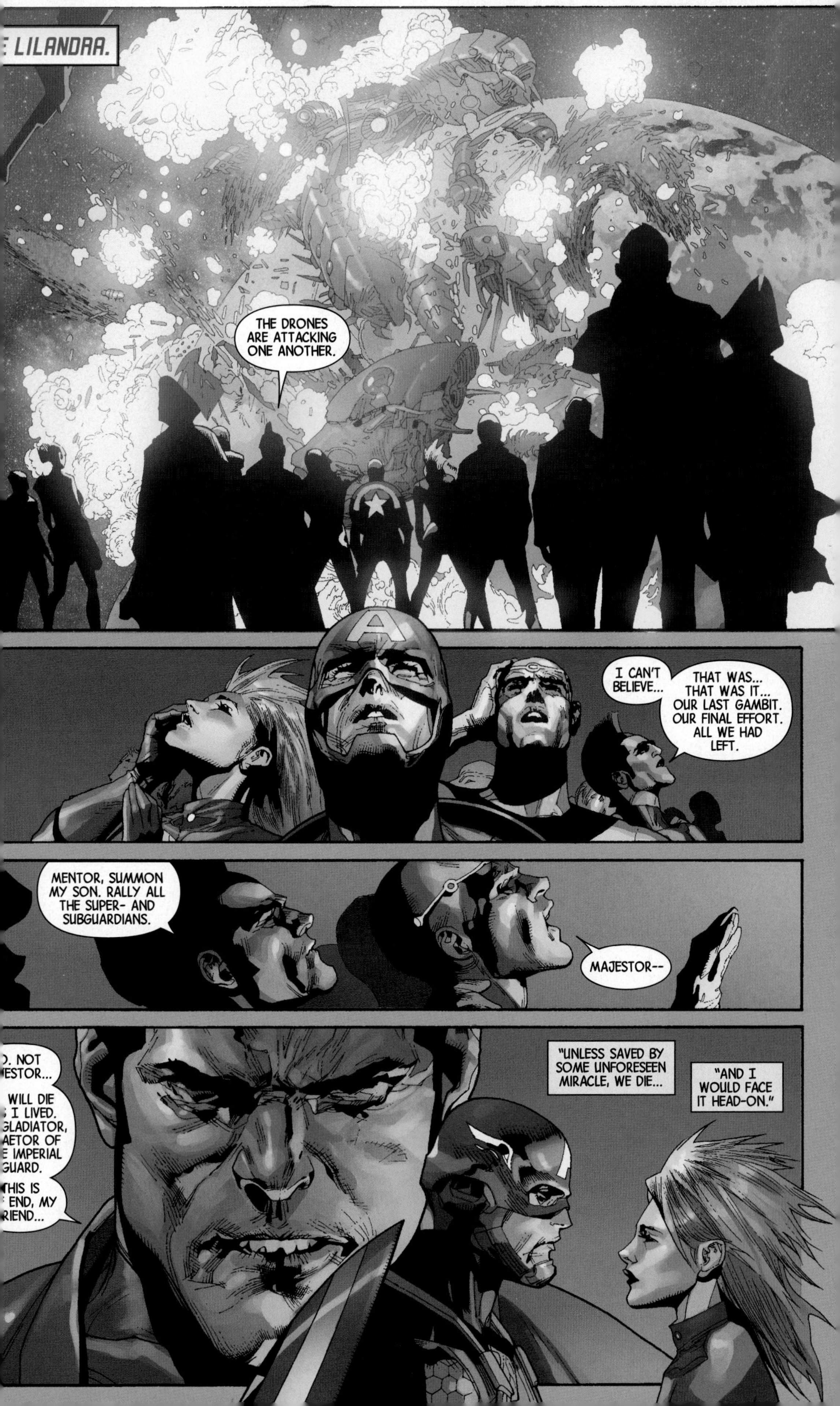

E LILANDRA.
THE DRONES ARE ATTACKING ONE ANOTHER.
I CAN'T BELIEVE...
THAT WAS... THAT WAS IT... OUR LAST GAMBIT. OUR FINAL EFFORT. ALL WE HAD LEFT.
MENTOR, SUMMON MY SON. RALLY ALL THE SUPER- AND SUBGUARDIANS.
MAJESTOR--
D. NOT JESTOR...
WILL DIE I LIVED. GLADIATOR, AETOR OF E IMPERIAL GUARD.
THIS IS END, MY RIEND...
"UNLESS SAVED BY SOME UNFORESEEN MIRACLE, WE DIE...
"AND I WOULD FACE IT HEAD-ON."

THE PROMISE
FULFILLED

◆

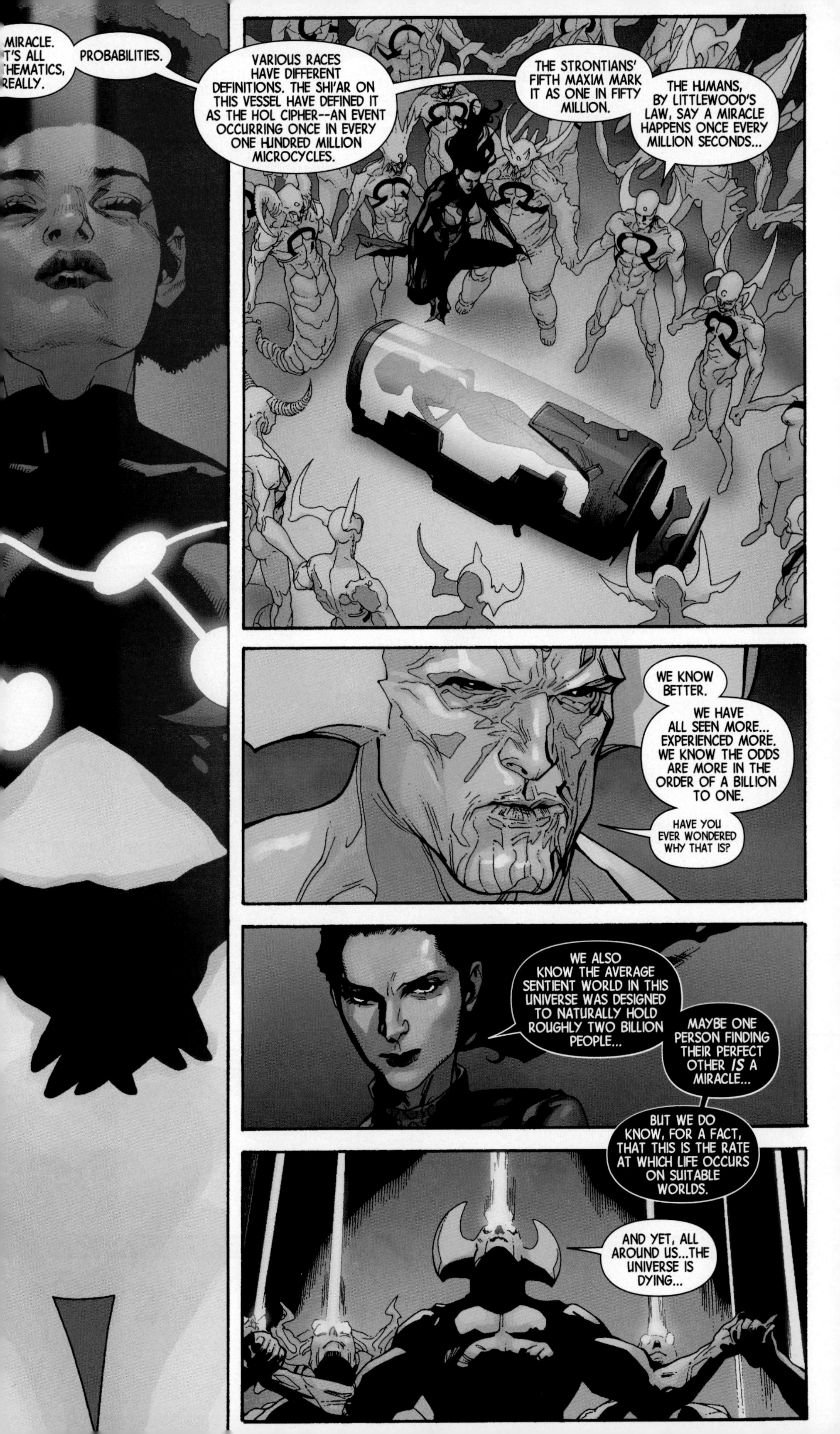
MIRACLE. IT'S ALL THEMATICS, REALLY.
PROBABILITIES.
VARIOUS RACES HAVE DIFFERENT DEFINITIONS. THE SHI'AR ON THIS VESSEL HAVE DEFINED IT AS THE HOL CIPHER--AN EVENT OCCURRING ONCE IN EVERY ONE HUNDRED MILLION MICROCYCLES.
THE STRONTIANS' FIFTH MAXIM MARK IT AS ONE IN FIFTY MILLION.
THE HUMANS, BY LITTLEWOOD'S LAW, SAY A MIRACLE HAPPENS ONCE EVERY MILLION SECONDS...
WE KNOW BETTER.
WE HAVE ALL SEEN MORE... EXPERIENCED MORE. WE KNOW THE ODDS ARE MORE IN THE ORDER OF A BILLION TO ONE.
HAVE YOU EVER WONDERED WHY THAT IS?
WE ALSO KNOW THE AVERAGE SENTIENT WORLD IN THIS UNIVERSE WAS DESIGNED TO NATURALLY HOLD ROUGHLY TWO BILLION PEOPLE...
MAYBE ONE PERSON FINDING THEIR PERFECT OTHER *IS* A MIRACLE...
BUT WE DO KNOW, FOR A FACT, THAT THIS IS THE RATE AT WHICH LIFE OCCURS ON SUITABLE WORLDS.
AND YET, ALL AROUND US...THE UNIVERSE IS DYING...

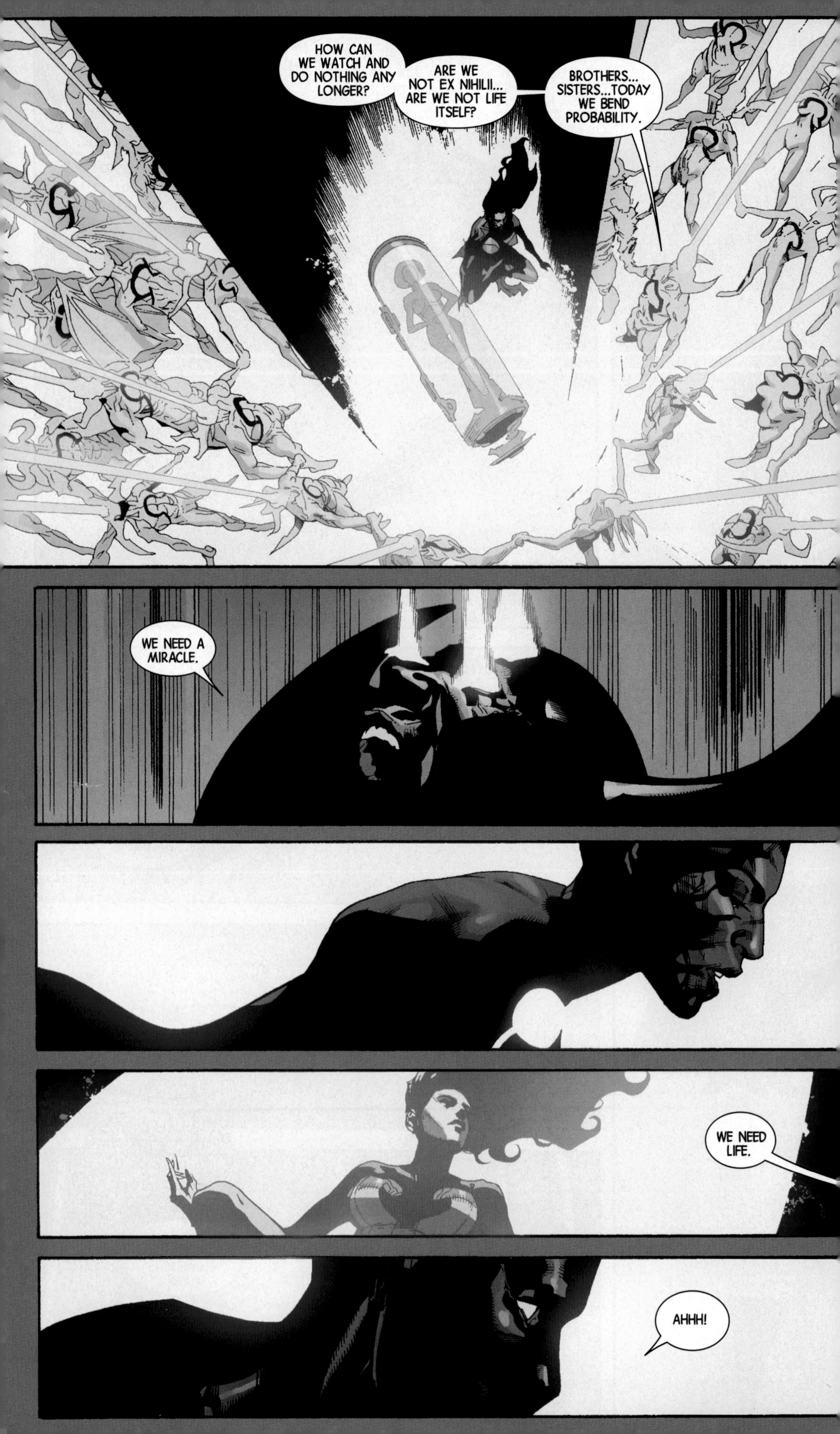
HOW CAN WE WATCH AND DO NOTHING ANY LONGER?
ARE WE NOT EX NIHILII... ARE WE NOT LIFE ITSELF?
BROTHERS... SISTERS...TODAY WE BEND PROBABILITY.
WE NEED A MIRACLE.
WE NEED LIFE.
AHHH!

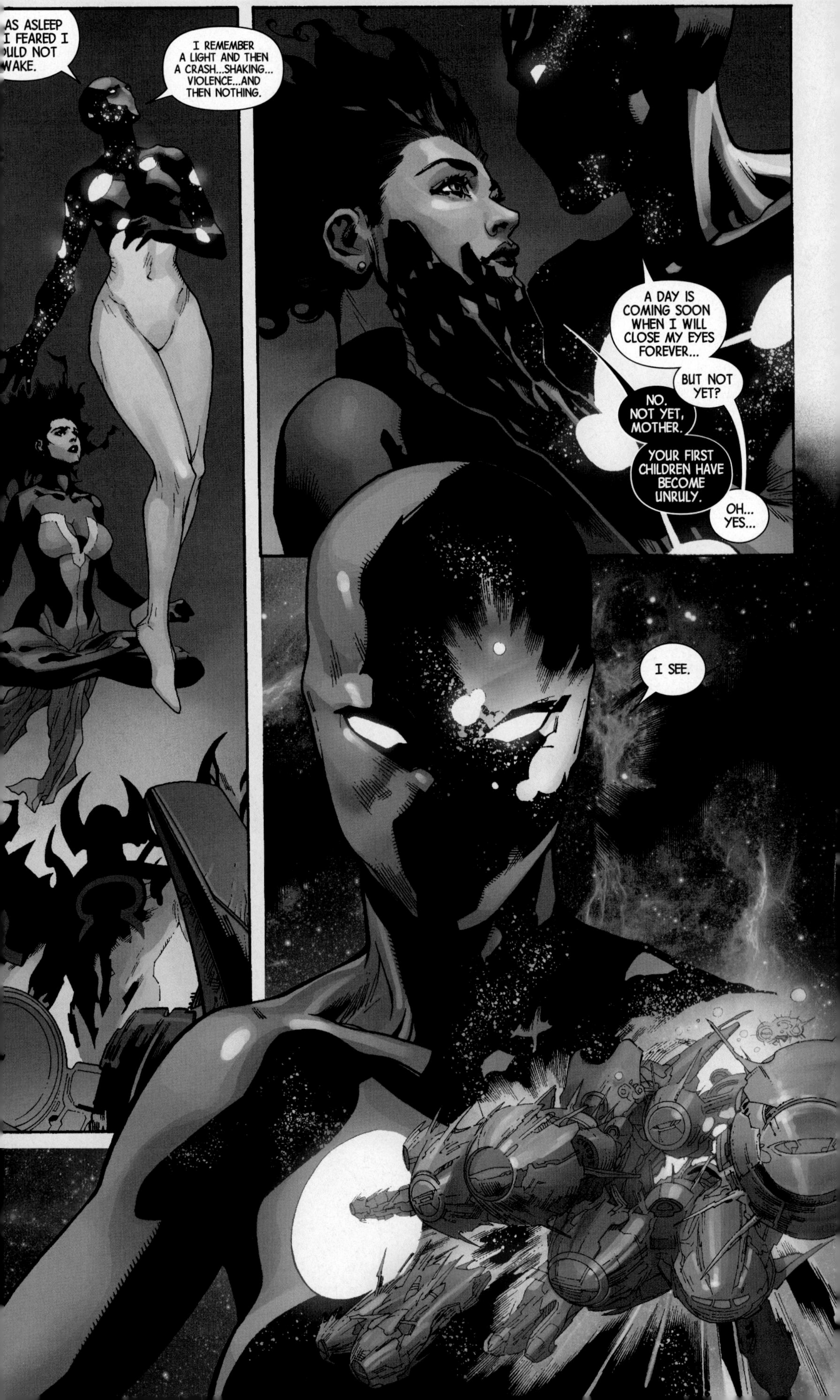
AS ASLEEP
I FEARED I
ULD NOT
WAKE.
I REMEMBER A LIGHT AND THEN A CRASH...SHAKING... VIOLENCE...AND THEN NOTHING.
A DAY IS COMING SOON WHEN I WILL CLOSE MY EYES FOREVER...
BUT NOT YET?
NO. NOT YET, MOTHER.
YOUR FIRST CHILDREN HAVE BECOME UNRULY.
OH... YES...
I SEE.

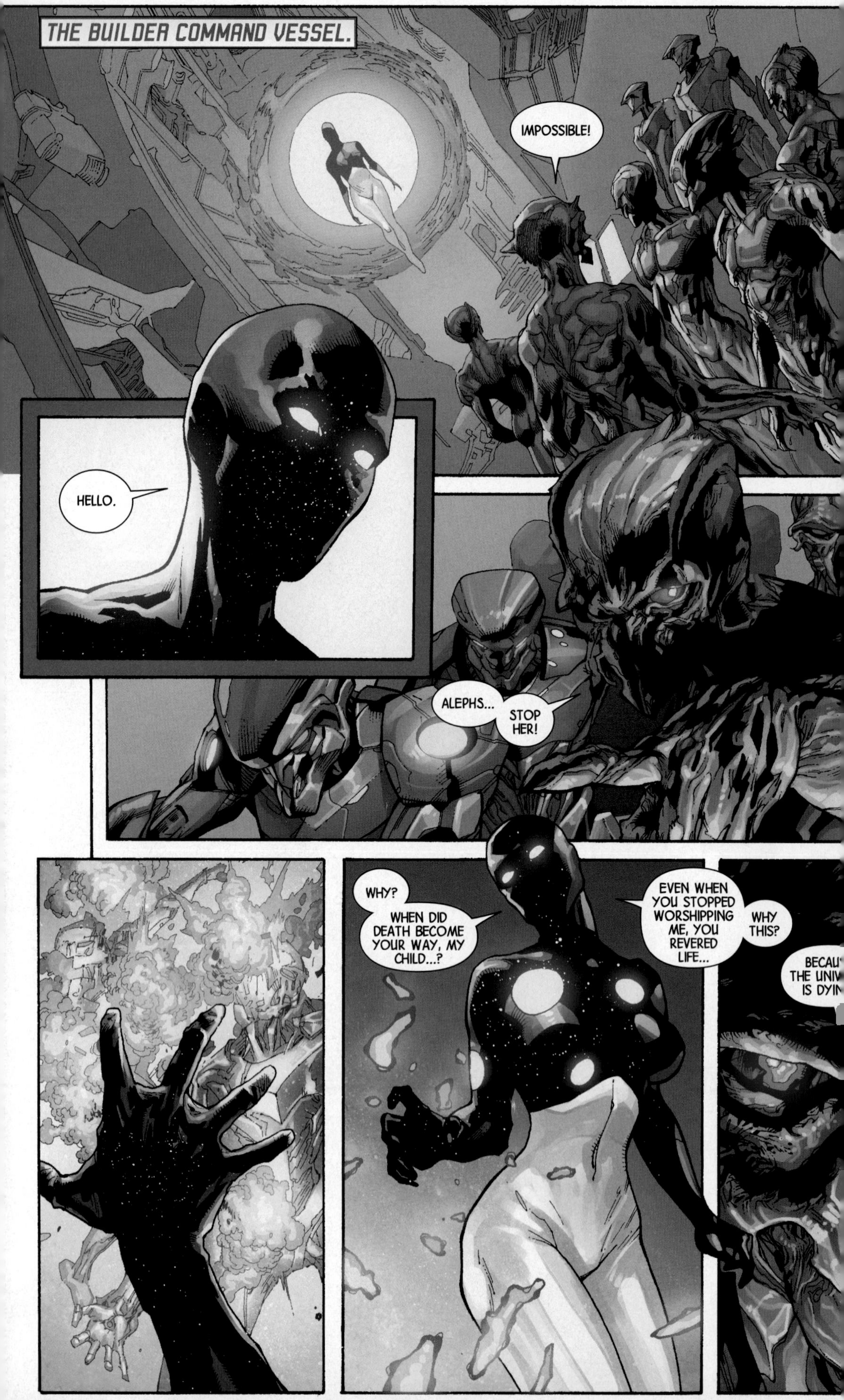
THE BUILDER COMMAND VESSEL.
IMPOSSIBLE!
HELLO.
ALEPHS...
STOP HER!
WHY?
WHEN DID DEATH BECOME YOUR WAY, MY CHILD...?
EVEN WHEN YOU STOPPED WORSHIPPING ME, YOU REVERED LIFE...
WHY THIS?

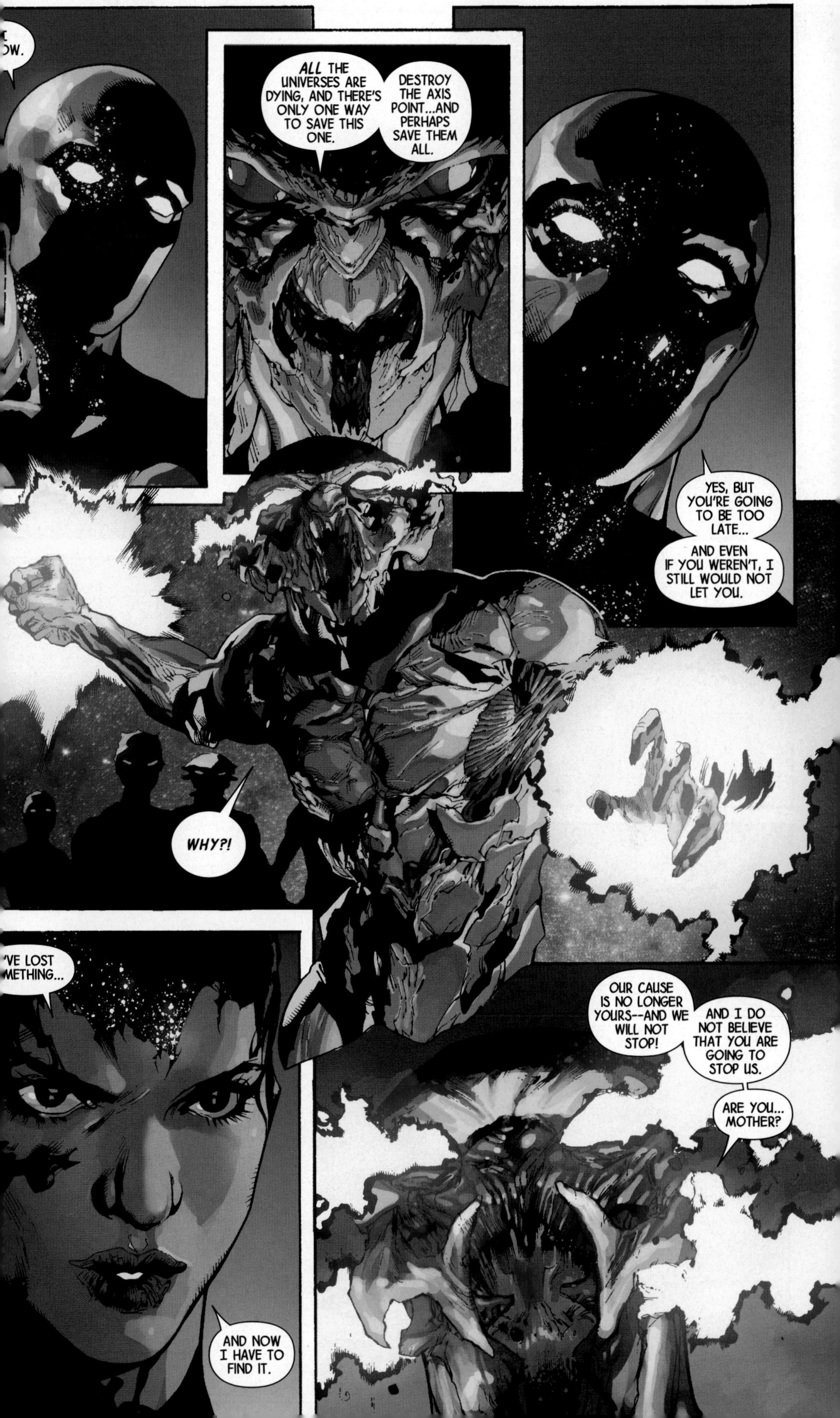

OW.
ALL THE UNIVERSES ARE DYING, AND THERE'S ONLY ONE WAY TO SAVE THIS ONE.
DESTROY THE AXIS POINT...AND PERHAPS SAVE THEM ALL.
YES, BUT YOU'RE GOING TO BE TOO LATE...
AND EVEN IF YOU WEREN'T, I STILL WOULD NOT LET YOU.
WHY?!
'VE LOST METHING...
AND NOW I HAVE TO FIND IT.
OUR CAUSE IS NO LONGER YOURS--AND WE WILL NOT STOP!
AND I DO NOT BELIEVE THAT YOU ARE GOING TO STOP US.
ARE YOU... MOTHER?

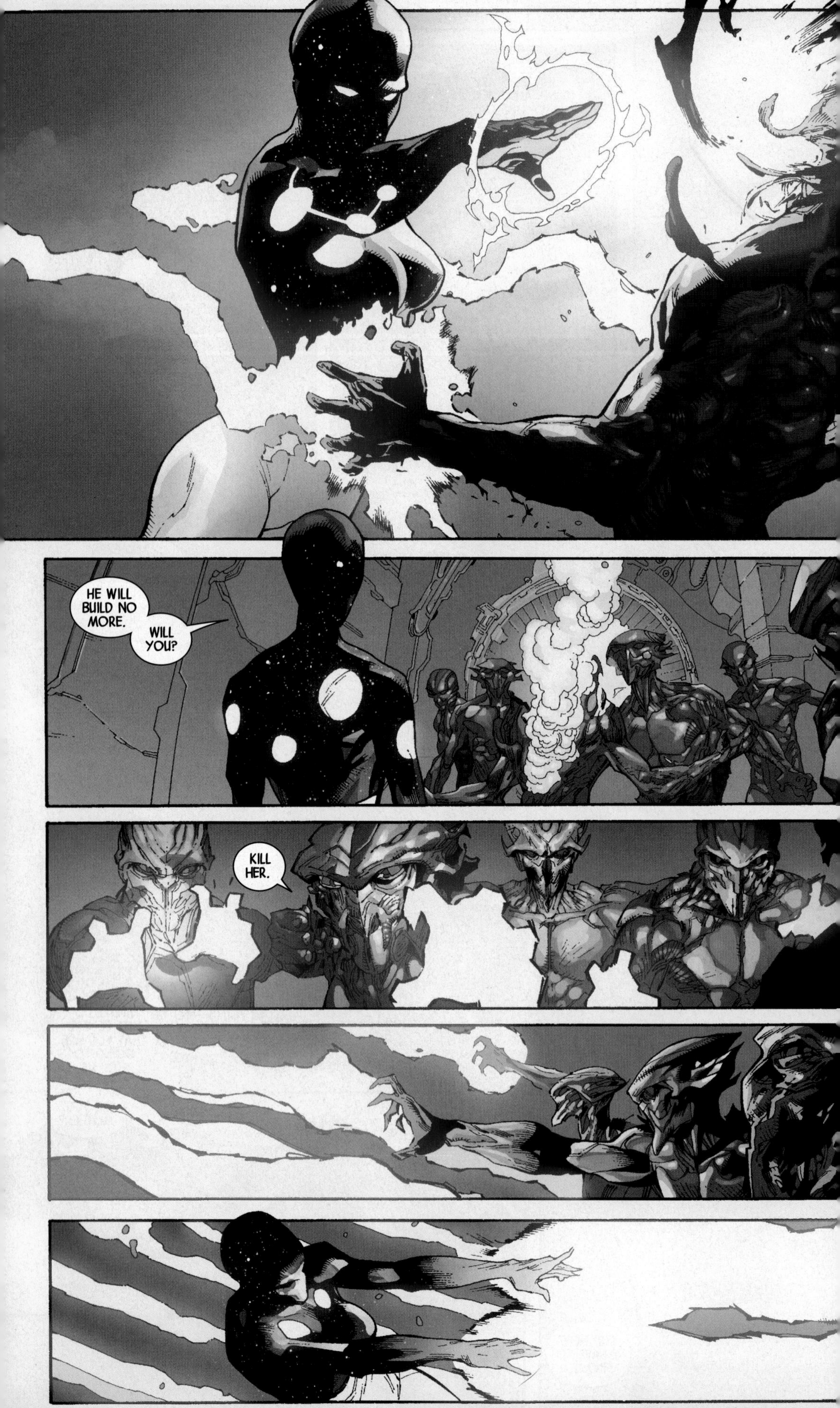
HE WILL BUILD NO MORE.
WILL YOU?
KILL HER.

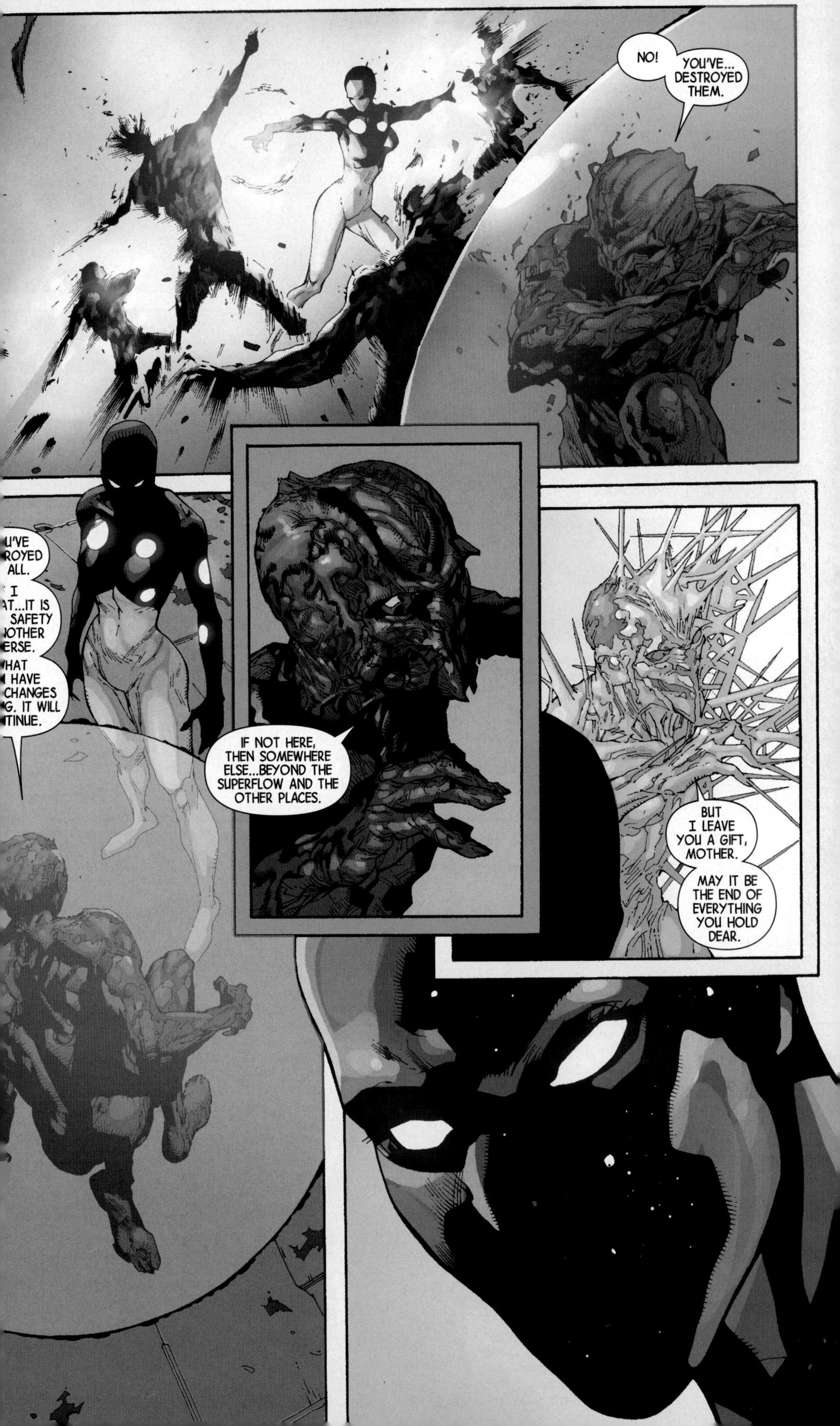

NO!
YOU'VE... DESTROYED THEM.
U'VE ROYED ALL.
I AT...IT IS SAFETY OTHER ERSE.
HAT HAVE CHANGES G. IT WILL TINUE.
IF NOT HERE, THEN SOMEWHERE ELSE...BEYOND THE SUPERFLOW AND THE OTHER PLACES.
BUT I LEAVE YOU A GIFT, MOTHER.
MAY IT BE THE END OF EVERYTHING YOU HOLD DEAR.

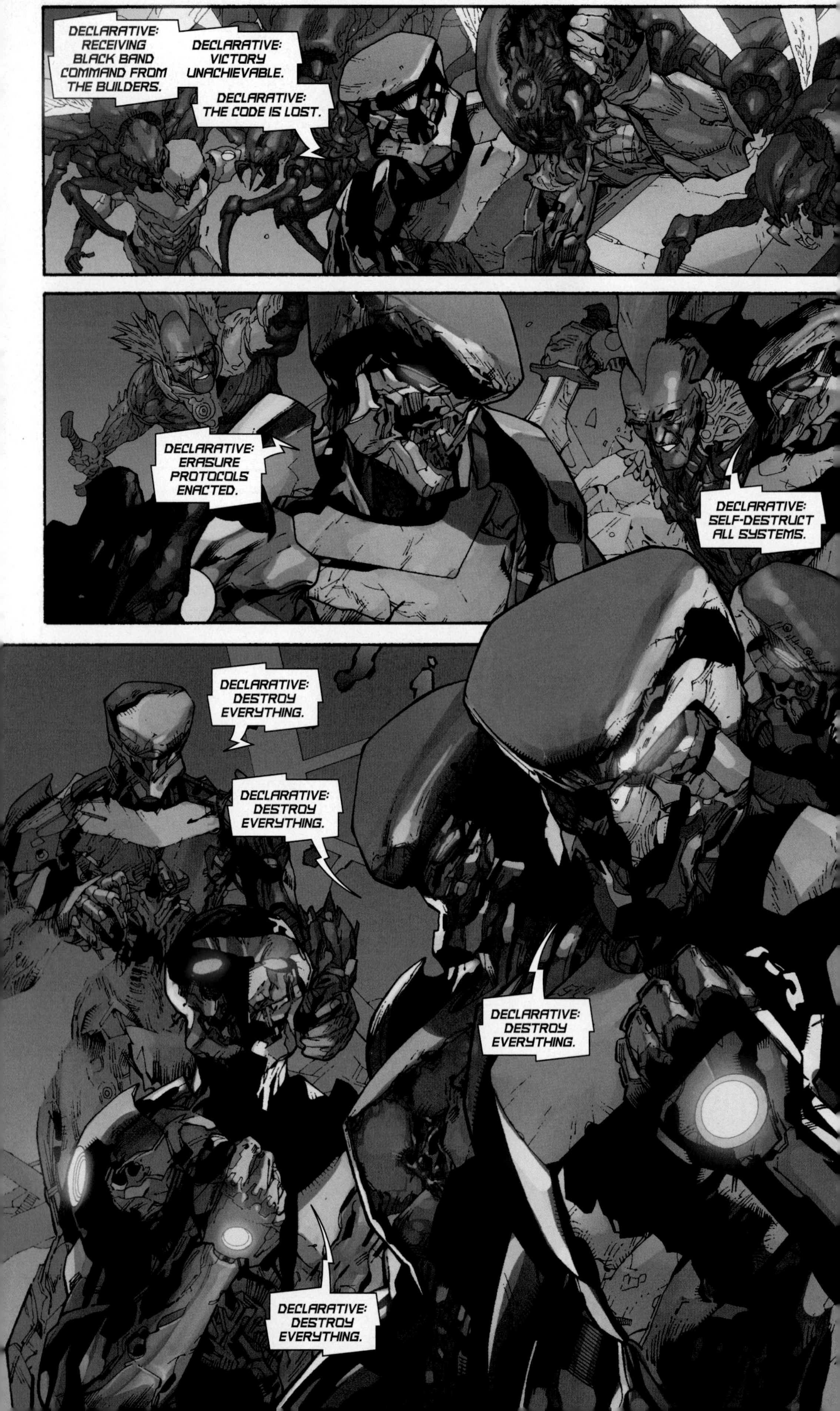
DECLARATIVE: RECEIVING BLACK BAND COMMAND FROM THE BUILDERS.
DECLARATIVE: VICTORY UNACHIEVABLE.
DECLARATIVE: THE CODE IS LOST.
DECLARATIVE: ERASURE PROTOCOLS ENACTED.
DECLARATIVE: SELF-DESTRUCT ALL SYSTEMS.
DECLARATIVE: DESTROY EVERYTHING.
DECLARATIVE: DESTROY EVERYTHING.
DECLARATIVE: DESTROY EVERYTHING.
DECLARATIVE: DESTROY EVERYTHING.

"TO THE EARTH..."

PREVIOUSLY IN INFINITY

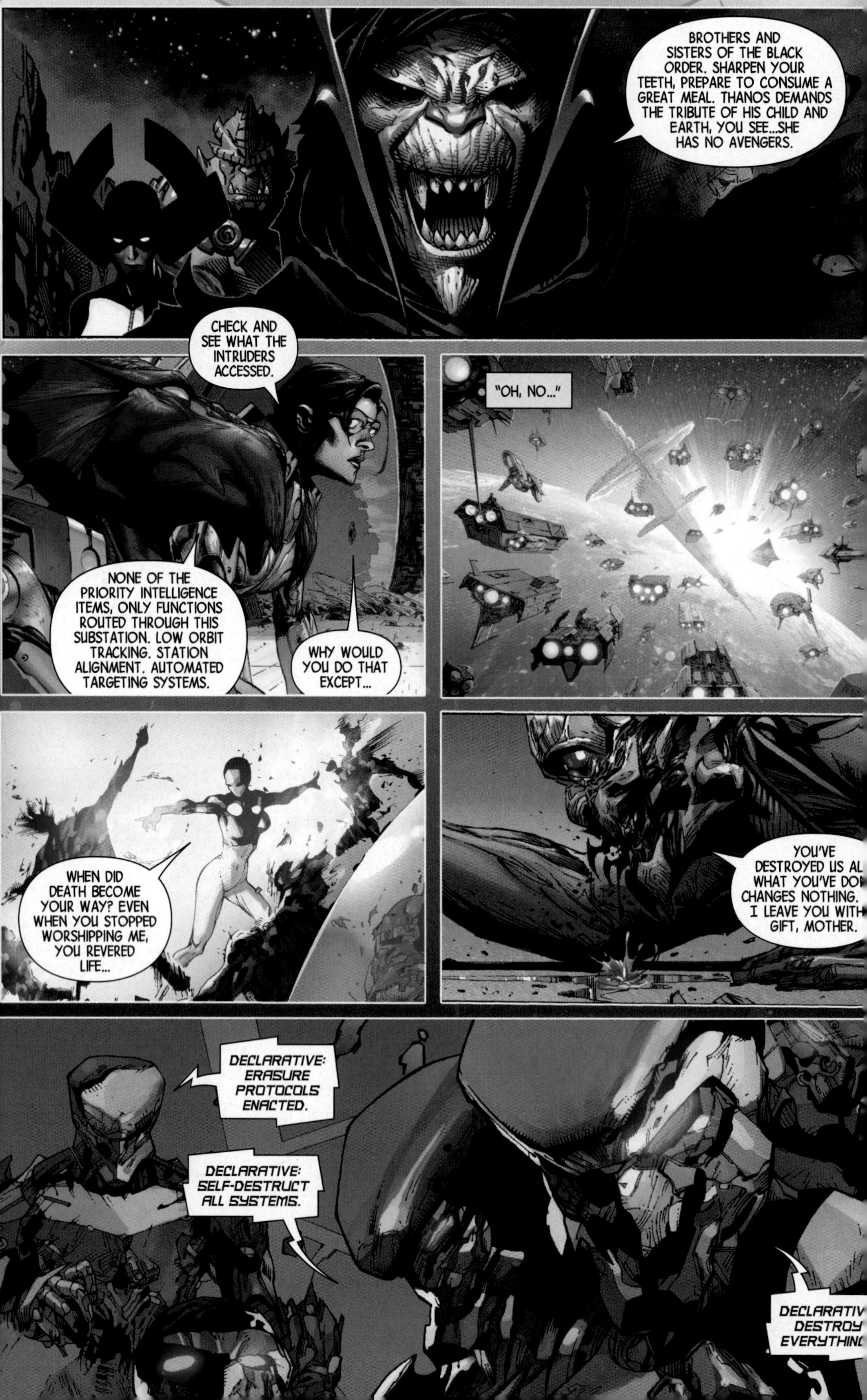
BROTHERS AND SISTERS OF THE BLACK ORDER. SHARPEN YOUR TEETH, PREPARE TO CONSUME A GREAT MEAL. THANOS DEMANDS THE TRIBUTE OF HIS CHILD AND EARTH, YOU SEE...SHE HAS NO AVENGERS.
CHECK AND SEE WHAT THE INTRUDERS ACCESSED.
NONE OF THE PRIORITY INTELLIGENCE ITEMS, ONLY FUNCTIONS ROUTED THROUGH THIS SUBSTATION. LOW ORBIT TRACKING. STATION ALIGNMENT. AUTOMATED TARGETING SYSTEMS.
WHY WOULD YOU DO THAT EXCEPT...
"OH, NO..."
WHEN DID DEATH BECOME YOUR WAY? EVEN WHEN YOU STOPPED WORSHIPPING ME, YOU REVERED LIFE...
YOU'VE DESTROYED US AL WHAT YOU'VE DO CHANGES NOTHING. I LEAVE YOU WITH GIFT, MOTHER.
DECLARATIVE: ERASURE PROTOCOLS ENACTED.
DECLARATIVE: SELF-DESTRUCT ALL SYSTEMS.
DECLARATIV DESTROY EVERYTHIN

◆ CAST ◆

THE AVENGERS

CAPTAIN AMERICA

CAPTAIN MARVEL

THOR

HULK/ BRUCE BANNER

CANNONBALL

SUNSPOT

SMASHER

HYPERION

FALCON

IRON MAN

SHANG CHI

SPIDER-WOMAN

MANIFOLD

THE BLACK ORDER/CULL OBSIDIAN

BLACK DWARF

GLADIATOR

RONAN THE ACCUSER

ANNIHILUS

KL'RT, SUPER-SKRULL

SHI'AR IMPERIAL GUARD

MENTOR

STARBOLT

ORACLE

MANTA

WARSTAR

HOMECOMING

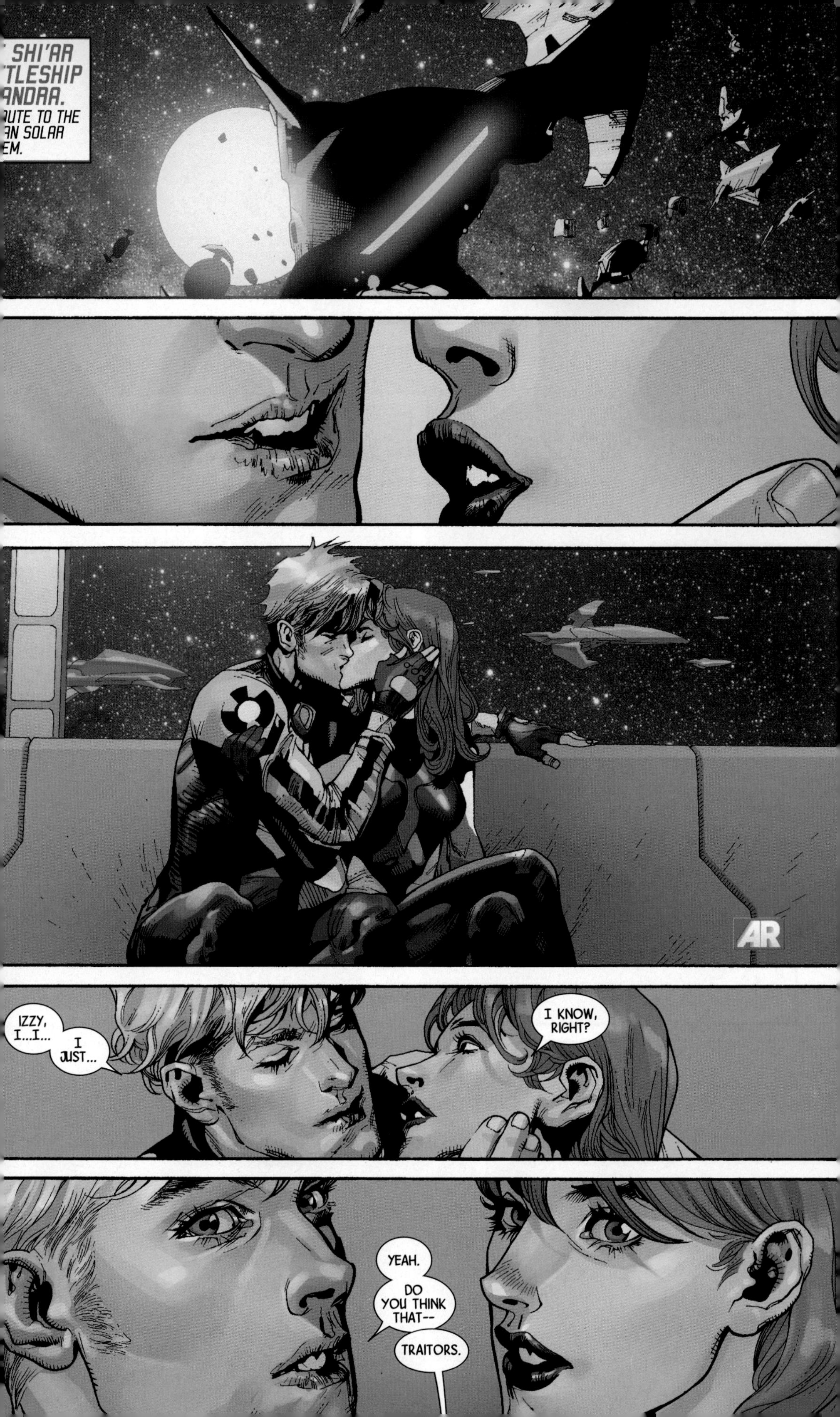
SHI'AR
TLESHIP
ANDRA.
UTE TO THE
AN SOLAR
EM.
IZZY, I...I...
I JUST...
I KNOW, RIGHT?
YEAH.
DO YOU THINK THAT--
TRAITORS.

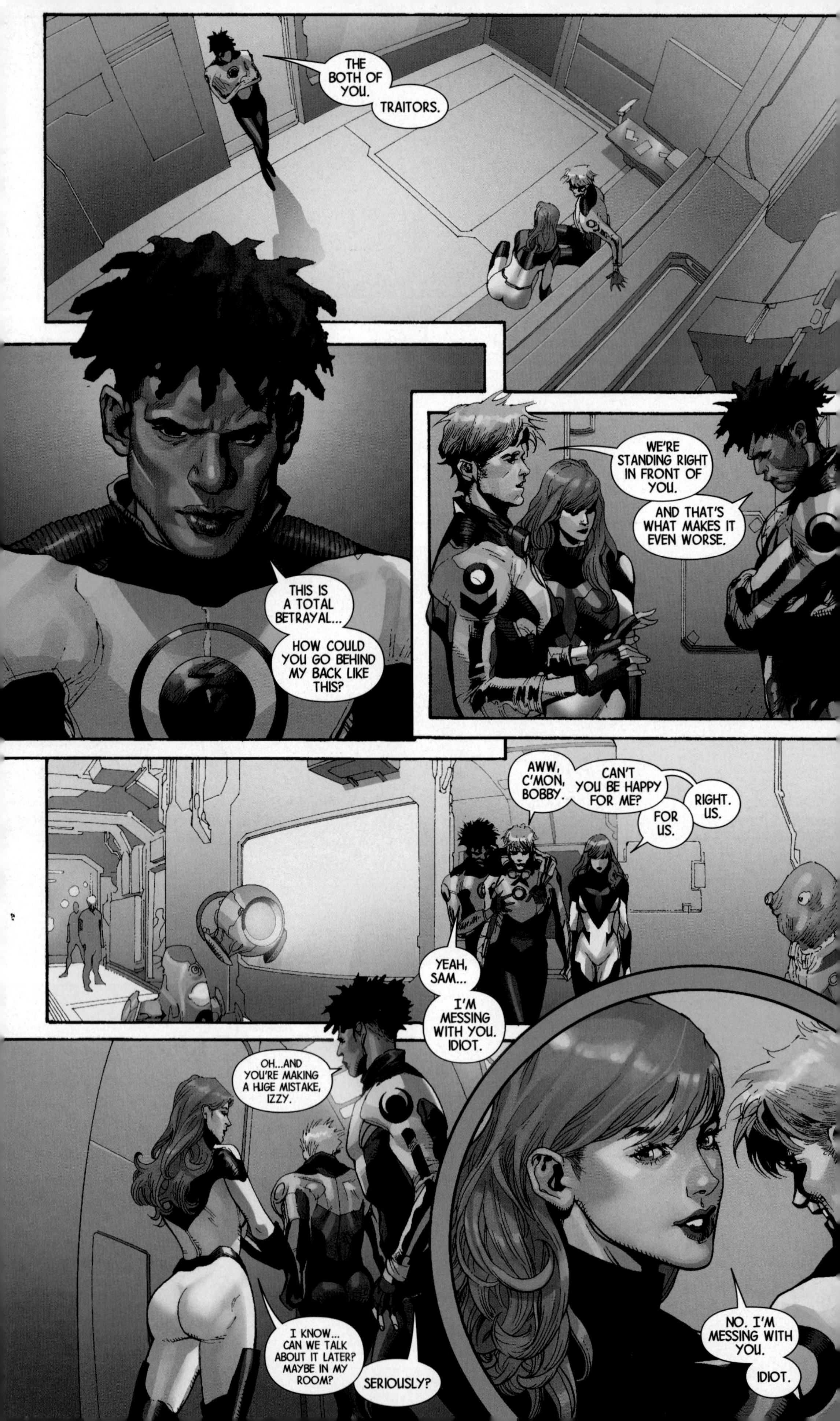
THE BOTH OF YOU.
TRAITORS.
THIS IS A TOTAL BETRAYAL...
HOW COULD YOU GO BEHIND MY BACK LIKE THIS?
WE'RE STANDING RIGHT IN FRONT OF YOU.
AND THAT'S WHAT MAKES IT EVEN WORSE.
AWW, C'MON, BOBBY.
CAN'T YOU BE HAPPY FOR ME?
FOR US.
RIGHT. US.
YEAH, SAM...
I'M MESSING WITH YOU. IDIOT.
OH...AND YOU'RE MAKING A HUGE MISTAKE, IZZY.
I KNOW... CAN WE TALK ABOUT IT LATER? MAYBE IN MY ROOM?
SERIOUSLY?
NO. I'M MESSING WITH YOU.
IDIOT.

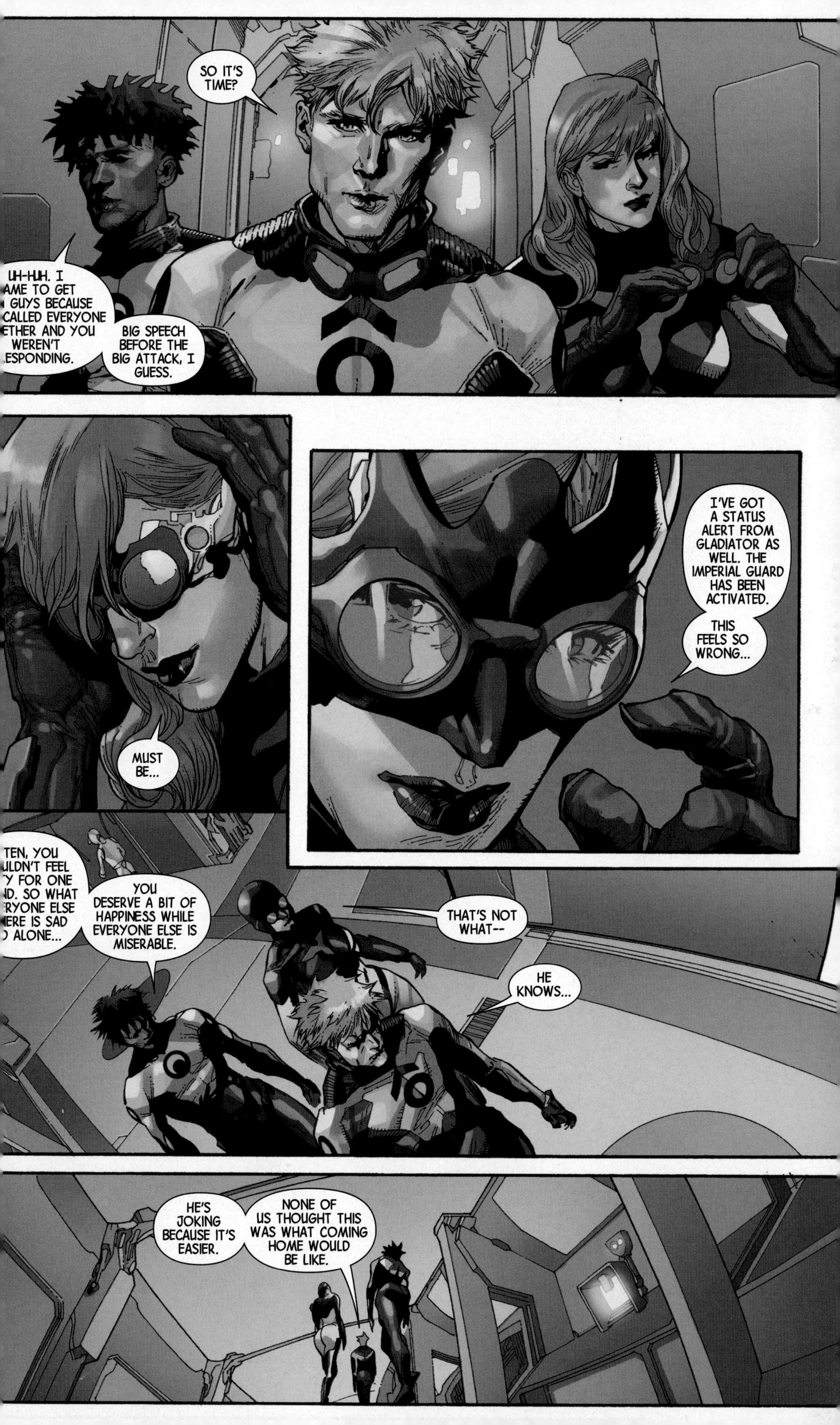
SO IT'S TIME?
UH-HUH. I AME TO GET GUYS BECAUSE CALLED EVERYONE ETHER AND YOU WEREN'T ESPONDING.
BIG SPEECH BEFORE THE BIG ATTACK, I GUESS.
MUST BE...
I'VE GOT A STATUS ALERT FROM GLADIATOR AS WELL. THE IMPERIAL GUARD HAS BEEN ACTIVATED.
THIS FEELS SO WRONG...
TEN, YOU ULDN'T FEEL Y FOR ONE D. SO WHAT RYONE ELSE ERE IS SAD ALONE...
YOU DESERVE A BIT OF HAPPINESS WHILE EVERYONE ELSE IS MISERABLE.
THAT'S NOT WHAT--
HE KNOWS...
HE'S JOKING BECAUSE IT'S EASIER.
NONE OF US THOUGHT THIS WAS WHAT COMING HOME WOULD BE LIKE.

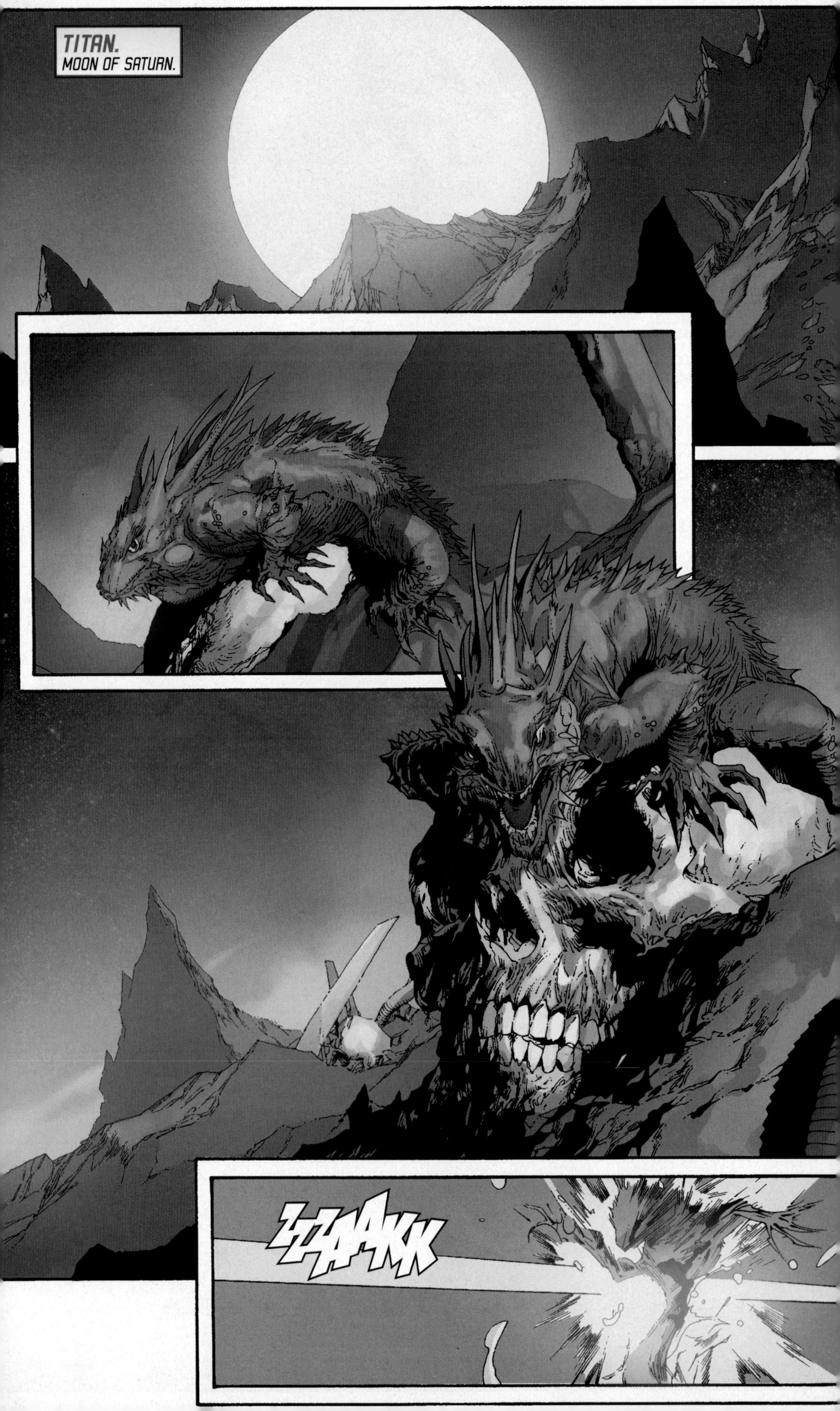
TITAN.
MOON OF SATURN.
ZZZAAKK

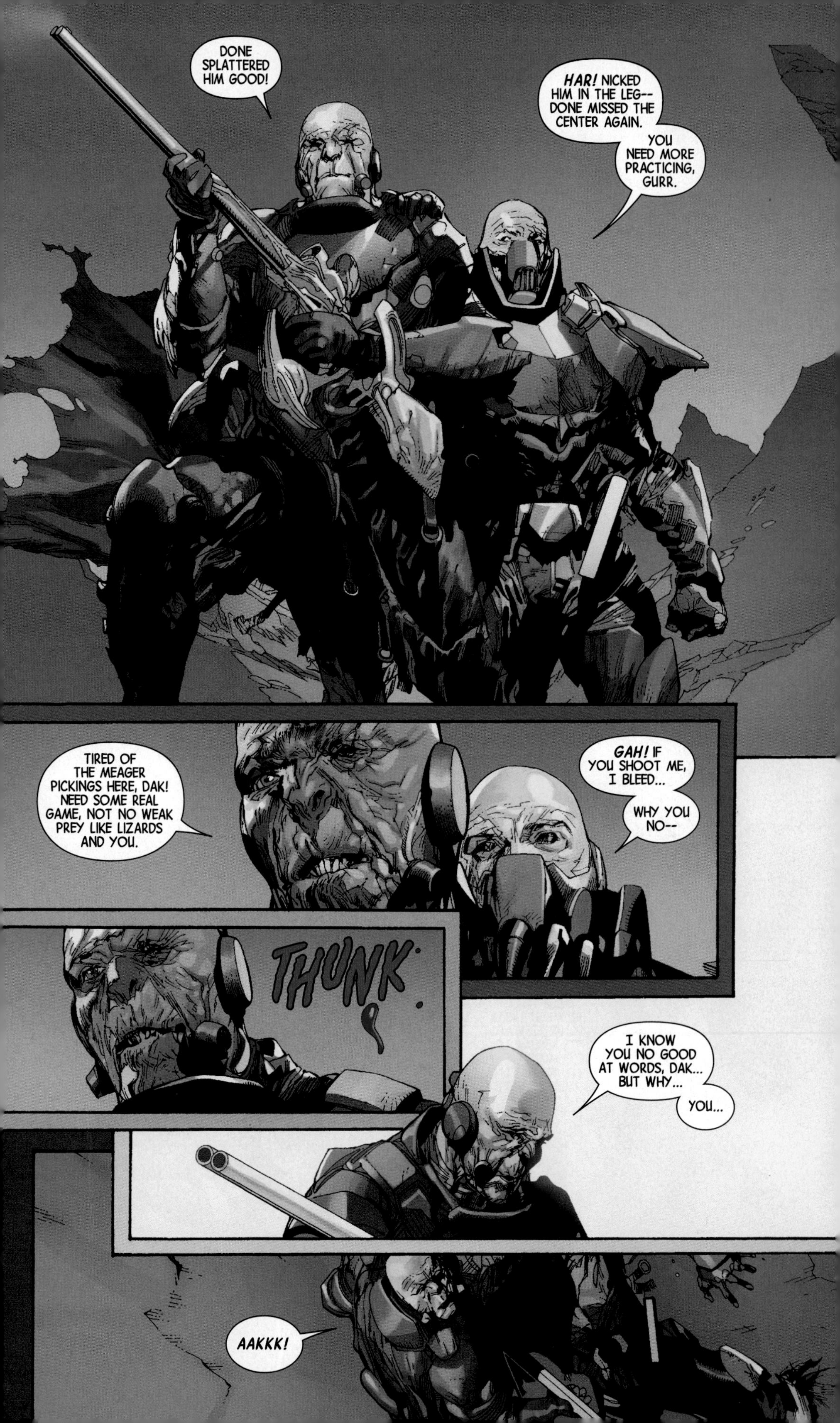
DONE SPLATTERED HIM GOOD!
HAR! NICKED HIM IN THE LEG-- DONE MISSED THE CENTER AGAIN.
YOU NEED MORE PRACTICING, GURR.
TIRED OF THE MEAGER PICKINGS HERE, DAK! NEED SOME REAL GAME, NOT NO WEAK PREY LIKE LIZARDS AND YOU.
GAH! IF YOU SHOOT ME, I BLEED...
WHY YOU NO--
THUNK
I KNOW YOU NO GOOD AT WORDS, DAK... BUT WHY...
YOU...
AAKKK!

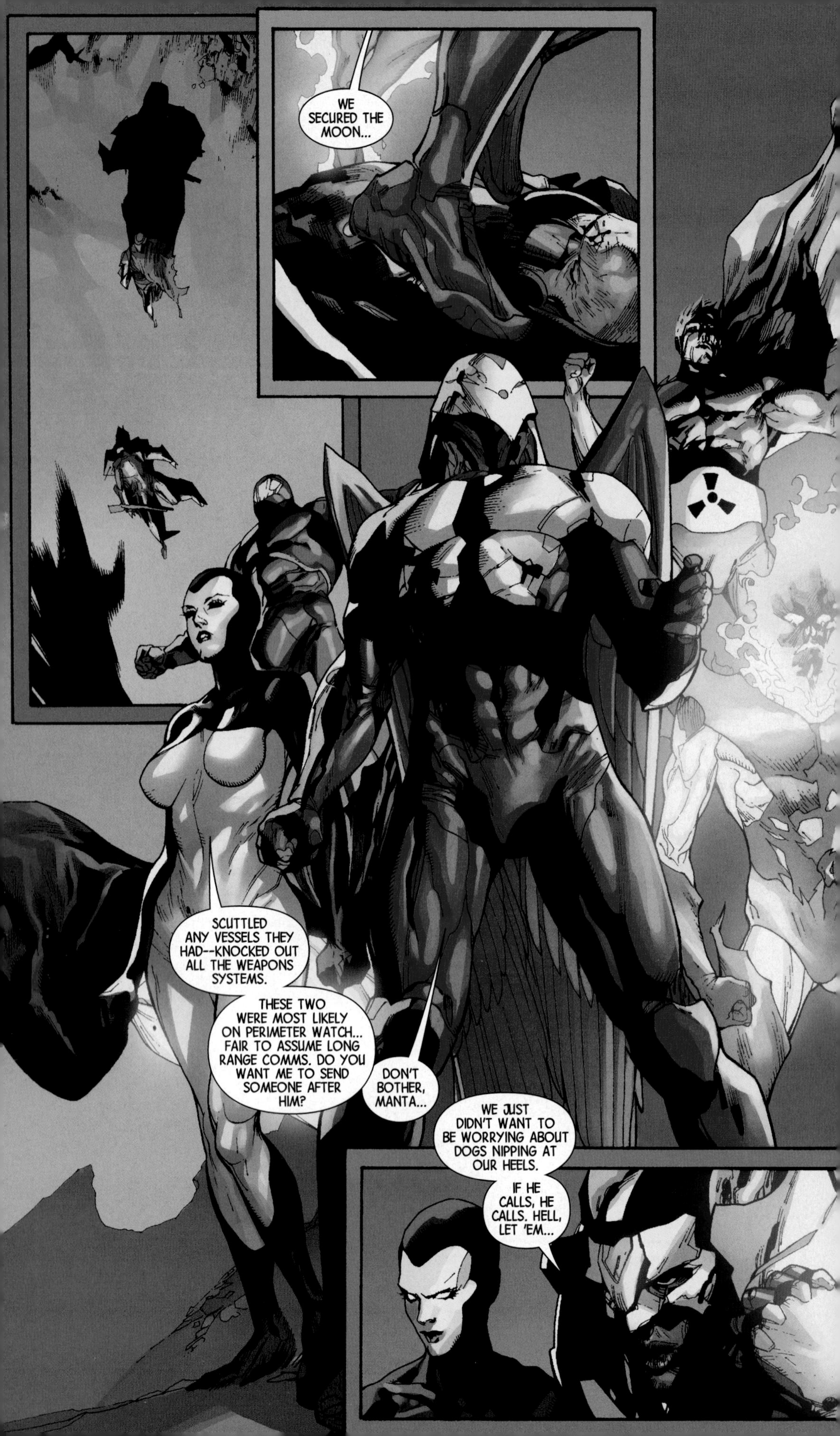
WE SECURED THE MOON...
SCUTTLED ANY VESSELS THEY HAD--KNOCKED OUT ALL THE WEAPONS SYSTEMS.
THESE TWO WERE MOST LIKELY ON PERIMETER WATCH... FAIR TO ASSUME LONG RANGE COMMS. DO YOU WANT ME TO SEND SOMEONE AFTER HIM?
DON'T BOTHER, MANTA...
WE JUST DIDN'T WANT TO BE WORRYING ABOUT DOGS NIPPING AT OUR HEELS.
IF HE CALLS, HE CALLS. HELL, LET 'EM...

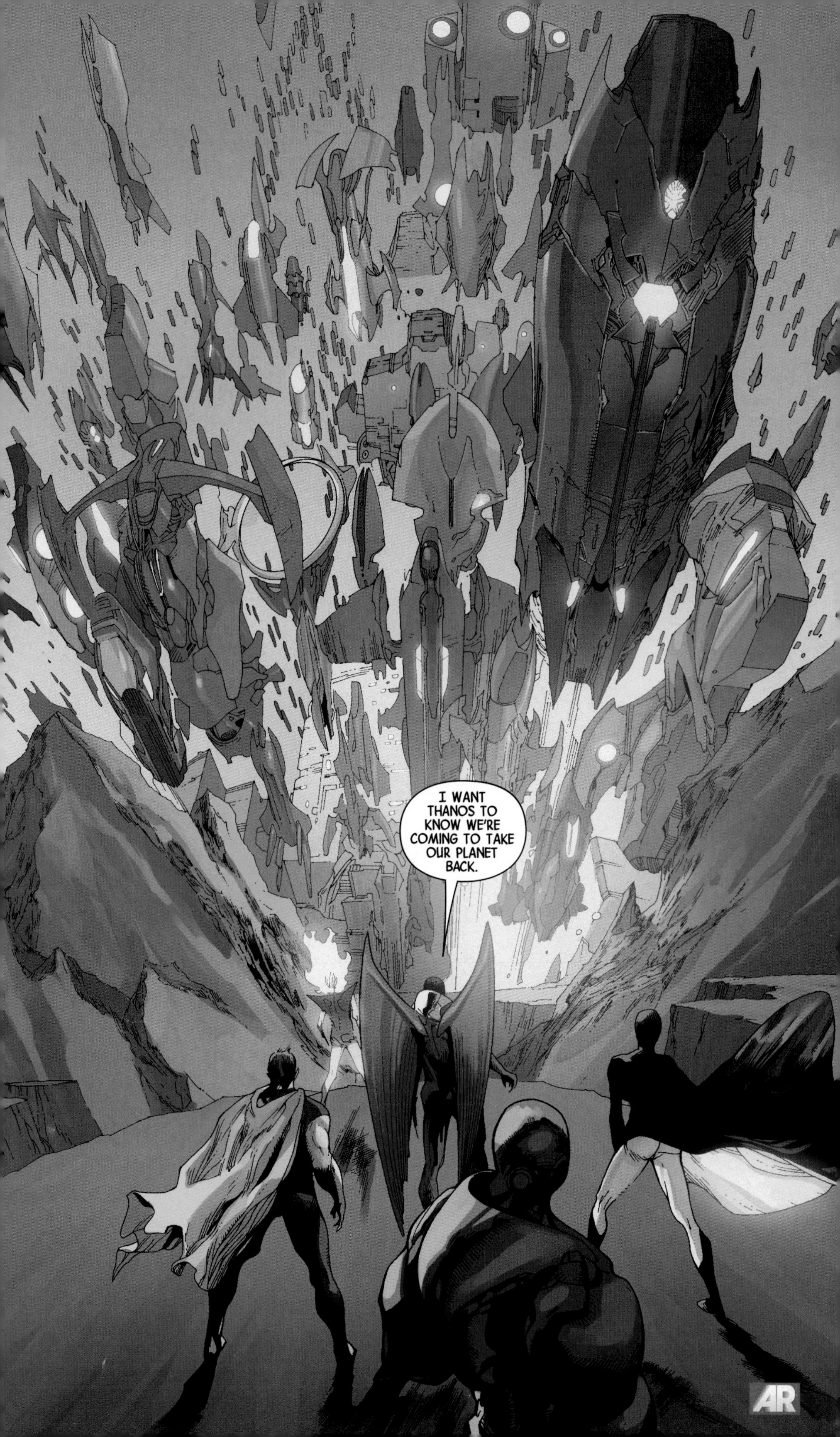
I WANT THANOS TO KNOW WE'RE COMING TO TAKE OUR PLANET BACK.

PLANS AND INTENTIONS

◆

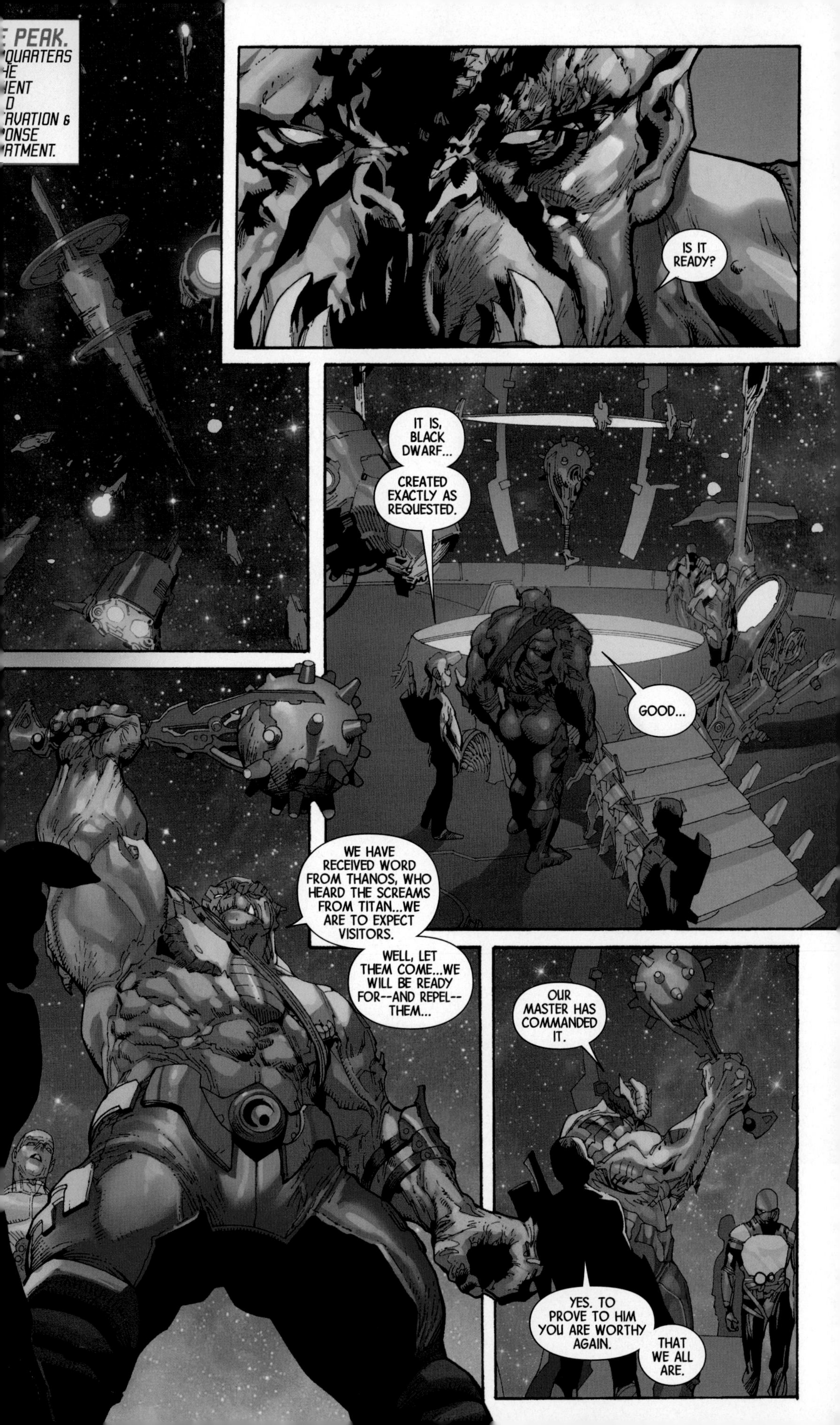

E PEAK.
QUARTERS
HE
IENT
D
RVATION &
ONSE
RTMENT.
IS IT READY?
IT IS, BLACK DWARF...
CREATED EXACTLY AS REQUESTED.
GOOD...
WE HAVE RECEIVED WORD FROM THANOS, WHO HEARD THE SCREAMS FROM TITAN...WE ARE TO EXPECT VISITORS.
WELL, LET THEM COME...WE WILL BE READY FOR--AND REPEL--THEM...
OUR MASTER HAS COMMANDED IT.
YES. TO PROVE TO HIM YOU ARE WORTHY AGAIN.
THAT WE ALL ARE.

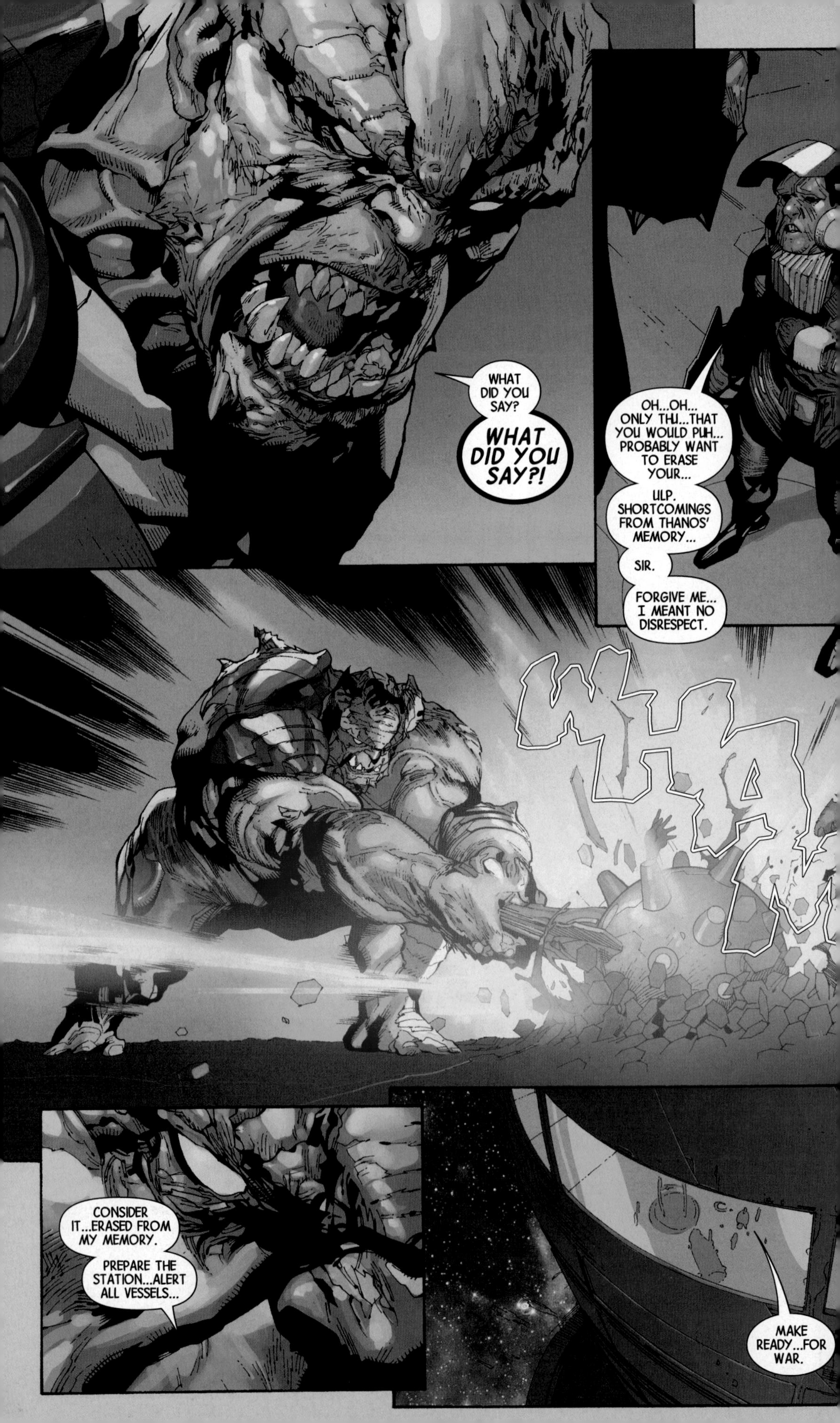
WHAT DID YOU SAY?
WHAT DID YOU SAY?!
OH...OH... ONLY THU...THAT YOU WOULD PUH... PROBABLY WANT TO ERASE YOUR...
ULP. SHORTCOMINGS FROM THANOS' MEMORY...
SIR.
FORGIVE ME... I MEANT NO DISRESPECT.
CONSIDER IT...ERASED FROM MY MEMORY.
PREPARE THE STATION...ALERT ALL VESSELS...
MAKE READY...FOR WAR.

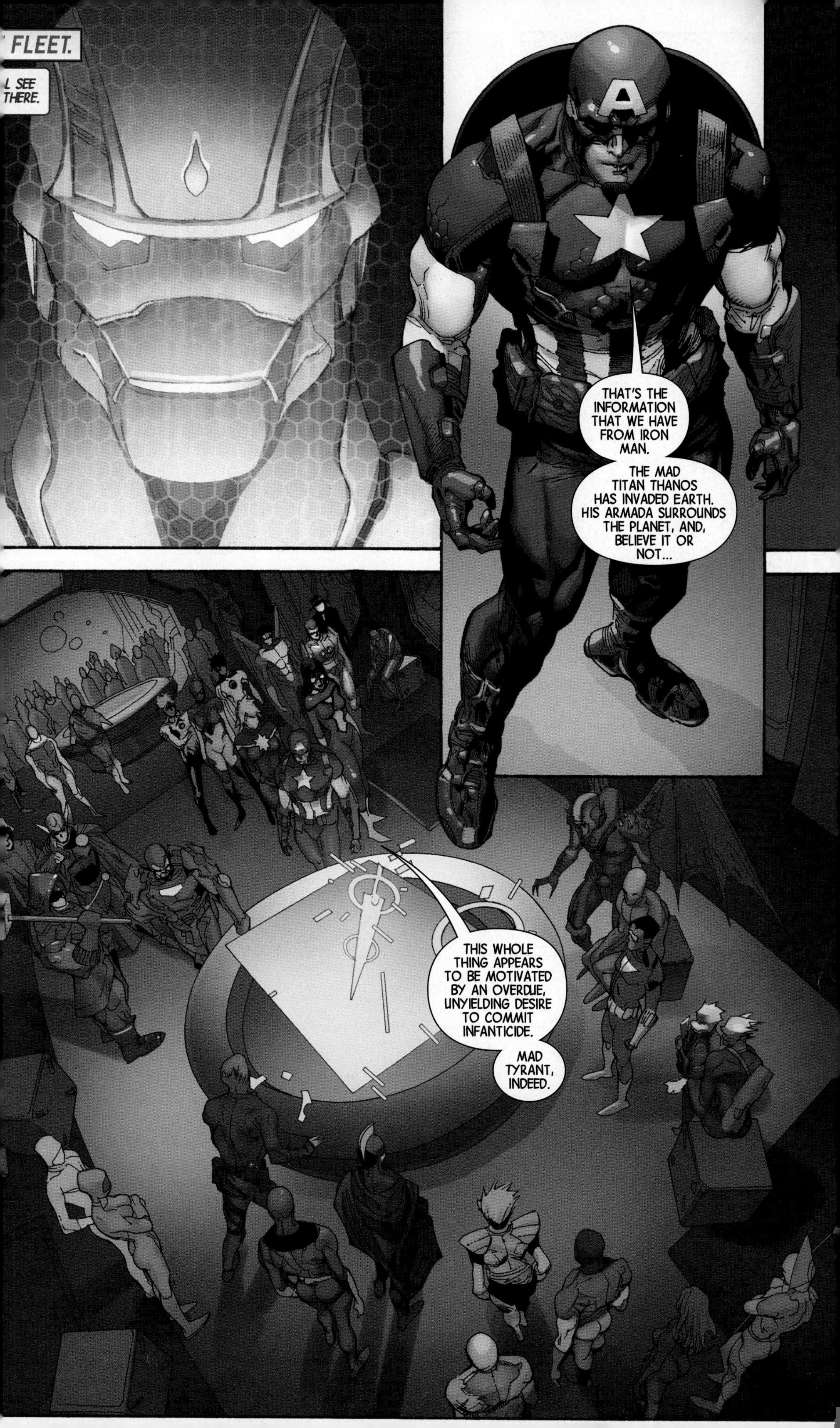
FLEET.
L SEE
THERE.
THAT'S THE INFORMATION THAT WE HAVE FROM IRON MAN.
THE MAD TITAN THANOS HAS INVADED EARTH. HIS ARMADA SURROUNDS THE PLANET, AND, BELIEVE IT OR NOT...
THIS WHOLE THING APPEARS TO BE MOTIVATED BY AN OVERDUE, UNYIELDING DESIRE TO COMMIT INFANTICIDE.
MAD TYRANT, INDEED.

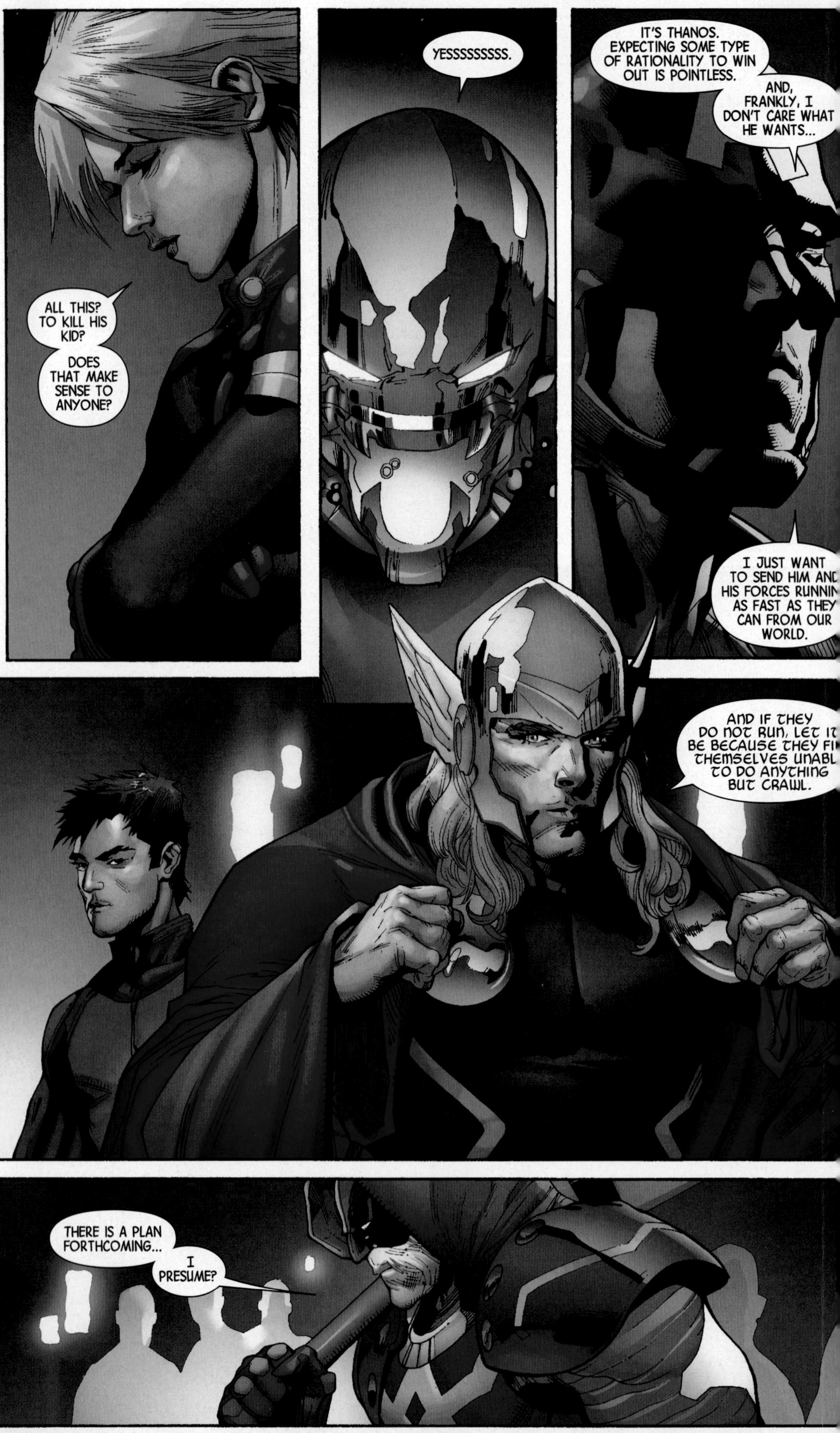
ALL THIS? TO KILL HIS KID?
DOES THAT MAKE SENSE TO ANYONE?
YESSSSSSSSS.
IT'S THANOS. EXPECTING SOME TYPE OF RATIONALITY TO WIN OUT IS POINTLESS.
AND, FRANKLY, I DON'T CARE WHAT HE WANTS...
I JUST WANT TO SEND HIM AND HIS FORCES RUNNIN AS FAST AS THEY CAN FROM OUR WORLD.
AND IF THEY DO NOT RUN, LET IT BE BECAUSE THEY FI THEMSELVES UNABL TO DO ANYTHING BUT CRAWL.
THERE IS A PLAN FORTHCOMING...
I PRESUME?

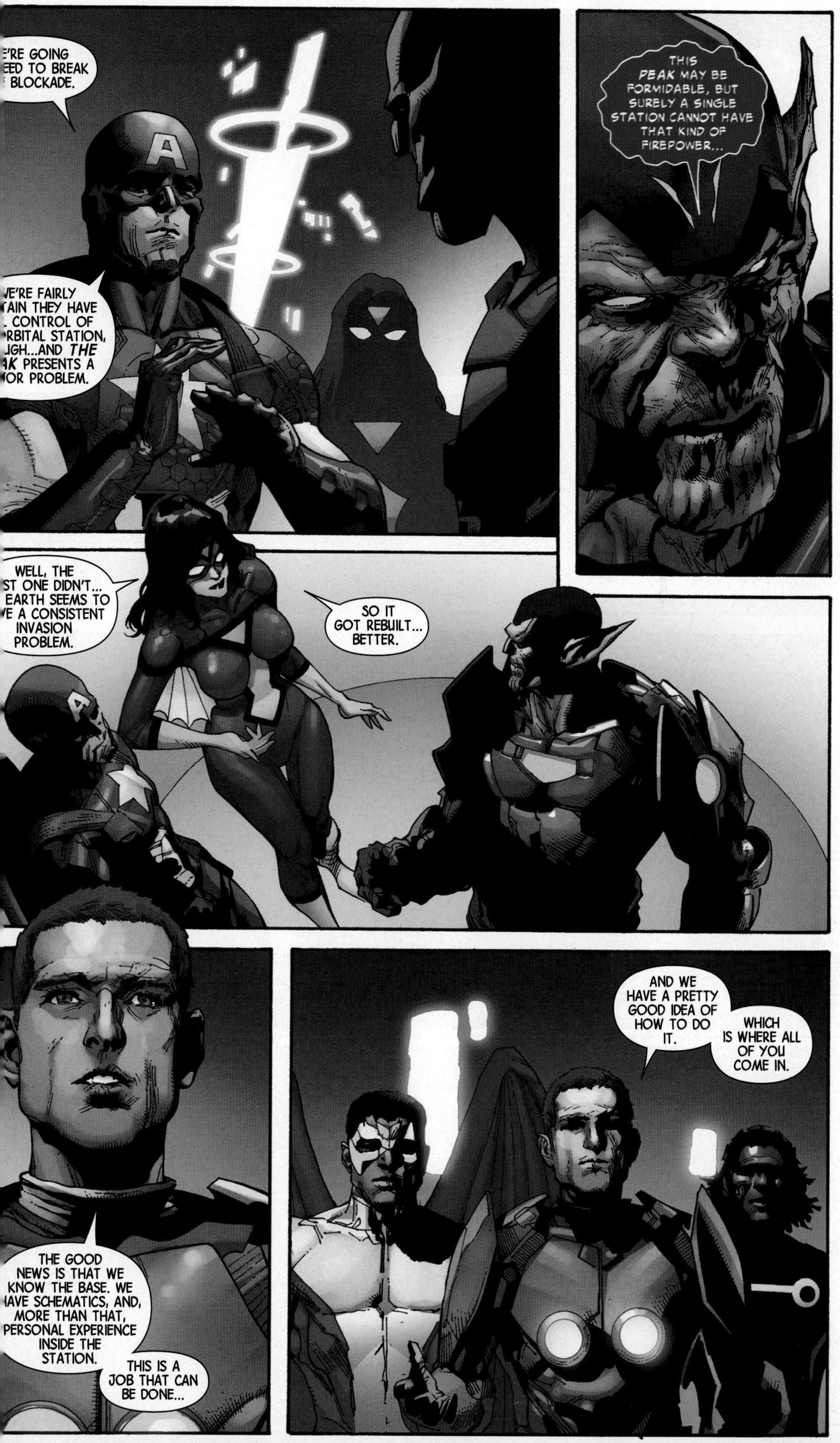
E'RE GOING
EED TO BREAK
BLOCKADE.
THIS
PEAK MAY BE
FORMIDABLE, BUT
SURELY A SINGLE
STATION CANNOT HAVE
THAT KIND OF
FIREPOWER...
E'RE FAIRLY
AIN THEY HAVE
CONTROL OF
RBITAL STATION,
UGH...AND THE
AK PRESENTS A
OR PROBLEM.
WELL, THE
ST ONE DIDN'T...
EARTH SEEMS TO
E A CONSISTENT
INVASION
PROBLEM.
SO IT
GOT REBUILT...
BETTER.
THE GOOD
NEWS IS THAT WE
KNOW THE BASE. WE
AVE SCHEMATICS, AND,
MORE THAN THAT,
PERSONAL EXPERIENCE
INSIDE THE
STATION.
THIS IS A
JOB THAT CAN
BE DONE...
AND WE
HAVE A PRETTY
GOOD IDEA OF
HOW TO DO
IT.
WHICH
IS WHERE ALL
OF YOU
COME IN.

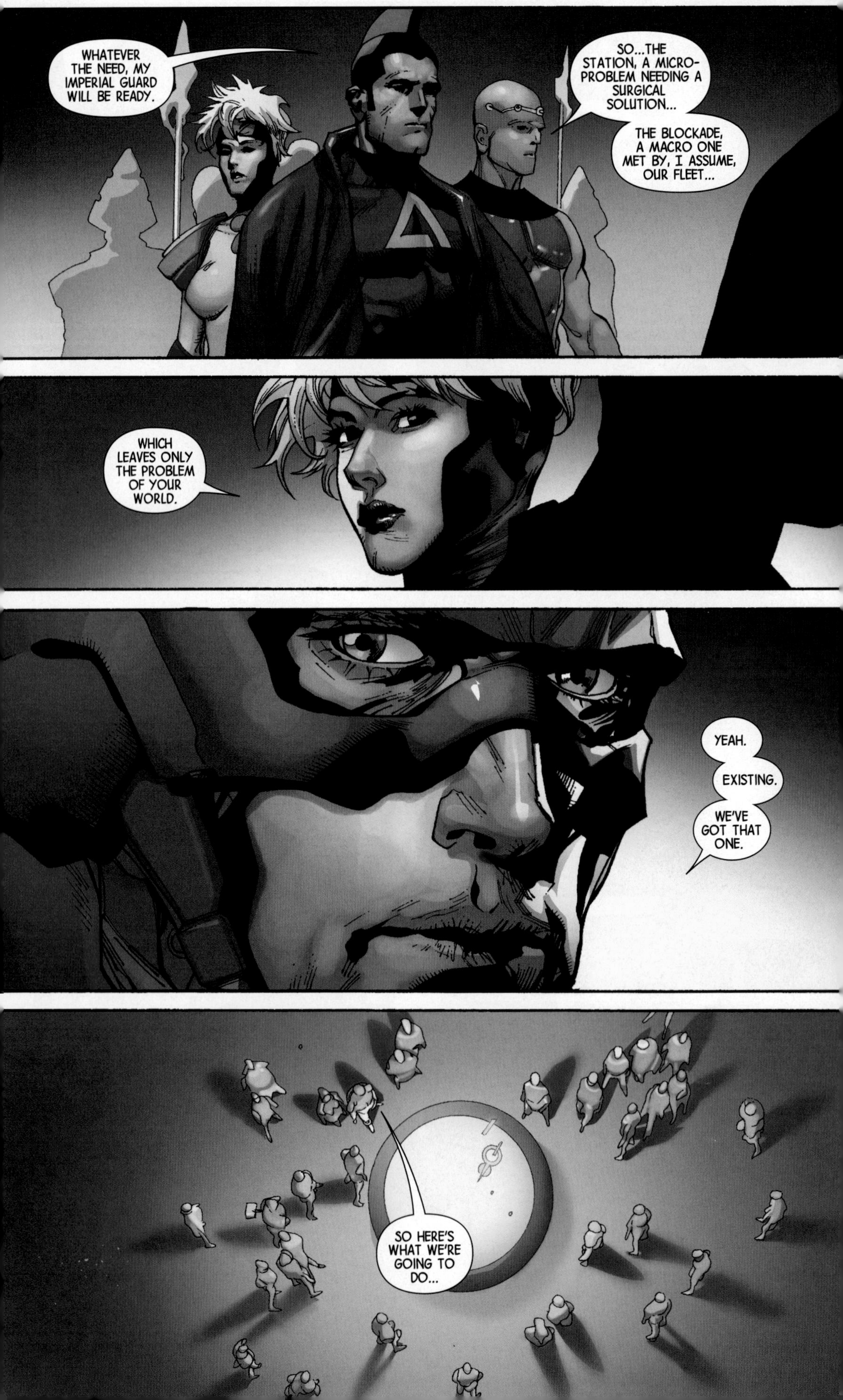
WHATEVER THE NEED, MY IMPERIAL GUARD WILL BE READY.
SO...THE STATION, A MICRO-PROBLEM NEEDING A SURGICAL SOLUTION...
THE BLOCKADE, A MACRO ONE MET BY, I ASSUME, OUR FLEET...
WHICH LEAVES ONLY THE PROBLEM OF YOUR WORLD.
YEAH.
EXISTING.
WE'VE GOT THAT ONE.
SO HERE'S WHAT WE'RE GOING TO DO...

A GREATER PURPOSE

◆

JUMP'S COMPLETED. ON OUR FINAL APPROACH NOW. A FORERUNNER HAS CONFIRMED WHAT THE SHI'AR LONG RANGE SCANS PICKED UP.

WE'RE BASICALLY GOING TO BE CRASHING A BLOCKADE.

AS EXPECTED. NUMBERS?

THE COUNCIL WORLDS SPARED WHAT THEY COULD IN THE HOPES THAT WE WOULD OVERWHELM THE PIRATES...SEND THEM RUNNING WHEN THEY SAW WHAT WAS COMING.

BUT THEY'VE GOT ABOUT WHAT WE HAVE...

AND IN ADDITION TO THAT--

THEY'RE FRESH, RESTED...NOT BROKEN AND BEATEN.

LIKE BEASTS WAITING ON WOUNDED PREY.

SOMETHING YOU WANT TO SAY, EDEN?

I'M TIRED. I C BELIEVE WHAT JUST LIVED THRO AND NOW I H TO DO IT AGAIN...

AND THIS TIME WITH THE LIV OF MY FAM AND PEOPL AT STAKE

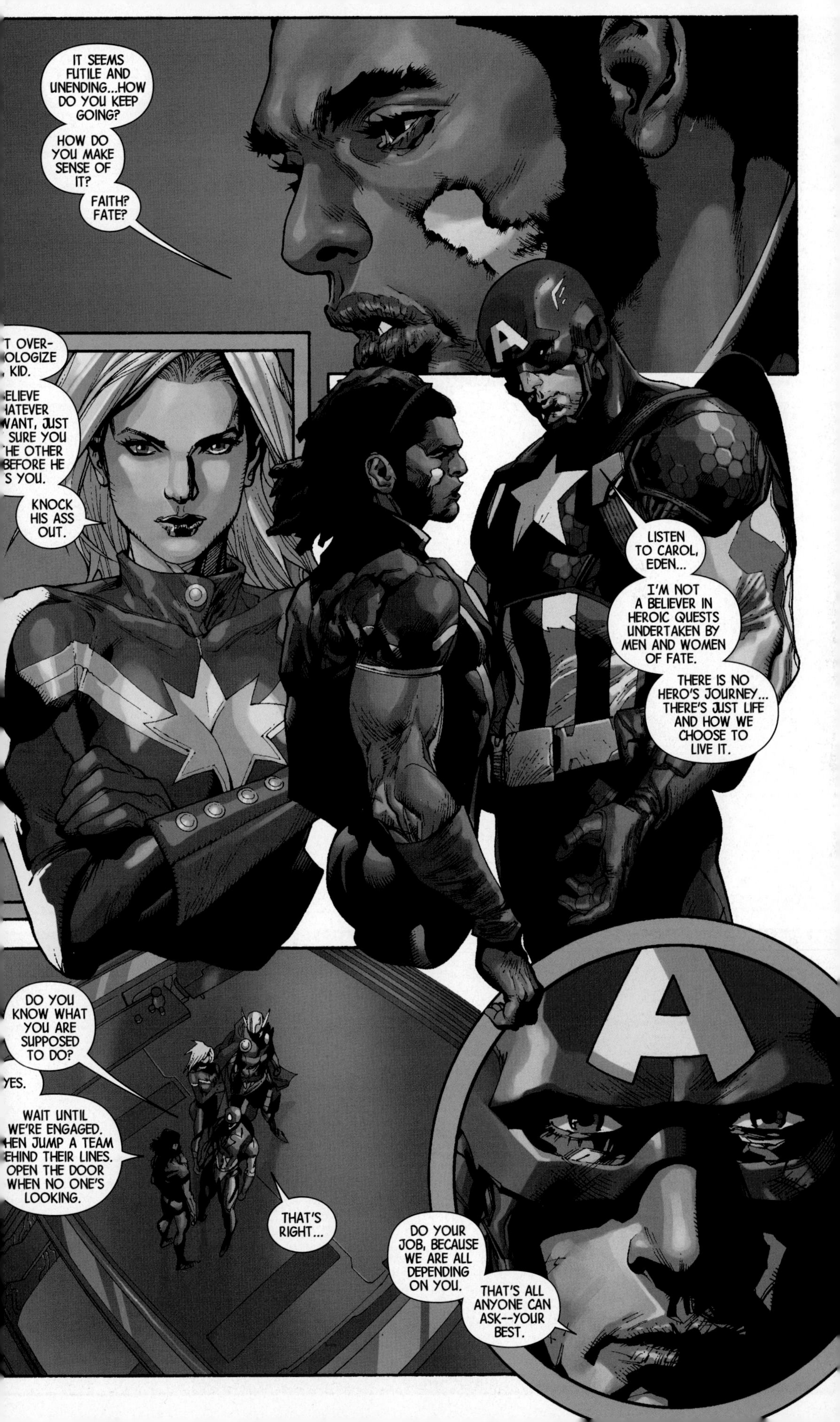

IT SEEMS FUTILE AND UNENDING...HOW DO YOU KEEP GOING?
HOW DO YOU MAKE SENSE OF IT?
FAITH? FATE?
T OVER- OLOGIZE , KID.
ELIEVE HATEVER WANT, JUST SURE YOU HE OTHER BEFORE HE S YOU.
KNOCK HIS ASS OUT.
LISTEN TO CAROL, EDEN...
I'M NOT A BELIEVER IN HEROIC QUESTS UNDERTAKEN BY MEN AND WOMEN OF FATE.
THERE IS NO HERO'S JOURNEY... THERE'S JUST LIFE AND HOW WE CHOOSE TO LIVE IT.
DO YOU KNOW WHAT YOU ARE SUPPOSED TO DO?
YES.
WAIT UNTIL WE'RE ENGAGED. HEN JUMP A TEAM EHIND THEIR LINES. OPEN THE DOOR WHEN NO ONE'S LOOKING.
THAT'S RIGHT...
DO YOUR JOB, BECAUSE WE ARE ALL DEPENDING ON YOU.
THAT'S ALL ANYONE CAN ASK--YOUR BEST.

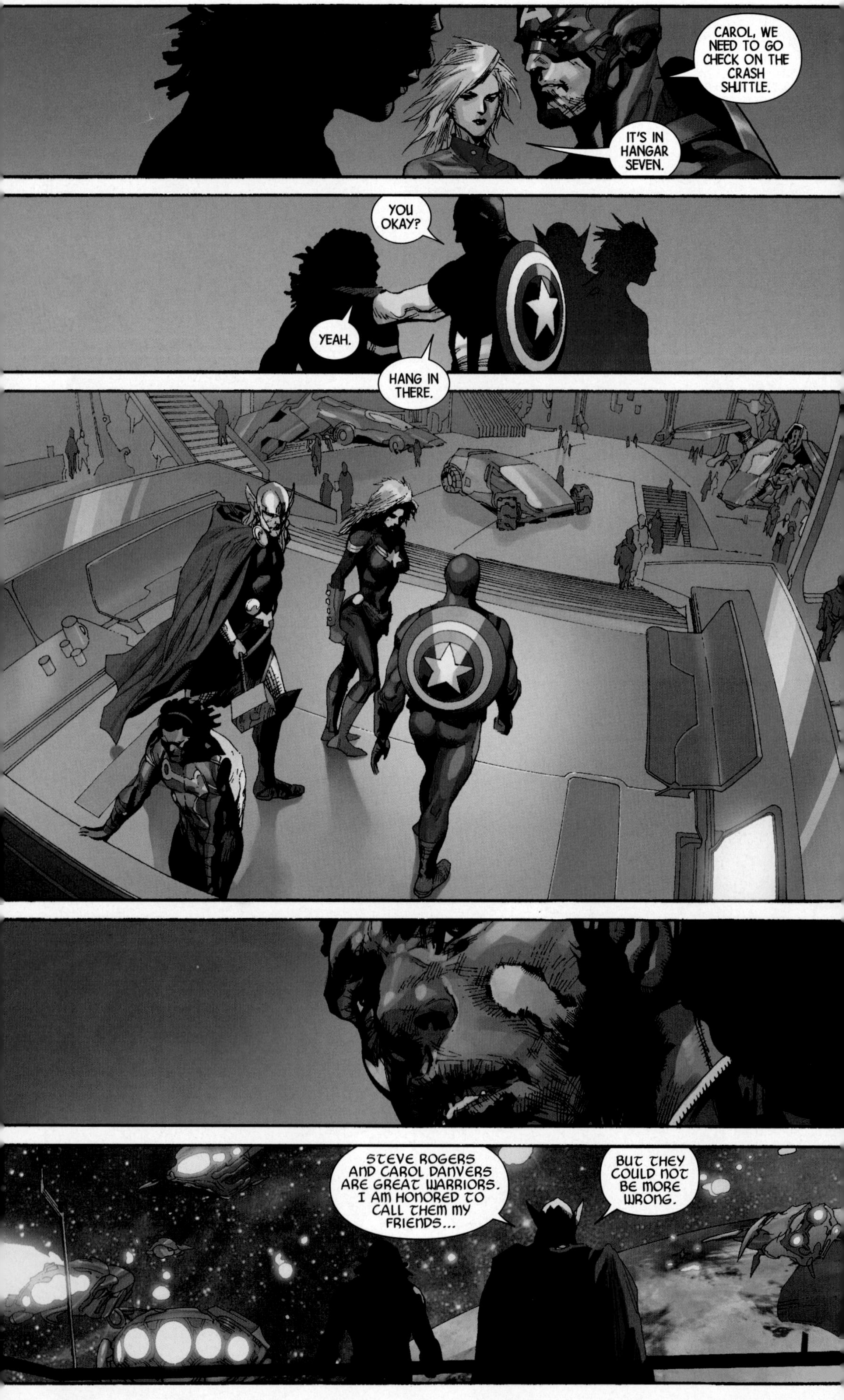
CAROL, WE NEED TO GO CHECK ON THE CRASH SHUTTLE.
IT'S IN HANGAR SEVEN.
YOU OKAY?
YEAH.
HANG IN THERE.
STEVE ROGERS AND CAROL DANVERS ARE GREAT WARRIORS. I AM HONORED TO CALL THEM MY FRIENDS...
BUT THEY COULD NOT BE MORE WRONG.

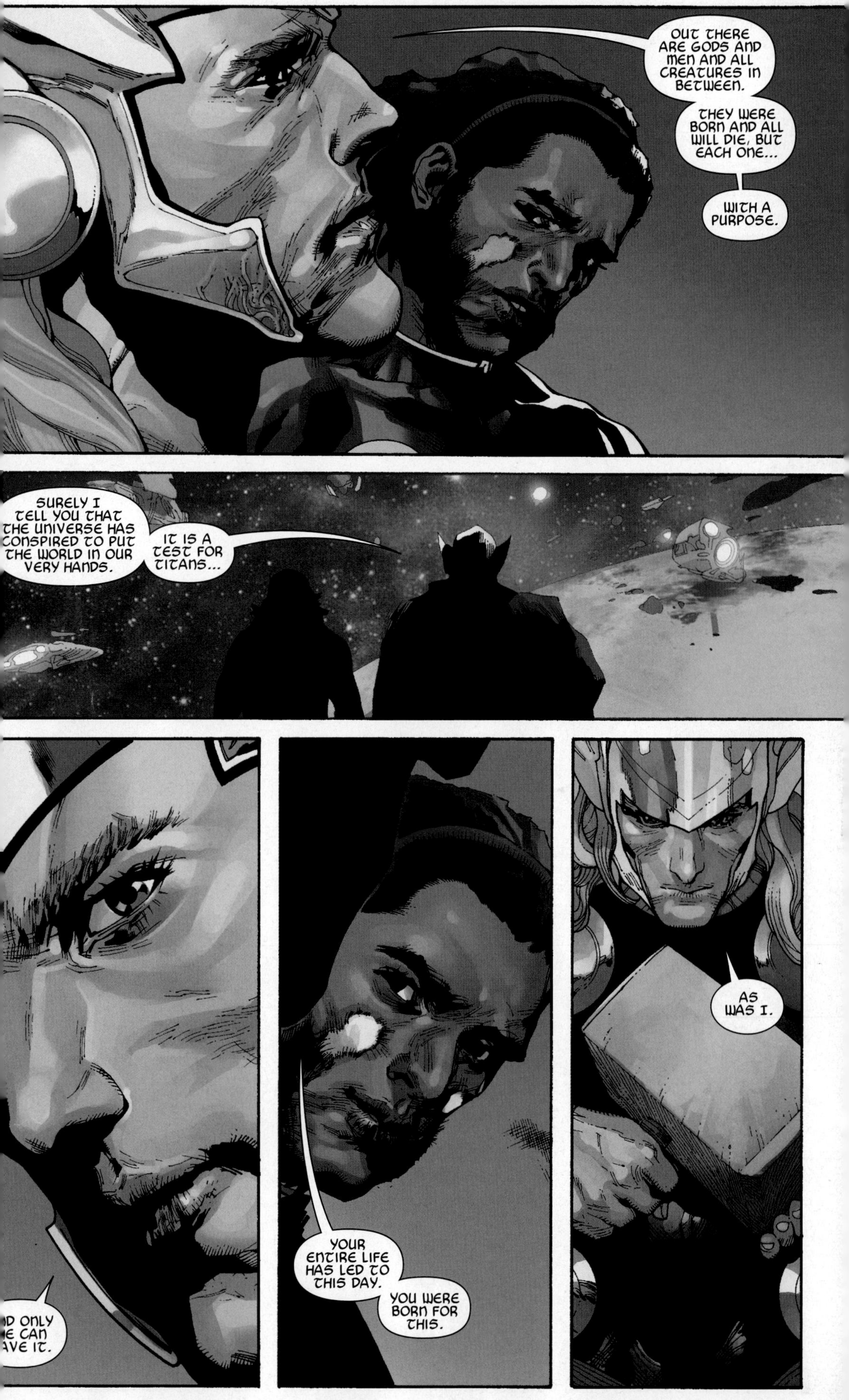
OUT THERE ARE GODS AND MEN AND ALL CREATURES IN BETWEEN.
THEY WERE BORN AND ALL WILL DIE, BUT EACH ONE...
WITH A PURPOSE.
SURELY I TELL YOU THAT THE UNIVERSE HAS CONSPIRED TO PUT THE WORLD IN OUR VERY HANDS.
IT IS A TEST FOR TITANS...
D ONLY E CAN AVE IT.
YOUR ENTIRE LIFE HAS LED TO THIS DAY.
YOU WERE BORN FOR THIS.
AS WAS I.

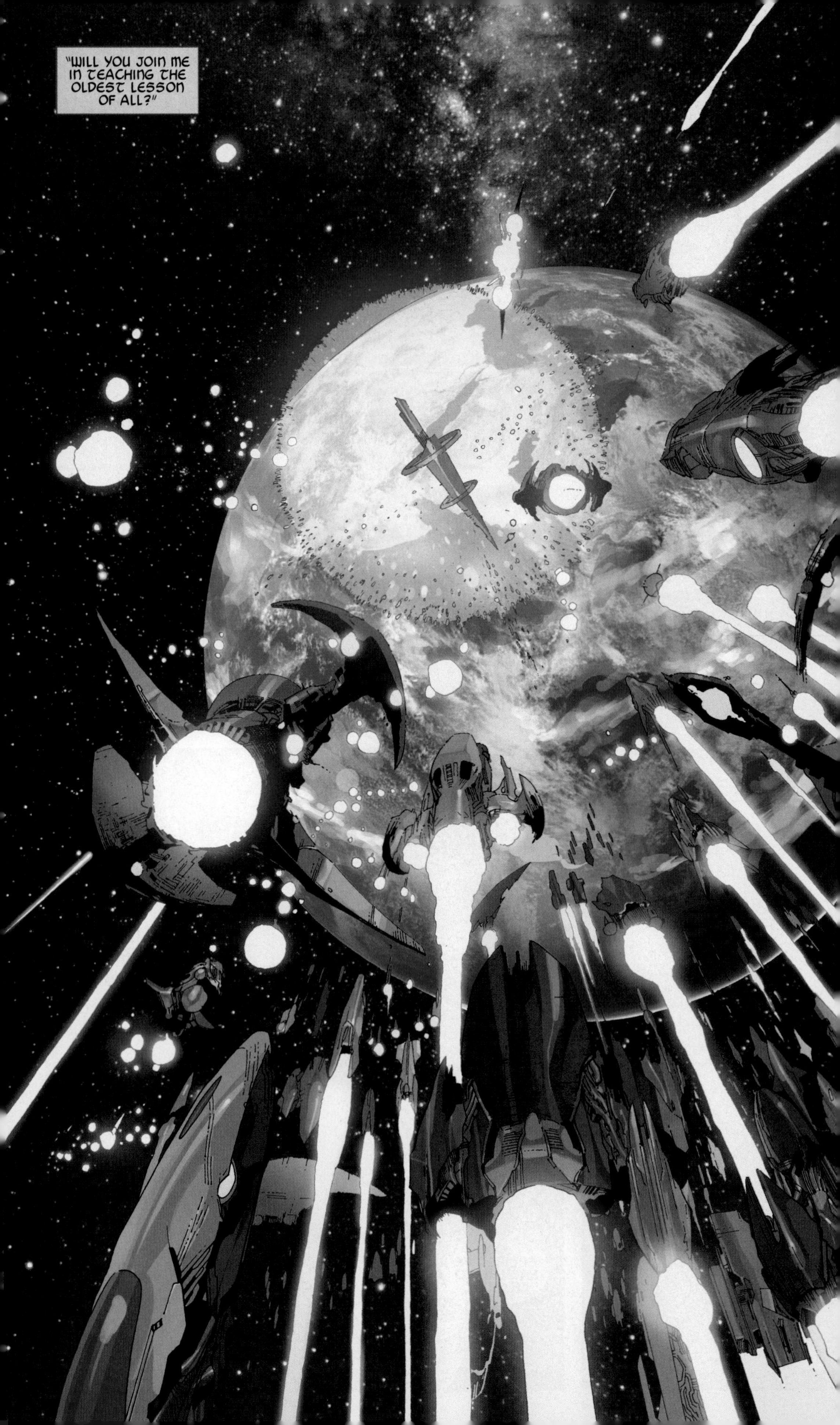
"WILL YOU JOIN ME IN TEACHING THE OLDEST LESSON OF ALL?"

"...TO THE VERY END"

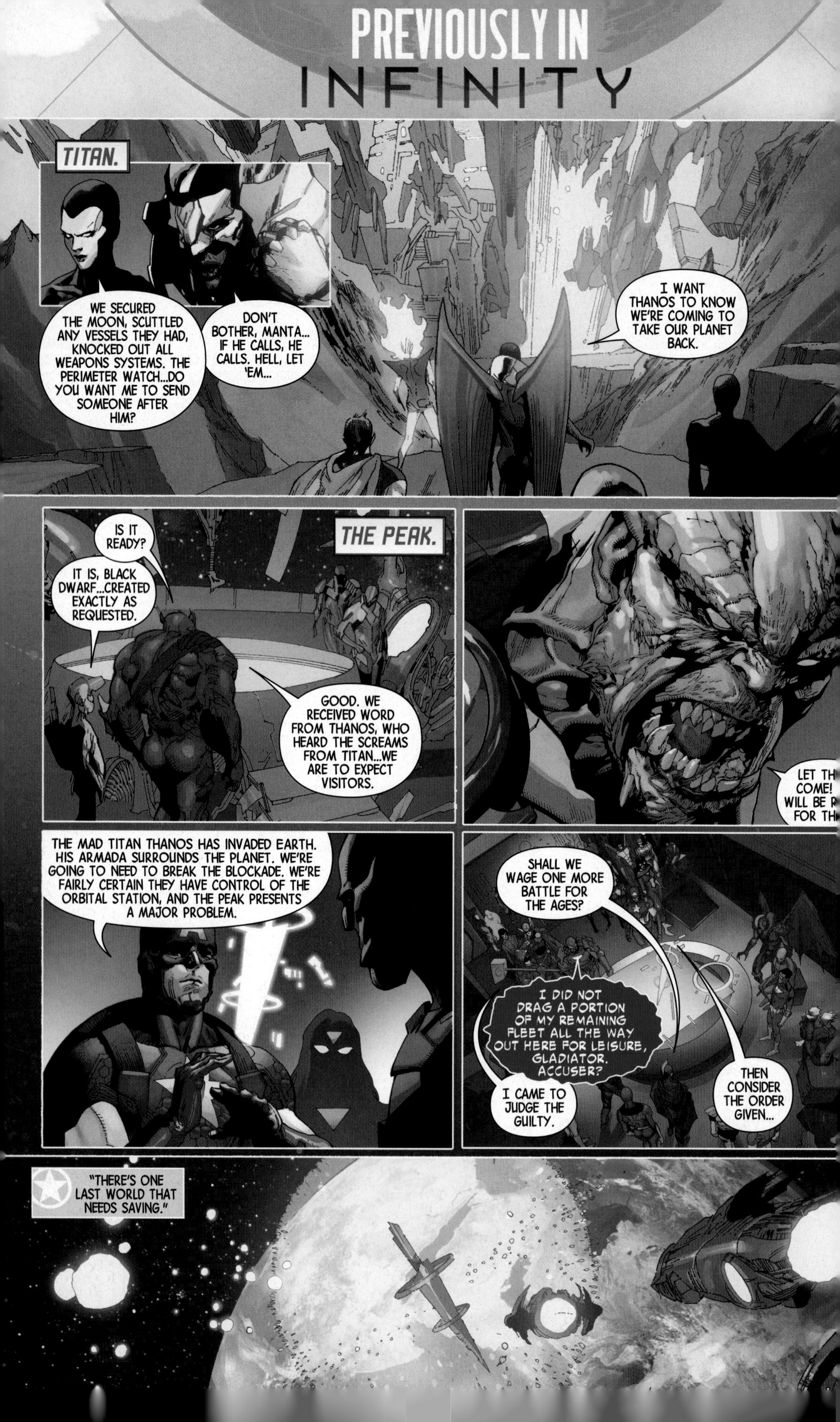
PREVIOUSLY IN
INFINITY
TITAN.
WE SECURED THE MOON, SCUTTLED ANY VESSELS THEY HAD, KNOCKED OUT ALL WEAPONS SYSTEMS. THE PERIMETER WATCH...DO YOU WANT ME TO SEND SOMEONE AFTER HIM?
DON'T BOTHER, MANTA... IF HE CALLS, HE CALLS. HELL, LET 'EM...
I WANT THANOS TO KNOW WE'RE COMING TO TAKE OUR PLANET BACK.
THE PEAK.
IS IT READY?
IT IS, BLACK DWARF...CREATED EXACTLY AS REQUESTED.
GOOD. WE RECEIVED WORD FROM THANOS, WHO HEARD THE SCREAMS FROM TITAN...WE ARE TO EXPECT VISITORS.
LET TH COME! WILL BE R FOR TH
THE MAD TITAN THANOS HAS INVADED EARTH. HIS ARMADA SURROUNDS THE PLANET. WE'RE GOING TO NEED TO BREAK THE BLOCKADE. WE'RE FAIRLY CERTAIN THEY HAVE CONTROL OF THE ORBITAL STATION, AND THE PEAK PRESENTS A MAJOR PROBLEM.
SHALL WE WAGE ONE MORE BATTLE FOR THE AGES?
I DID NOT DRAG A PORTION OF MY REMAINING FLEET ALL THE WAY OUT HERE FOR LEISURE, GLADIATOR. ACCUSER?
I CAME TO JUDGE THE GUILTY.
THEN CONSIDER THE ORDER GIVEN...
"THERE'S ONE LAST WORLD THAT NEEDS SAVING."

CAST

THE AVENGERS

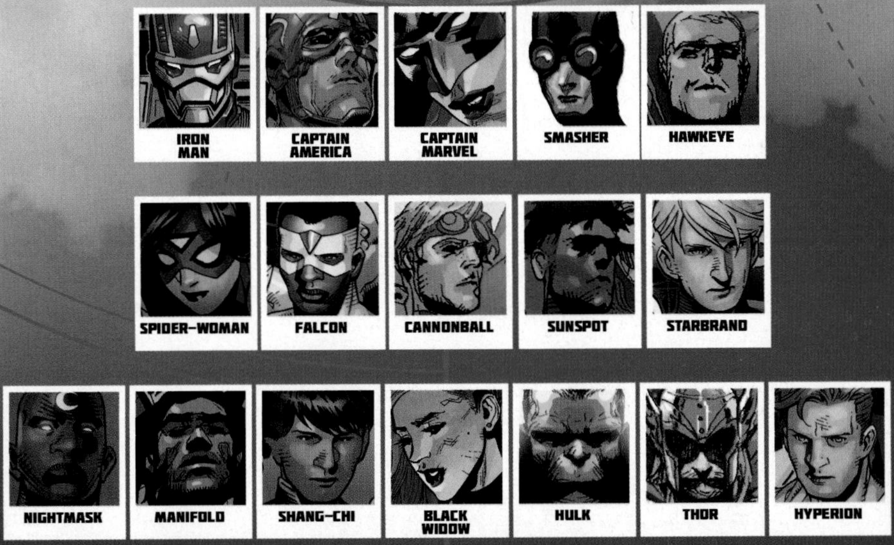
IRON MAN
CAPTAIN AMERICA
CAPTAIN MARVEL
SMASHER
HAWKEYE
SPIDER-WOMAN
FALCON
CANNONBALL
SUNSPOT
STARBRAND
NIGHTMASK
MANIFOLD
SHANG-CHI
BLACK WIDOW
HULK
THOR
HYPERION

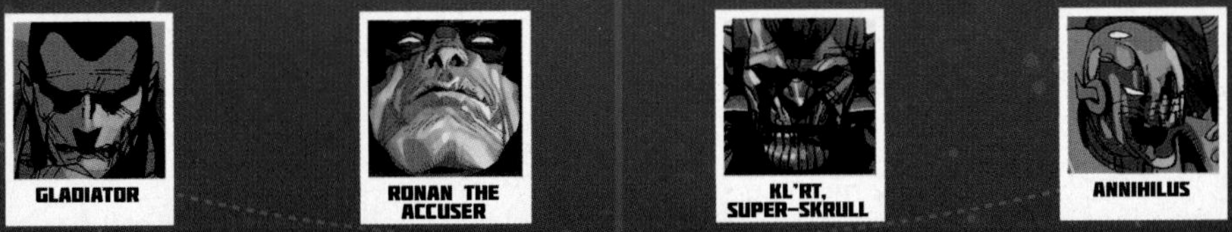
GLADIATOR
RONAN THE ACCUSER
KL'RT, SUPER-SKRULL
ANNIHILUS

SHI'AR IMPERIAL GUARD

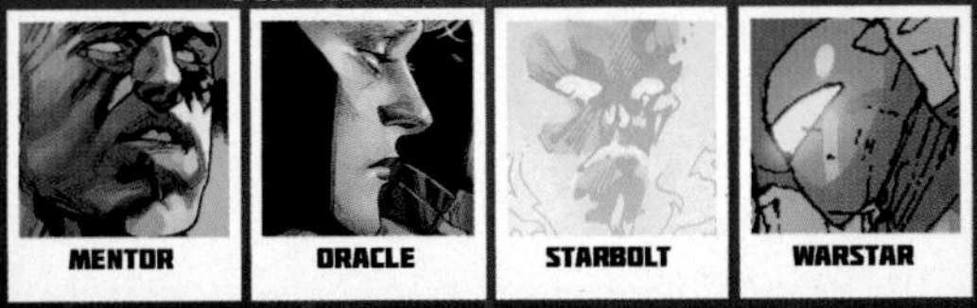
MENTOR
ORACLE
STARBOLT
WARSTAR

GUARDIANS OF THE GALAXY

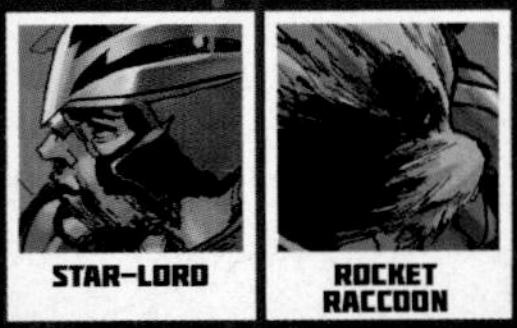
STAR-LORD
ROCKET RACCOON

THE BLACK ORDER/CULL OBSIDIAN

A WORD FROM THE HEAVENS

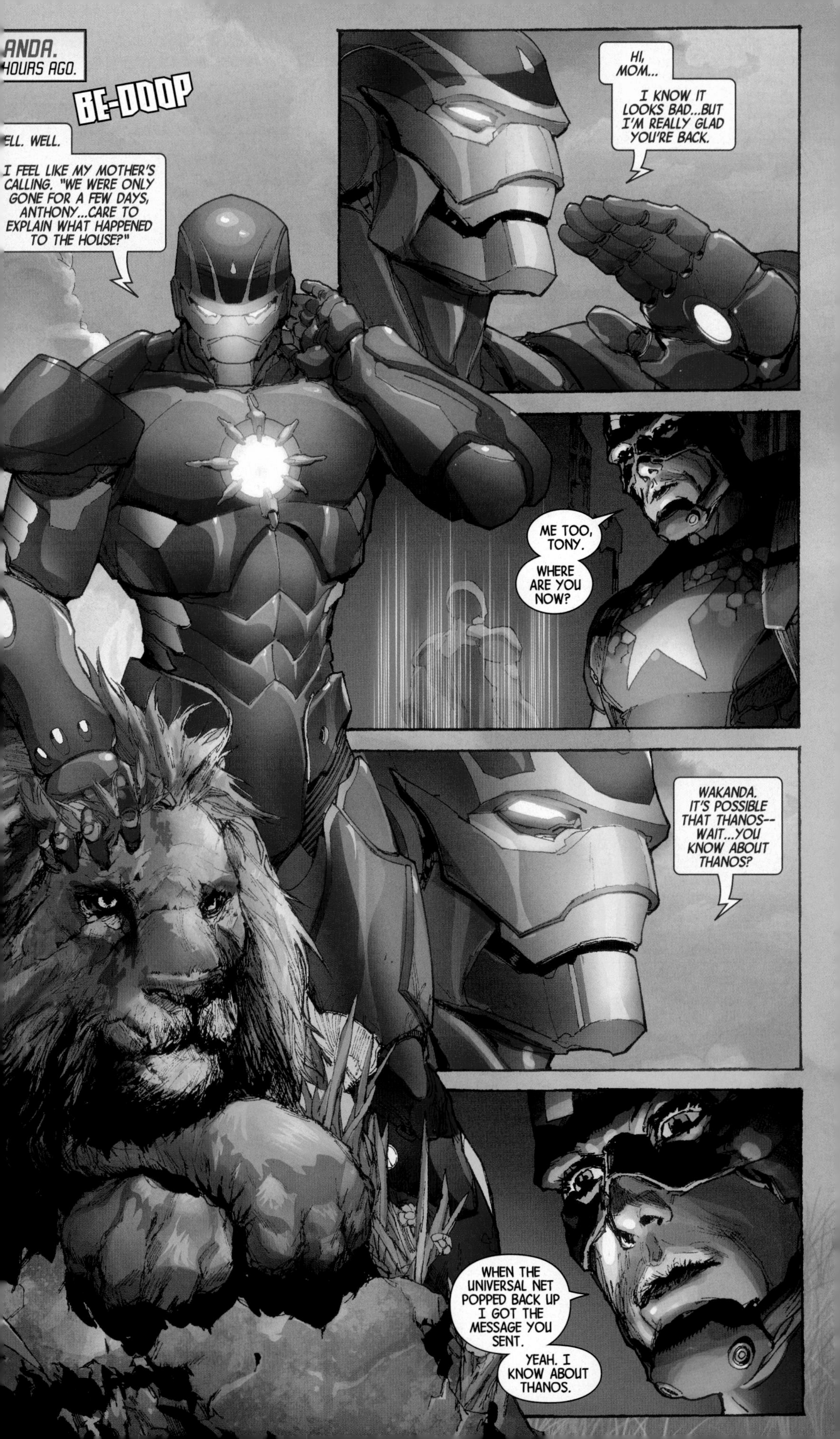
ANDA.
HOURS AGO.
BE-DOOP
ELL. WELL.
I FEEL LIKE MY MOTHER'S CALLING. "WE WERE ONLY GONE FOR A FEW DAYS, ANTHONY...CARE TO EXPLAIN WHAT HAPPENED TO THE HOUSE?"
HI, MOM...
I KNOW IT LOOKS BAD...BUT I'M REALLY GLAD YOU'RE BACK.
ME TOO, TONY.
WHERE ARE YOU NOW?
WAKANDA. IT'S POSSIBLE THAT THANOS-- WAIT...YOU KNOW ABOUT THANOS?
WHEN THE UNIVERSAL NET POPPED BACK UP I GOT THE MESSAGE YOU SENT.
YEAH. I KNOW ABOUT THANOS.

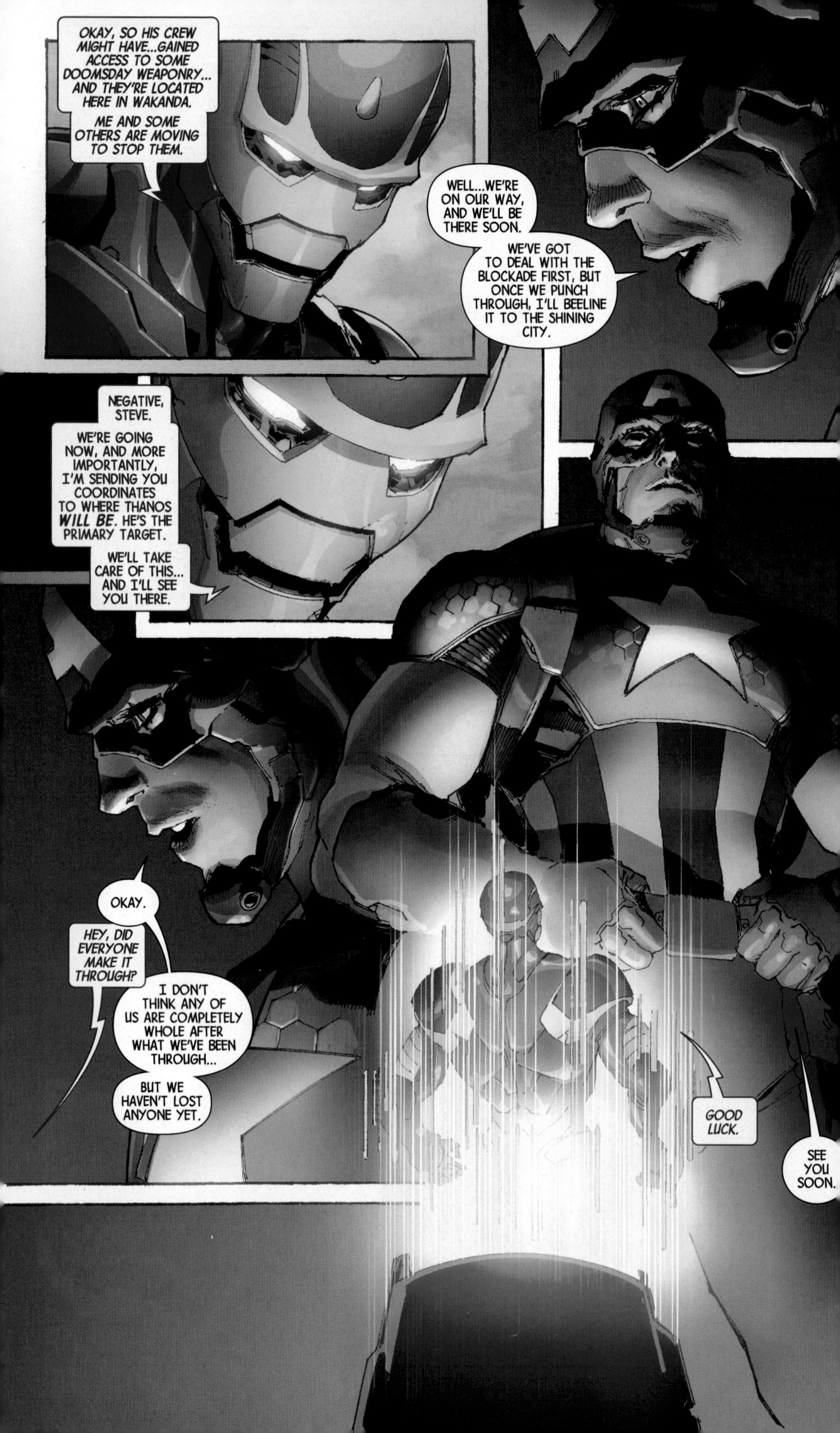
OKAY, SO HIS CREW MIGHT HAVE...GAINED ACCESS TO SOME DOOMSDAY WEAPONRY... AND THEY'RE LOCATED HERE IN WAKANDA.
ME AND SOME OTHERS ARE MOVING TO STOP THEM.
WELL...WE'RE ON OUR WAY, AND WE'LL BE THERE SOON.
WE'VE GOT TO DEAL WITH THE BLOCKADE FIRST, BUT ONCE WE PUNCH THROUGH, I'LL BEELINE IT TO THE SHINING CITY.
NEGATIVE, STEVE.
WE'RE GOING NOW, AND MORE IMPORTANTLY, I'M SENDING YOU COORDINATES TO WHERE THANOS *WILL BE*. HE'S THE PRIMARY TARGET.
WE'LL TAKE CARE OF THIS... AND I'LL SEE YOU THERE.
OKAY.
HEY, DID EVERYONE MAKE IT THROUGH?
I DON'T THINK ANY OF US ARE COMPLETELY WHOLE AFTER WHAT WE'VE BEEN THROUGH...
BUT WE HAVEN'T LOST ANYONE YET.
GOOD LUCK.
SEE YOU SOON.

HOMECOMING

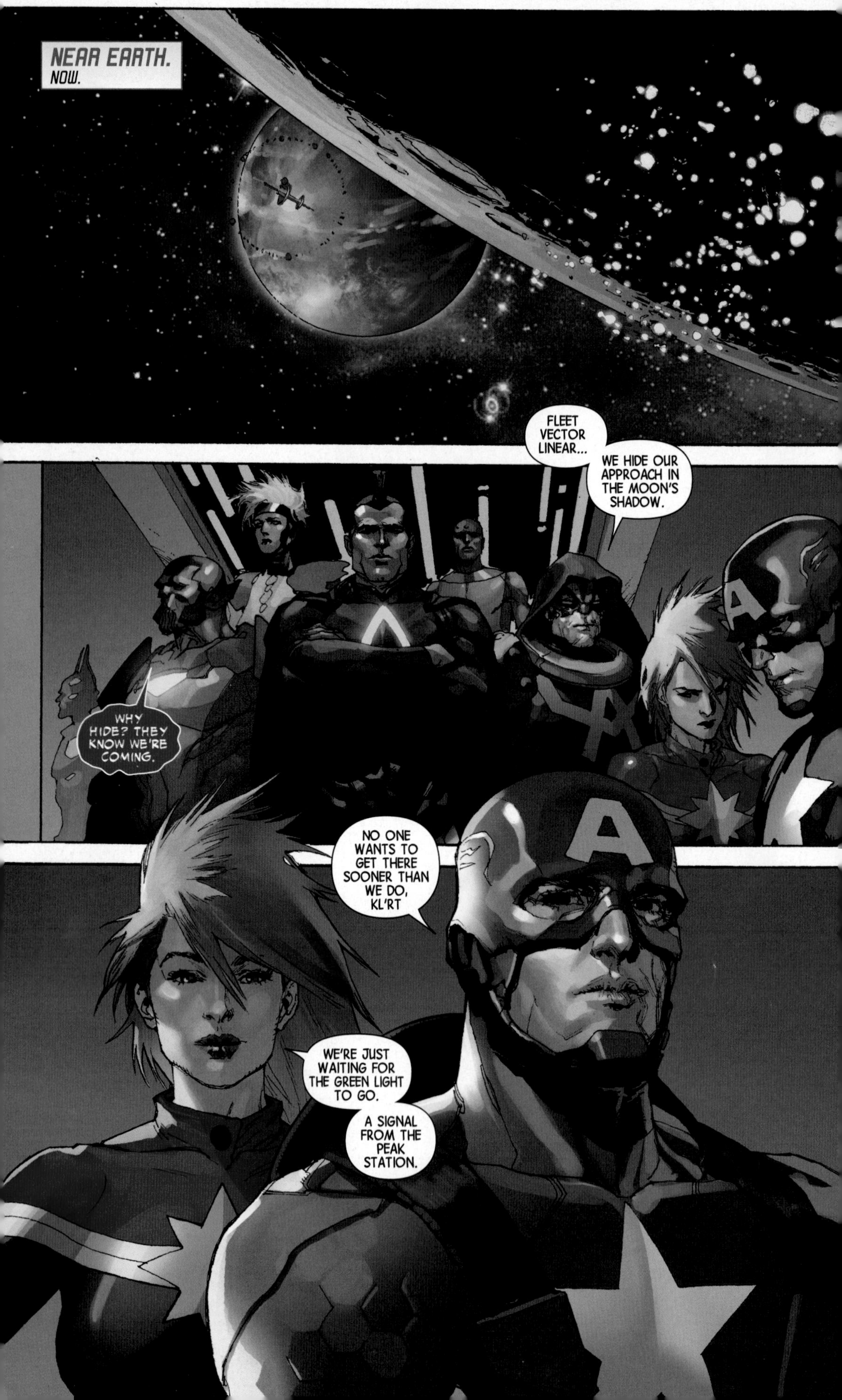
NEAR EARTH.
NOW.
FLEET VECTOR LINEAR...
WE HIDE OUR APPROACH IN THE MOON'S SHADOW.
WHY HIDE? THEY KNOW WE'RE COMING.
NO ONE WANTS TO GET THERE SOONER THAN WE DO, KL'RT
WE'RE JUST WAITING FOR THE GREEN LIGHT TO GO.
A SIGNAL FROM THE PEAK STATION.

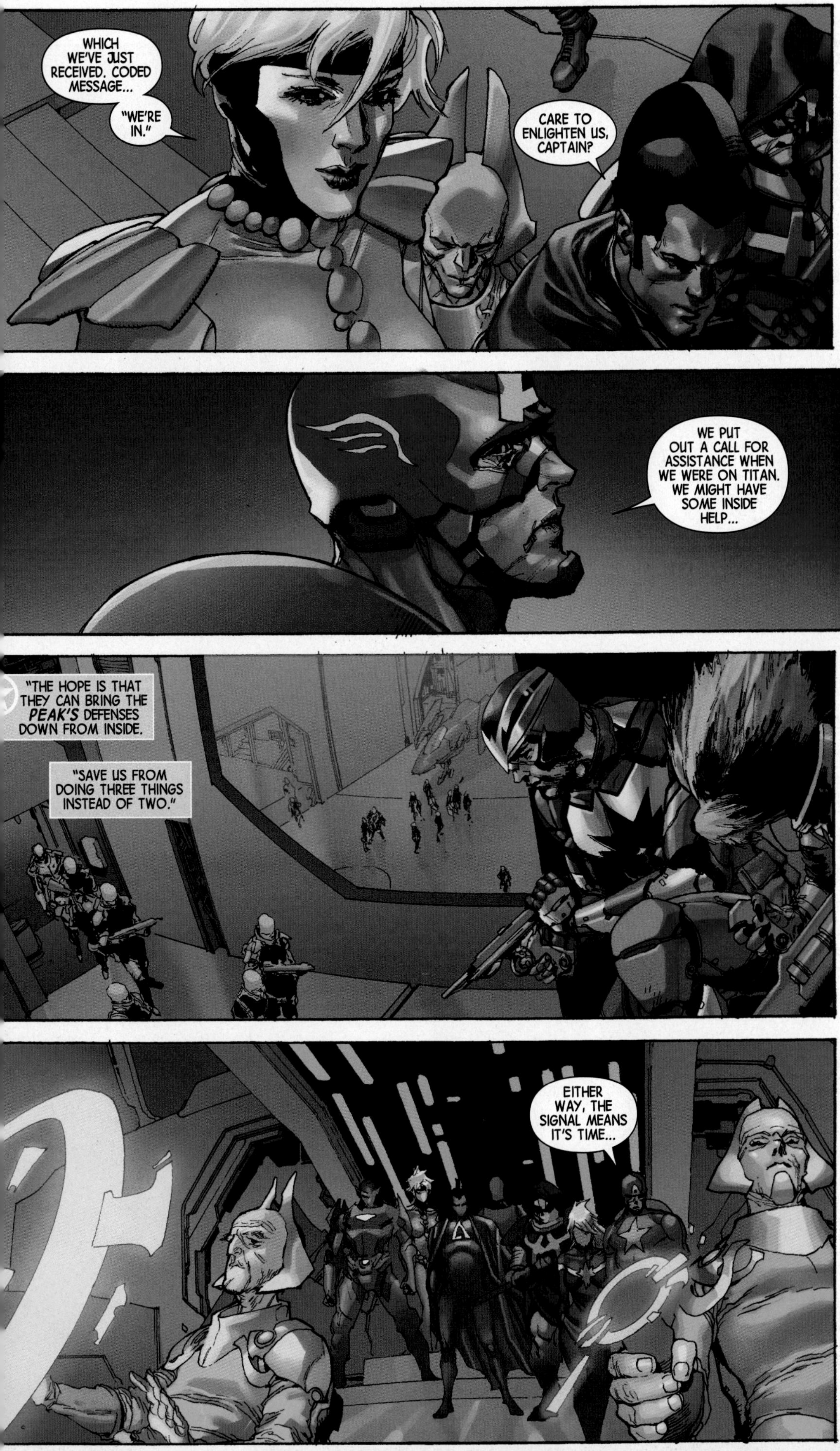
WHICH WE'VE JUST RECEIVED. CODED MESSAGE...
"WE'RE IN."
CARE TO ENLIGHTEN US, CAPTAIN?
WE PUT OUT A CALL FOR ASSISTANCE WHEN WE WERE ON TITAN. WE MIGHT HAVE SOME INSIDE HELP...
"THE HOPE IS THAT THEY CAN BRING THE PEAK'S DEFENSES DOWN FROM INSIDE.
"SAVE US FROM DOING THREE THINGS INSTEAD OF TWO."
EITHER WAY, THE SIGNAL MEANS IT'S TIME...

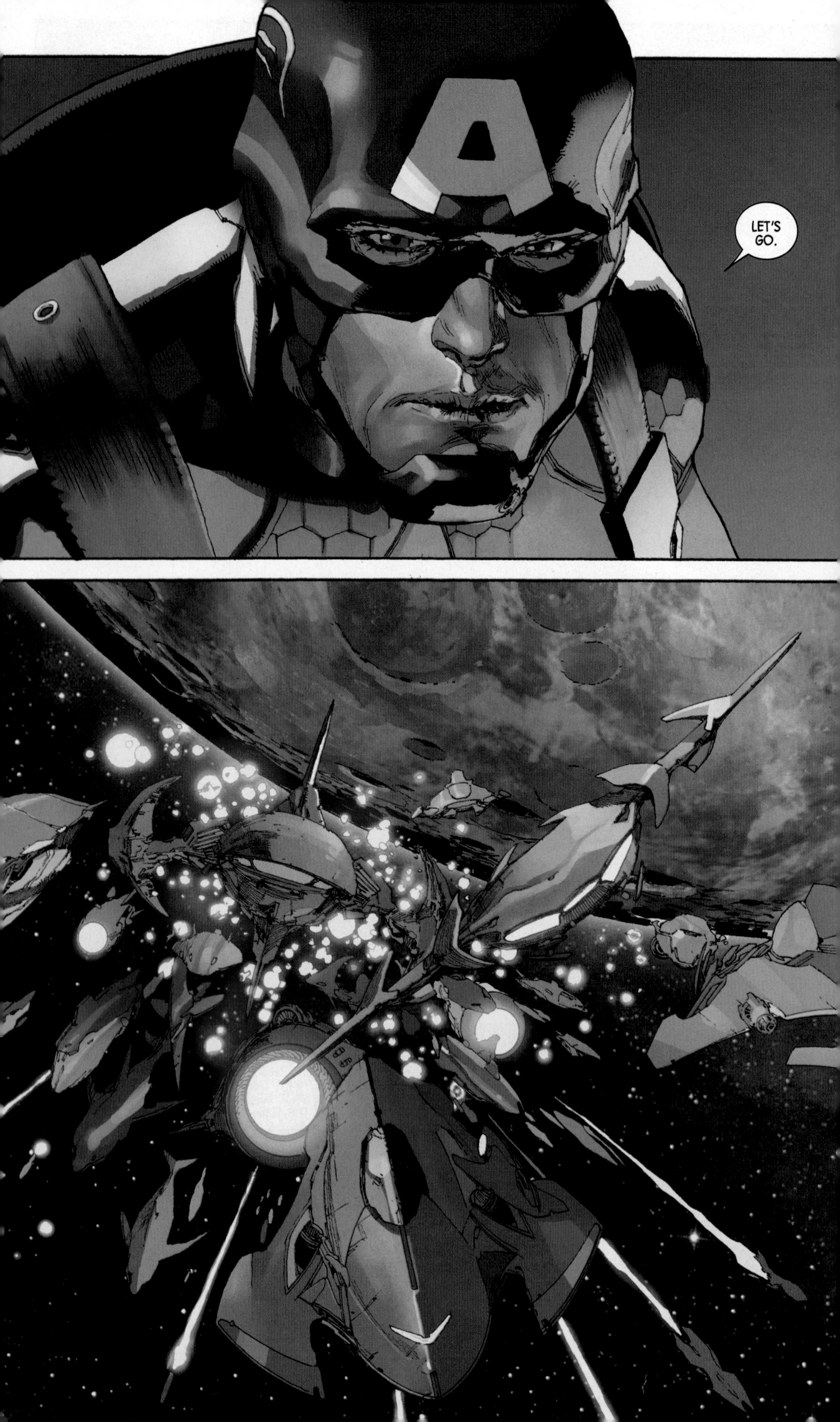
LET'S GO.

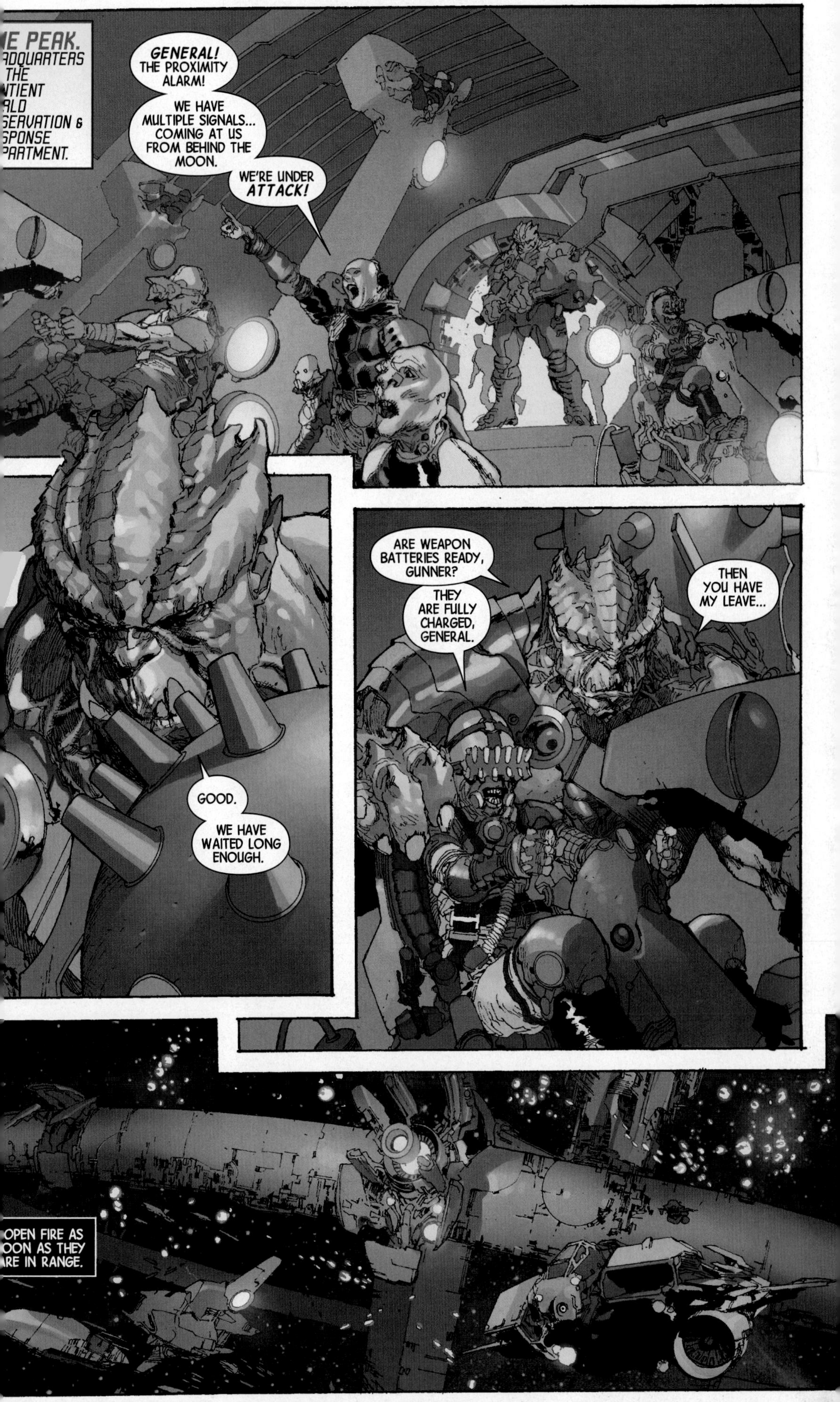

E PEAK. ADQUARTERS THE NTIENT RLD SERVATION & SPONSE PARTMENT.
GENERAL! THE PROXIMITY ALARM!
WE HAVE MULTIPLE SIGNALS... COMING AT US FROM BEHIND THE MOON.
WE'RE UNDER ATTACK!
GOOD.
WE HAVE WAITED LONG ENOUGH.
ARE WEAPON BATTERIES READY, GUNNER?
THEY ARE FULLY CHARGED, GENERAL.
THEN YOU HAVE MY LEAVE...
OPEN FIRE AS OON AS THEY RE IN RANGE.

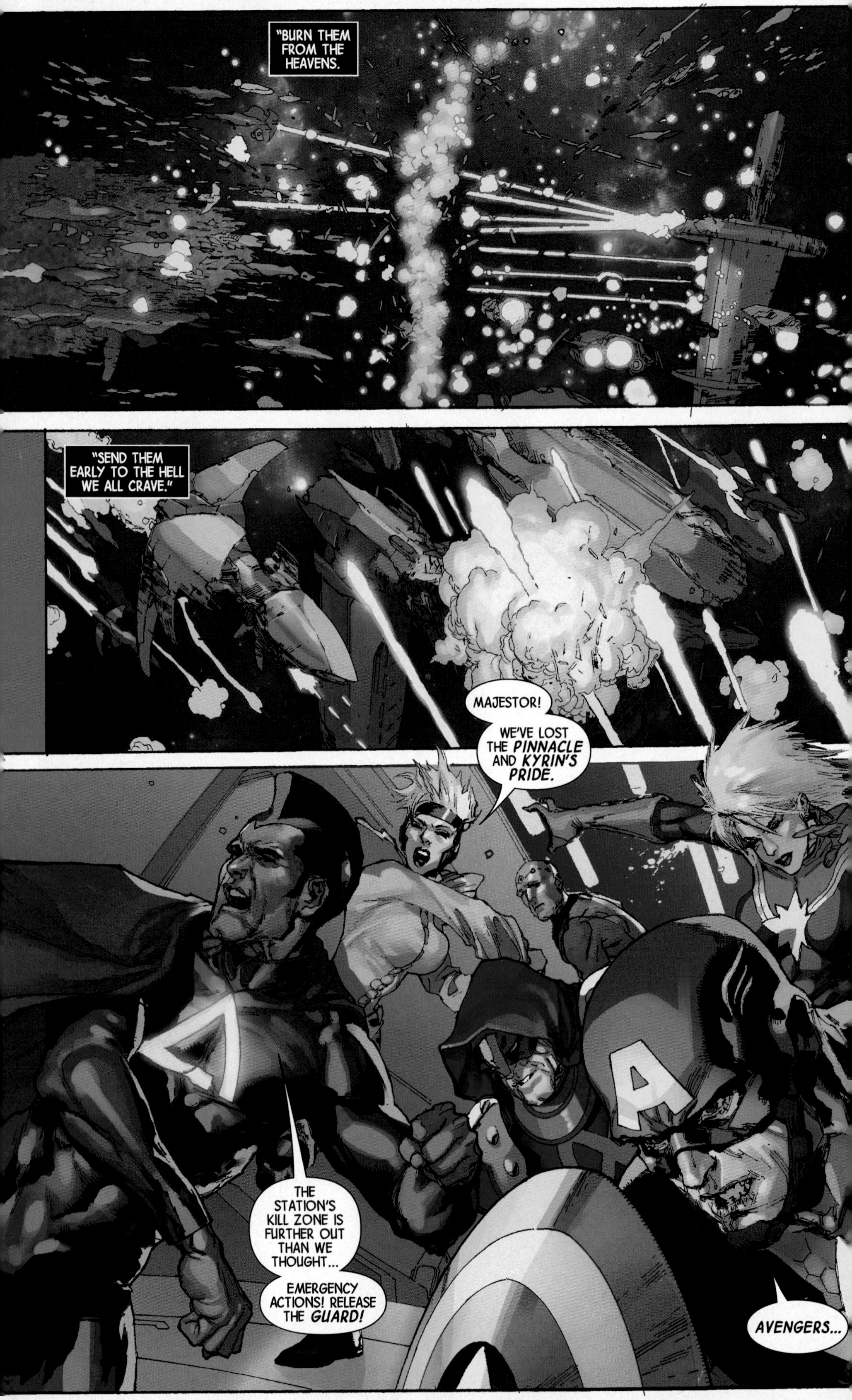
"BURN THEM FROM THE HEAVENS.
"SEND THEM EARLY TO THE HELL WE ALL CRAVE."
MAJESTOR!
WE'VE LOST THE *PINNACLE* AND *KYRIN'S PRIDE*.
THE STATION'S KILL ZONE IS FURTHER OUT THAN WE THOUGHT...
EMERGENCY ACTIONS! RELEASE THE *GUARD!*
AVENGERS...

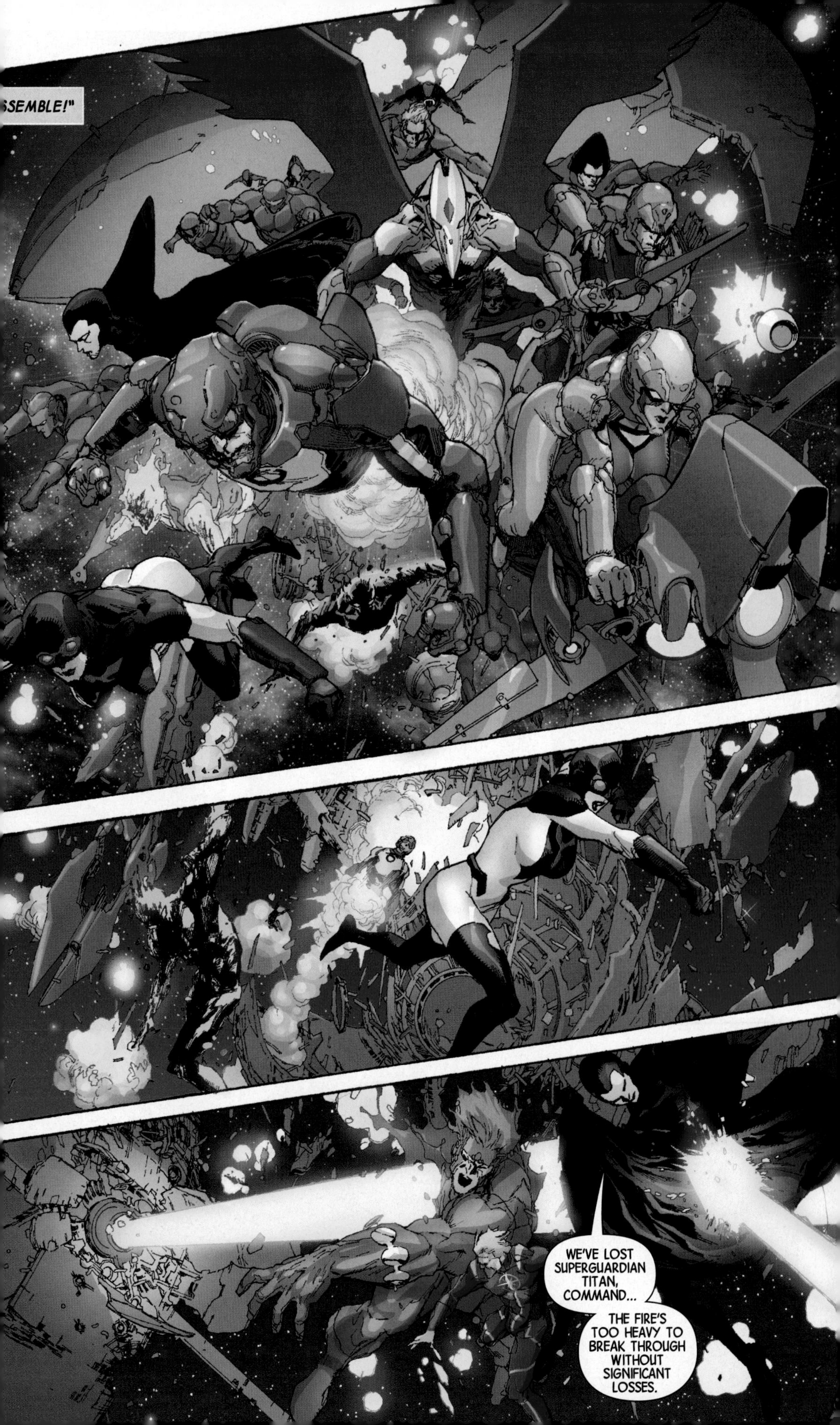
SSEMBLE!"
WE'VE LOST SUPERGUARDIAN TITAN, COMMAND...
THE FIRE'S TOO HEAVY TO BREAK THROUGH WITHOUT SIGNIFICANT LOSSES.

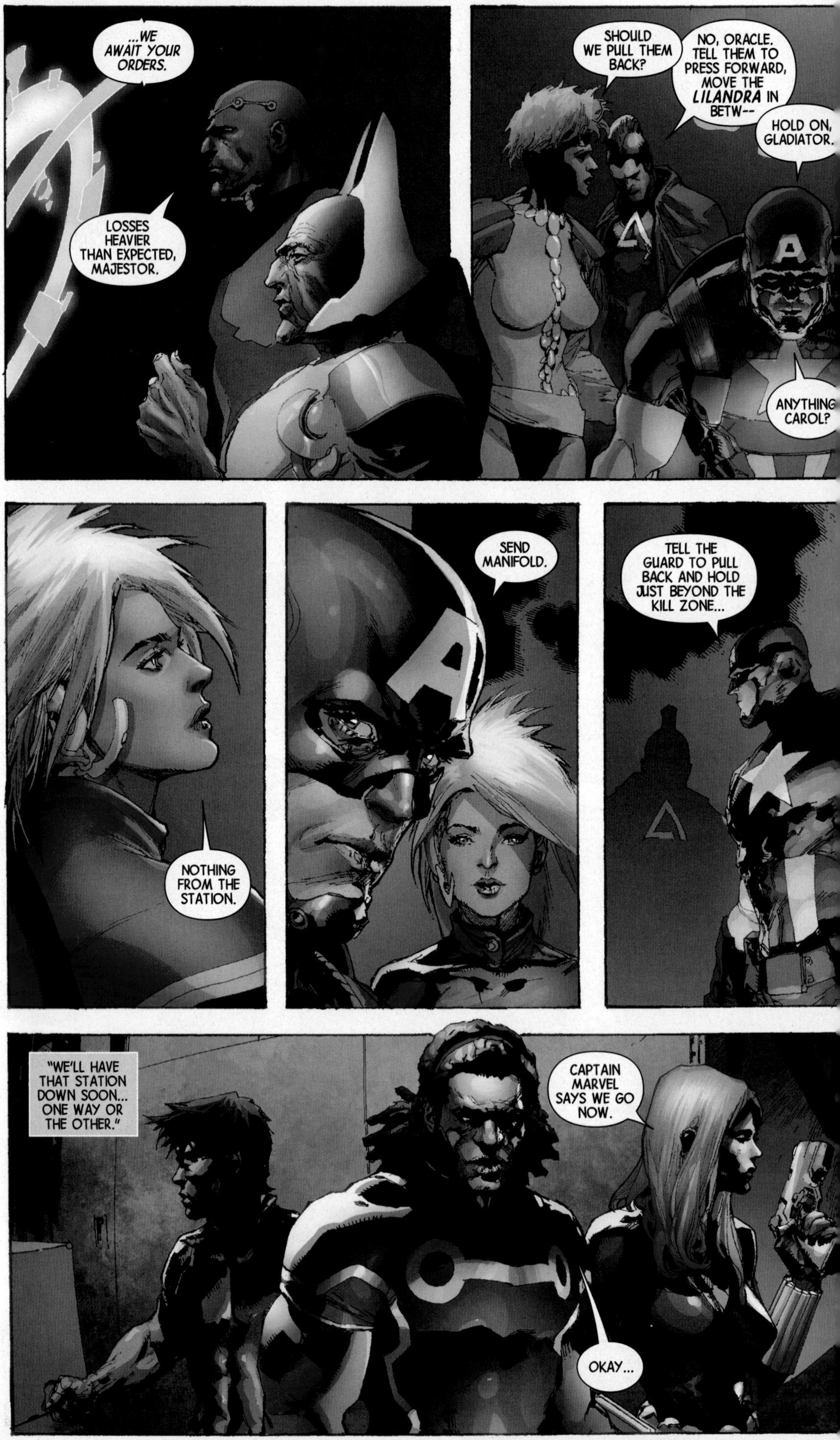
...WE AWAIT YOUR ORDERS.
LOSSES HEAVIER THAN EXPECTED, MAJESTOR.
SHOULD WE PULL THEM BACK?
NO, ORACLE. TELL THEM TO PRESS FORWARD, MOVE THE LILANDRA IN BETW--
HOLD ON, GLADIATOR.
ANYTHING CAROL?
NOTHING FROM THE STATION.
SEND MANIFOLD.
TELL THE GUARD TO PULL BACK AND HOLD JUST BEYOND THE KILL ZONE...
"WE'LL HAVE THAT STATION DOWN SOON... ONE WAY OR THE OTHER."
CAPTAIN MARVEL SAYS WE GO NOW.
OKAY...

HOLD ON TIGHT.

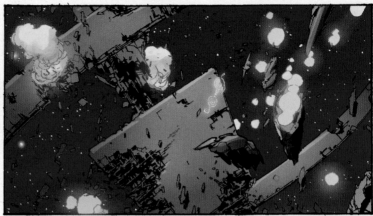

CONTACT.

MANIFOLD JUMP SUCCESSFUL.

THEY'RE IN.

THEN ALL THE PIECES ARE ON THE BOARD EXCEPT FOR US-- IT'S TIME TO LAUNCH...

TELL HYPERION TO SPIN UP THE ENGINES... WE'RE ON OUR WAY DOWN.

I'LL BE RIGHT BEHIND YOU, CAROL.

YOU DIDN'T HAVE TO...WHAT I MEAN IS...

I WANT TO THANK ALL OF YOU FOR THIS.

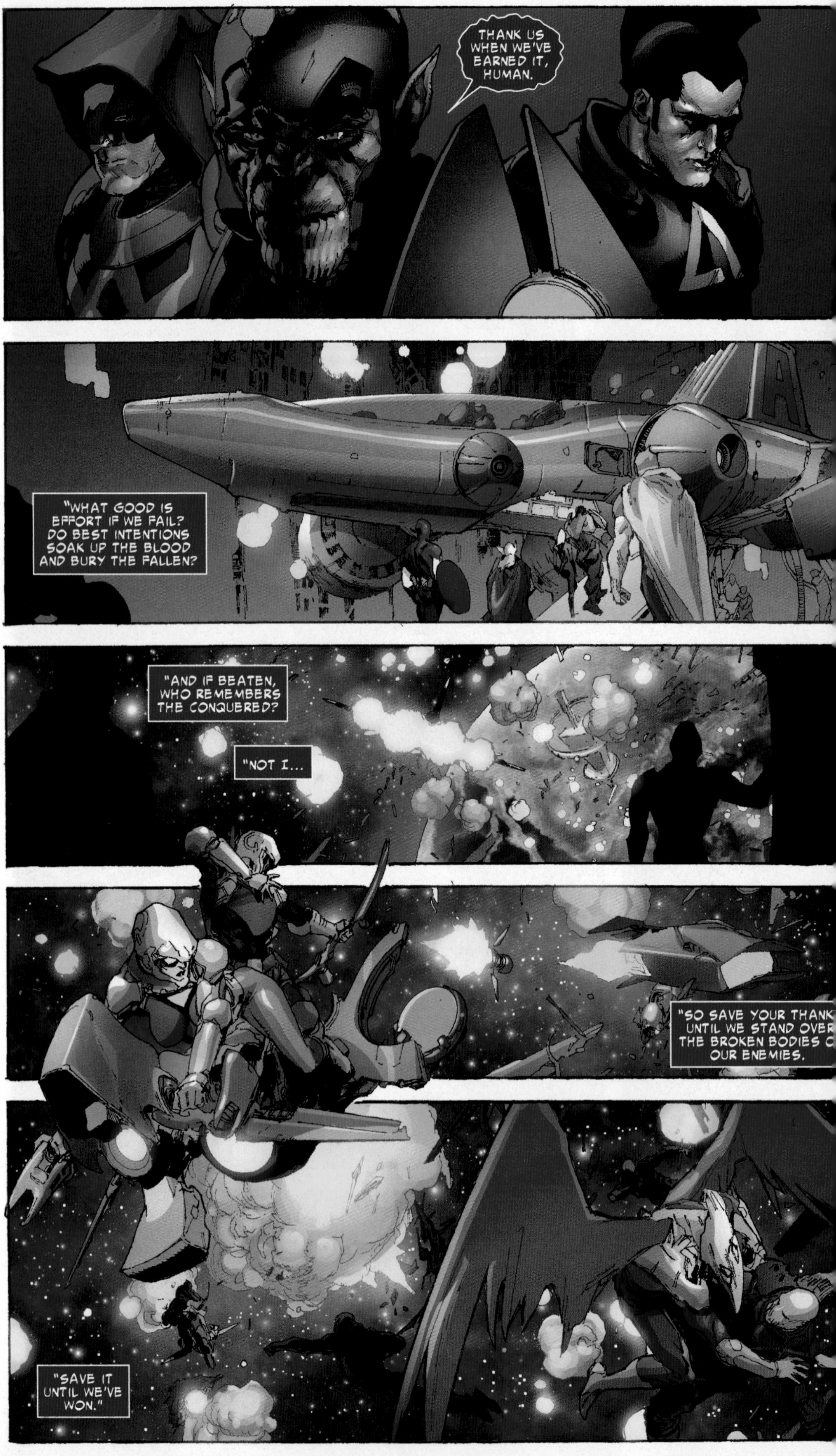
THANK US WHEN WE'VE EARNED IT, HUMAN.
"WHAT GOOD IS EFFORT IF WE FAIL? DO BEST INTENTIONS SOAK UP THE BLOOD AND BURY THE FALLEN?
"AND IF BEATEN, WHO REMEMBERS THE CONQUERED?
"NOT I...
"SO SAVE YOUR THANK UNTIL WE STAND OVER THE BROKEN BODIES O OUR ENEMIES.
"SAVE IT UNTIL WE'VE WON."

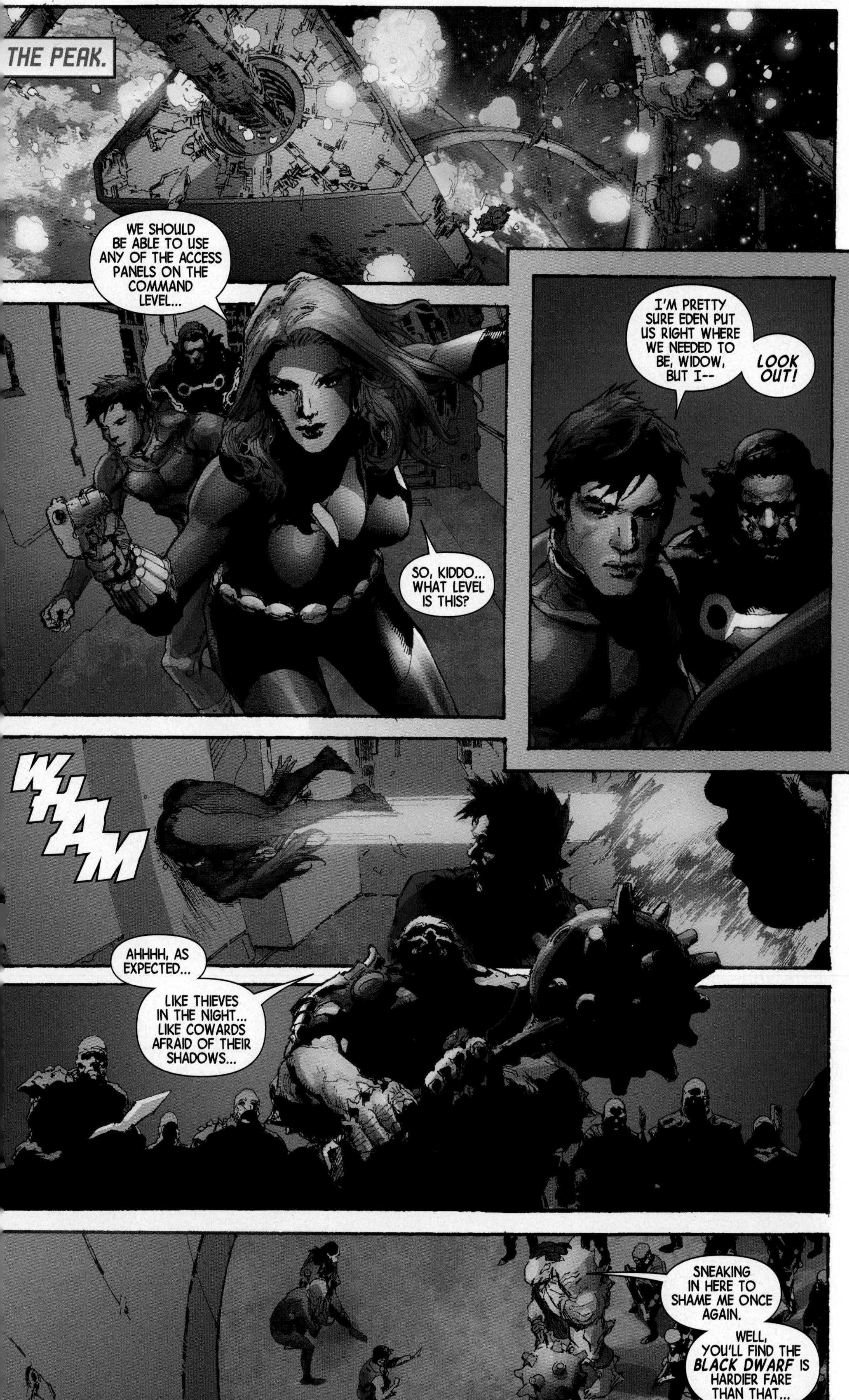
THE PEAK.
WE SHOULD BE ABLE TO USE ANY OF THE ACCESS PANELS ON THE COMMAND LEVEL...
SO, KIDDO... WHAT LEVEL IS THIS?
I'M PRETTY SURE EDEN PUT US RIGHT WHERE WE NEEDED TO BE, WIDOW, BUT I--
LOOK OUT!
WHAM
AHHHH, AS EXPECTED...
LIKE THIEVES IN THE NIGHT... LIKE COWARDS AFRAID OF THEIR SHADOWS...
SNEAKING IN HERE TO SHAME ME ONCE AGAIN.
WELL, YOU'LL FIND THE *BLACK DWARF* IS HARDIER FARE THAN THAT...

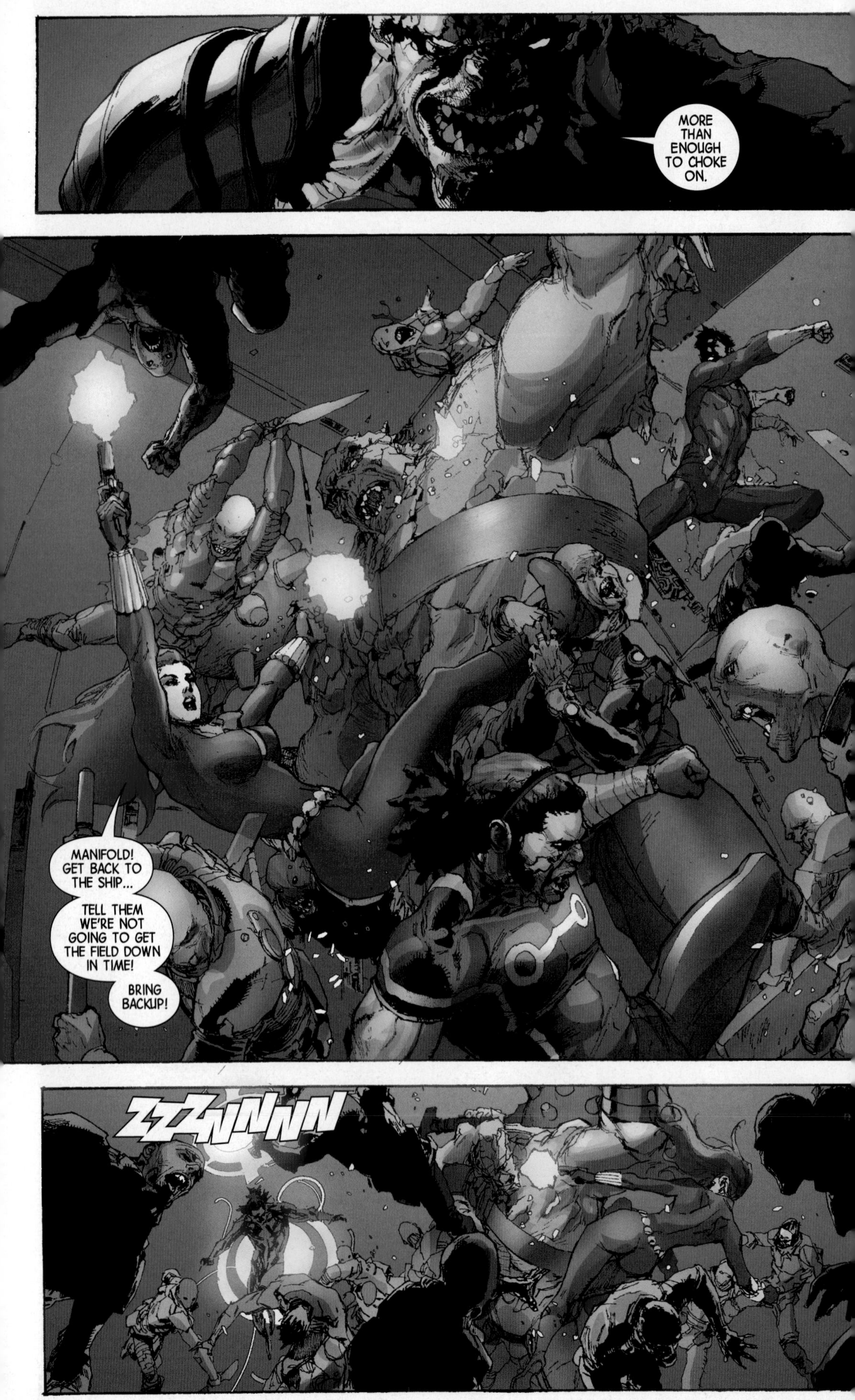
MORE THAN ENOUGH TO CHOKE ON.
MANIFOLD! GET BACK TO THE SHIP...
TELL THEM WE'RE NOT GOING TO GET THE FIELD DOWN IN TIME!
BRING BACKUP!
ZZZNNNNN

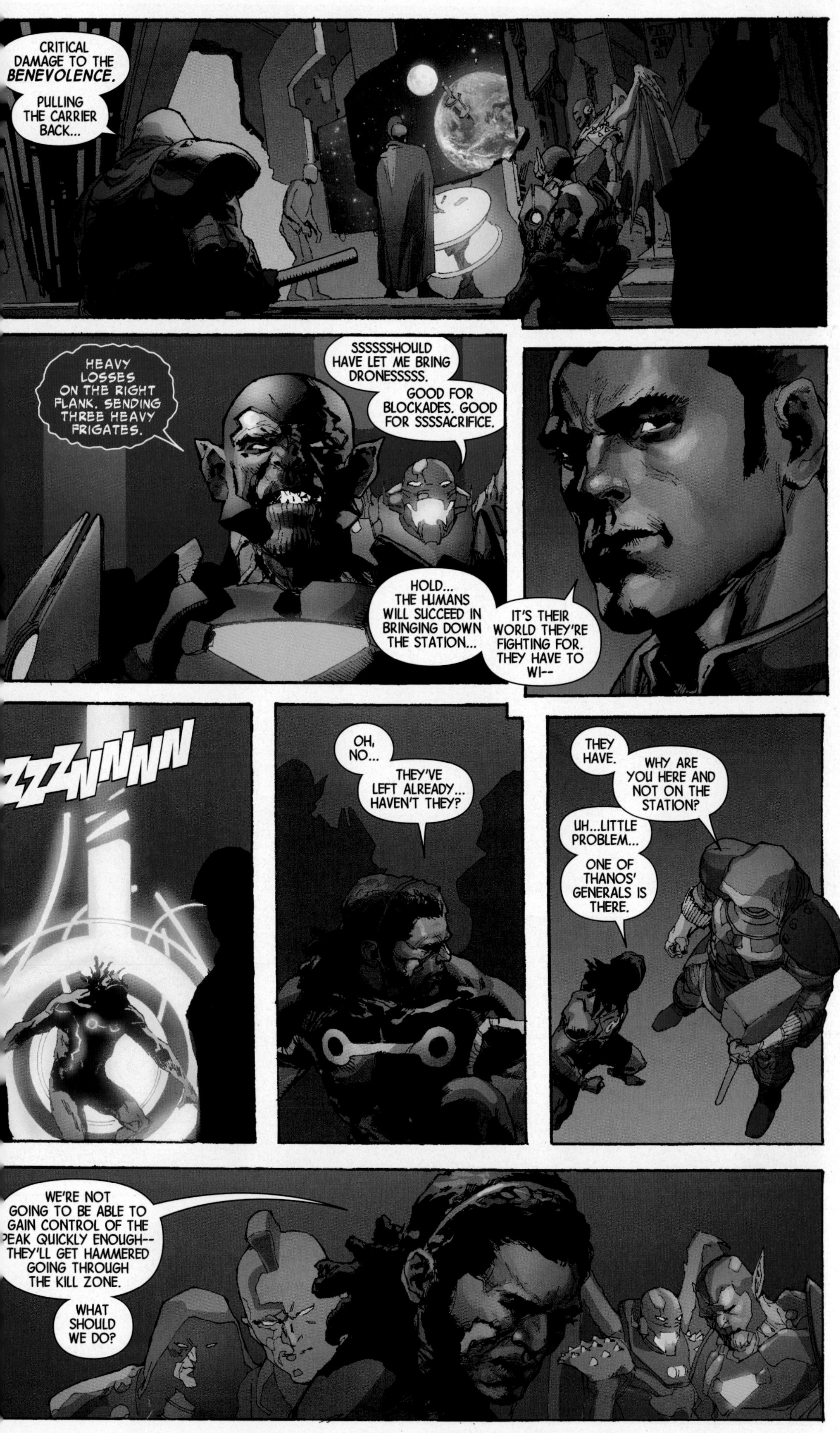
CRITICAL DAMAGE TO THE *BENEVOLENCE.*
PULLING THE CARRIER BACK...
HEAVY LOSSES ON THE RIGHT FLANK. SENDING THREE HEAVY FRIGATES.
SSSSSSHOULD HAVE LET ME BRING DRONESSSSS.
GOOD FOR BLOCKADES. GOOD FOR SSSSACRIFICE.
HOLD... THE HUMANS WILL SUCCEED IN BRINGING DOWN THE STATION...
IT'S THEIR WORLD THEY'RE FIGHTING FOR. THEY HAVE TO WI--
ZZZNNNNN
OH, NO...
THEY'VE LEFT ALREADY... HAVEN'T THEY?
THEY HAVE.
WHY ARE YOU HERE AND NOT ON THE STATION?
UH...LITTLE PROBLEM...
ONE OF THANOS' GENERALS IS THERE.
WE'RE NOT GOING TO BE ABLE TO GAIN CONTROL OF THE PEAK QUICKLY ENOUGH--THEY'LL GET HAMMERED GOING THROUGH THE KILL ZONE.
WHAT SHOULD WE DO?

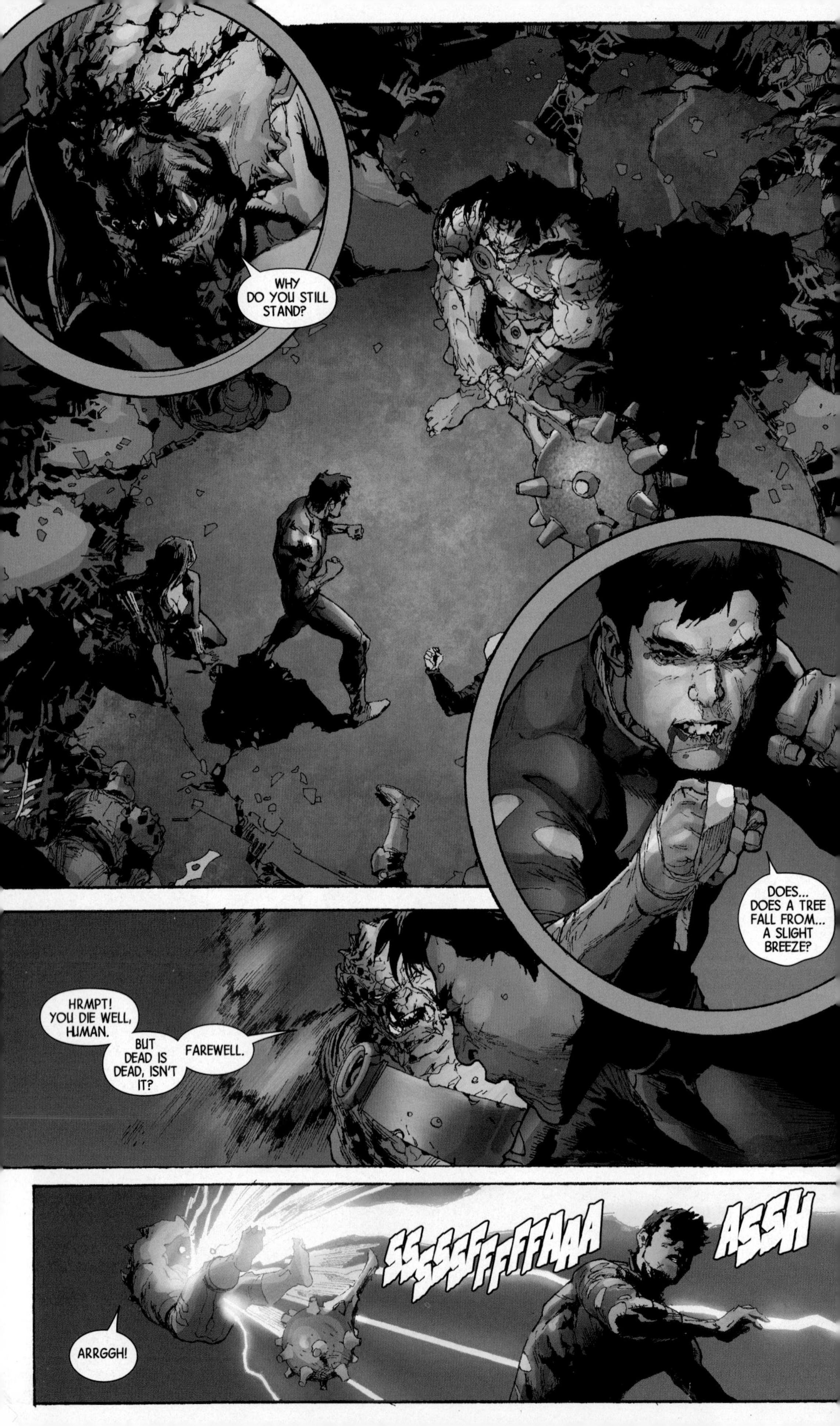
WHY DO YOU STILL STAND?
DOES... DOES A TREE FALL FROM... A SLIGHT BREEZE?
HRMPT! YOU DIE WELL, HUMAN.
BUT DEAD IS DEAD, ISN'T IT?
FAREWELL.
ARRGGH!
SSSSSFFFFFAAAASSH

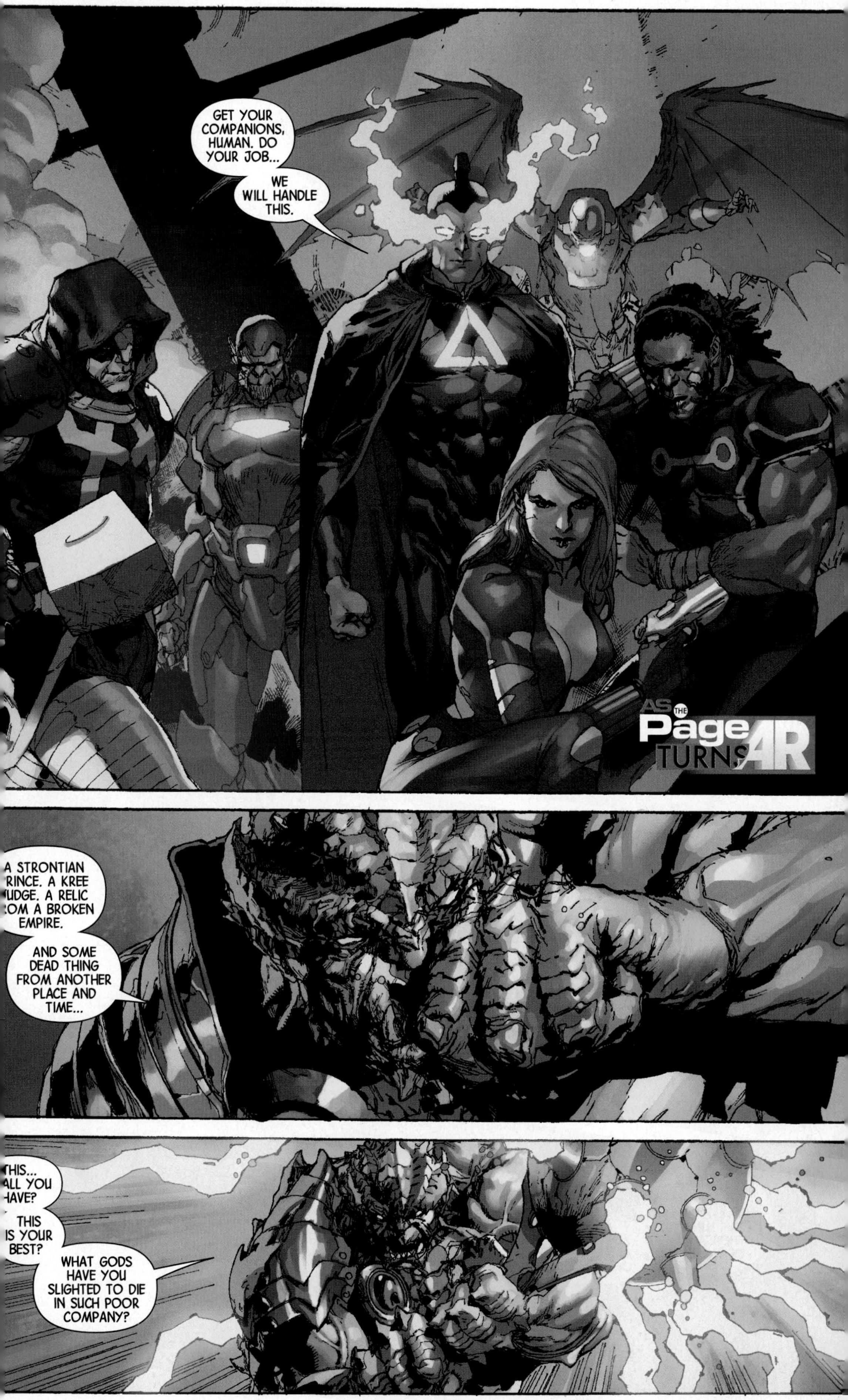

GET YOUR COMPANIONS, HUMAN. DO YOUR JOB...
WE WILL HANDLE THIS.
A STRONTIAN RINCE. A KREE UDGE. A RELIC OM A BROKEN EMPIRE.
AND SOME DEAD THING FROM ANOTHER PLACE AND TIME...
THIS... ALL YOU HAVE?
THIS IS YOUR BEST?
WHAT GODS HAVE YOU SLIGHTED TO DIE IN SUCH POOR COMPANY?

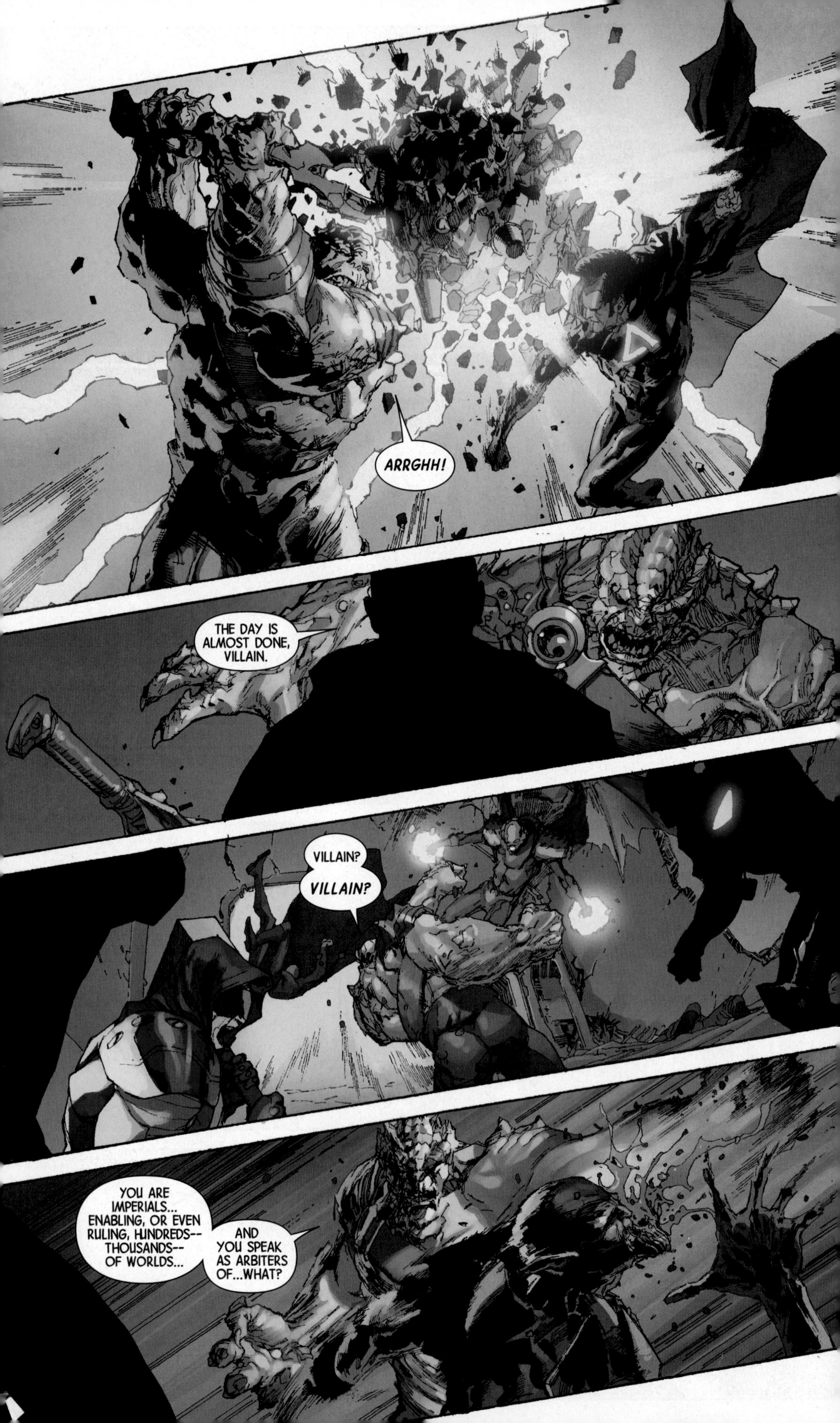
ARRGHH!
THE DAY IS ALMOST DONE, VILLAIN.
VILLAIN?
VILLAIN?
YOU ARE IMPERIALS... ENABLING, OR EVEN RULING, HUNDREDS-- THOUSANDS-- OF WORLDS...
AND YOU SPEAK AS ARBITERS OF...WHAT?

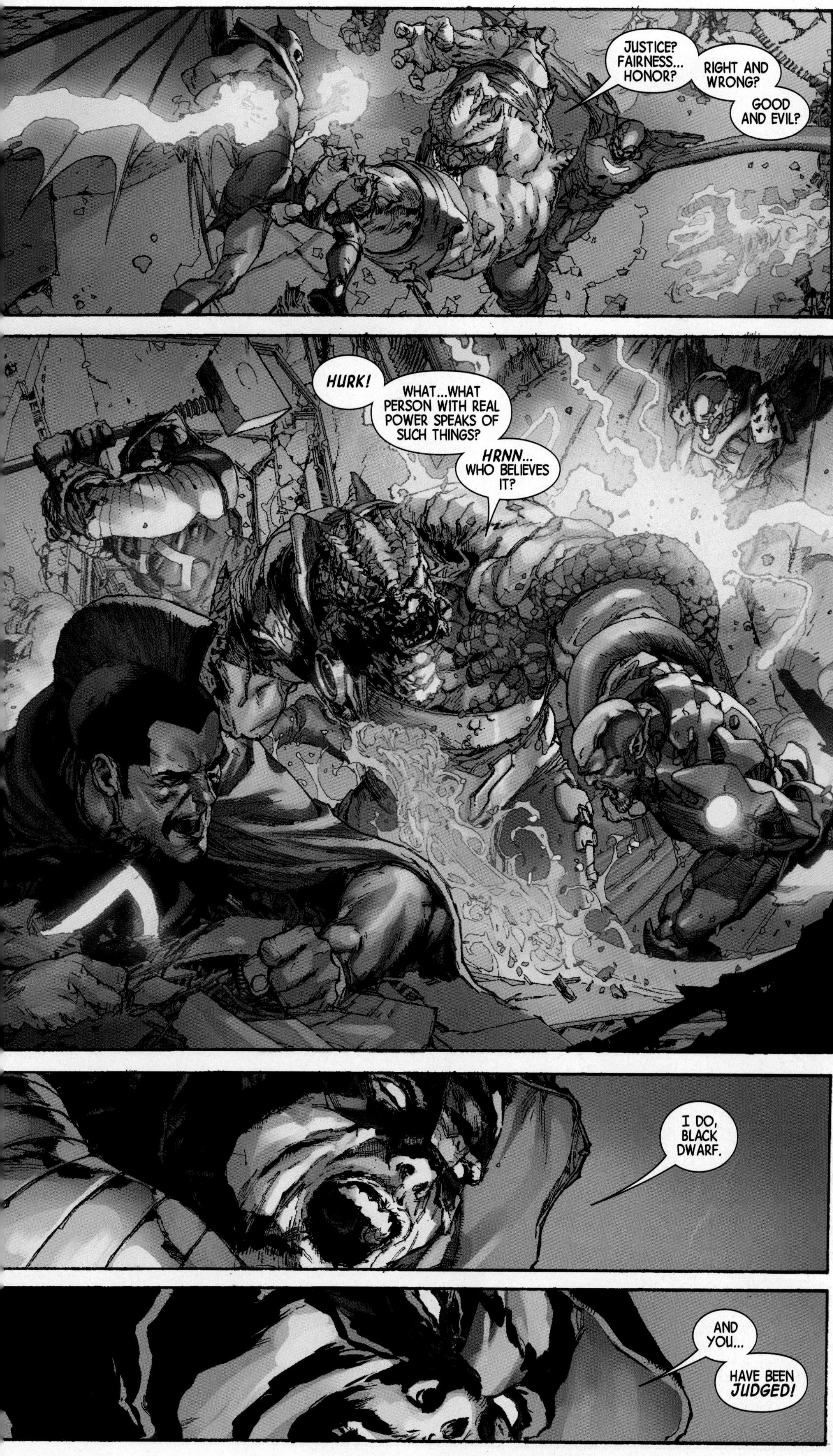
JUSTICE? FAIRNESS... HONOR?
RIGHT AND WRONG?
GOOD AND EVIL?
HURK!
WHAT...WHAT PERSON WITH REAL POWER SPEAKS OF SUCH THINGS?
HRNN... WHO BELIEVES IT?
I DO, BLACK DWARF.
AND YOU...
HAVE BEEN JUDGED!

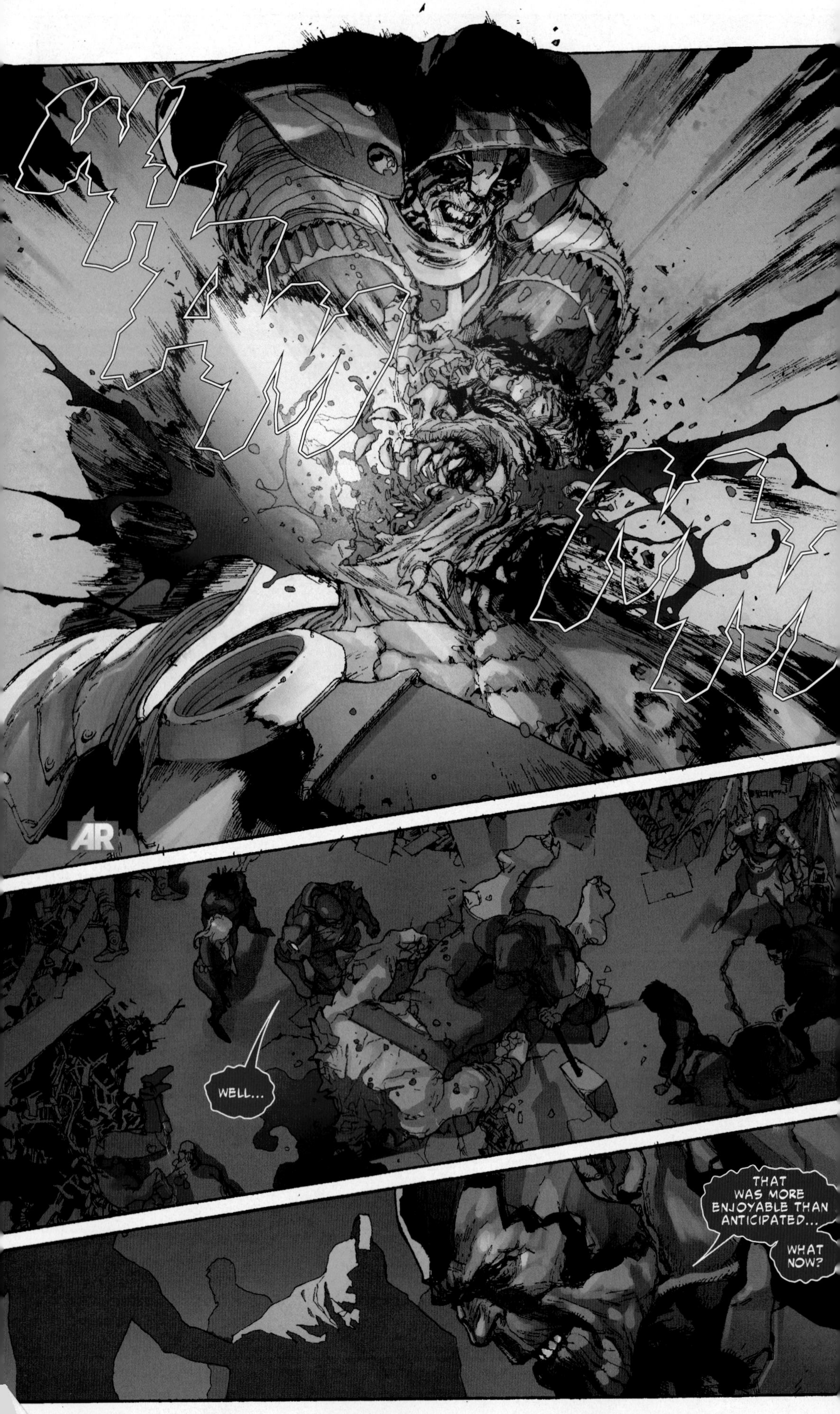
WELL...
THAT WAS MORE ENJOYABLE THAN ANTICIPATED...
WHAT NOW?

WE STILL HAVE THE IRATE FLEET TO SEND RUNNING...

"SO THAT IS WHAT WE WILL DO...

"WHILE THE AVENGERS FIGHT FOR EARTH...

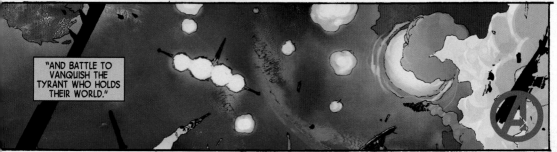

"AND BATTLE TO VANQUISH THE TYRANT WHO HOLDS THEIR WORLD."

#18

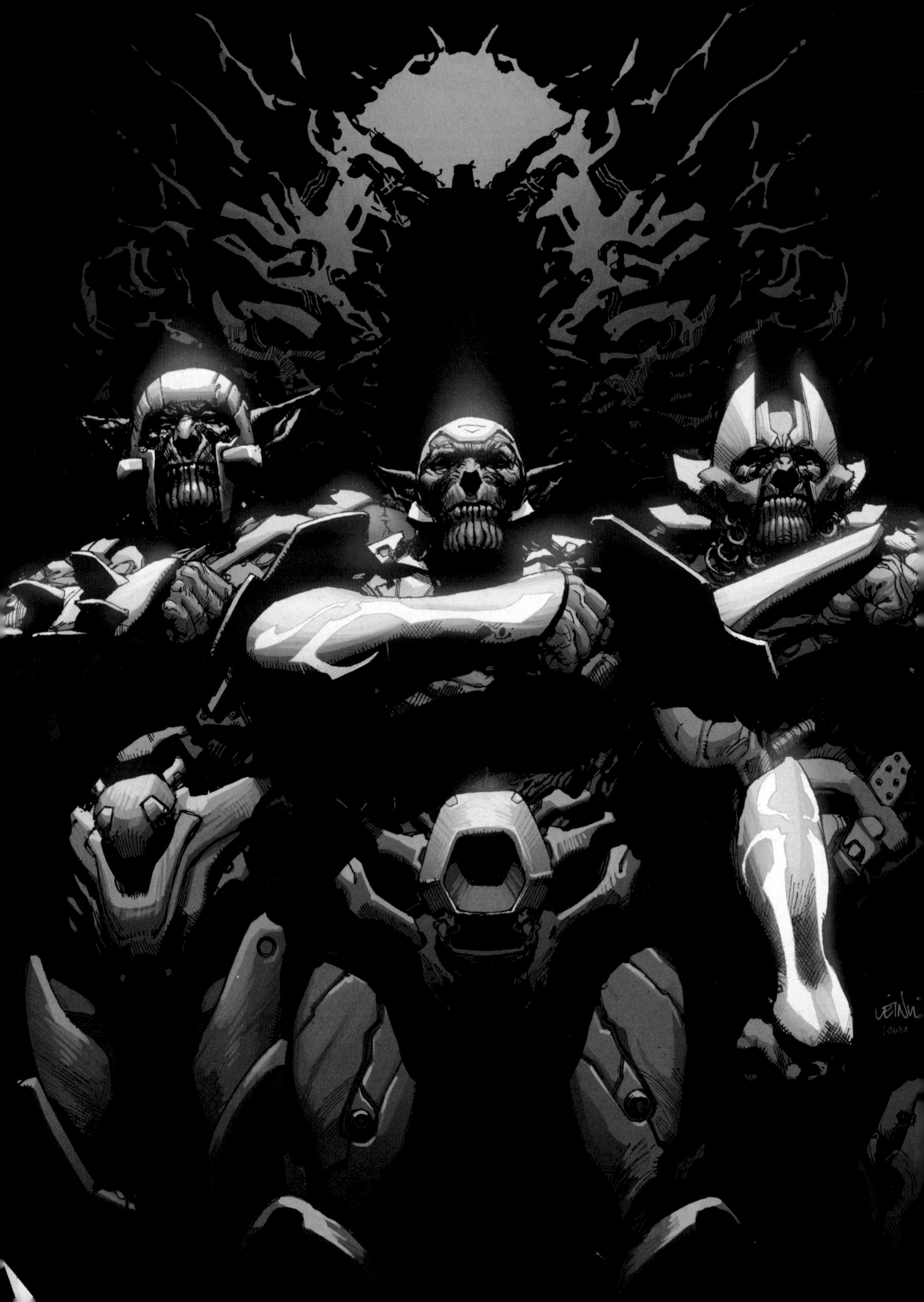

#19

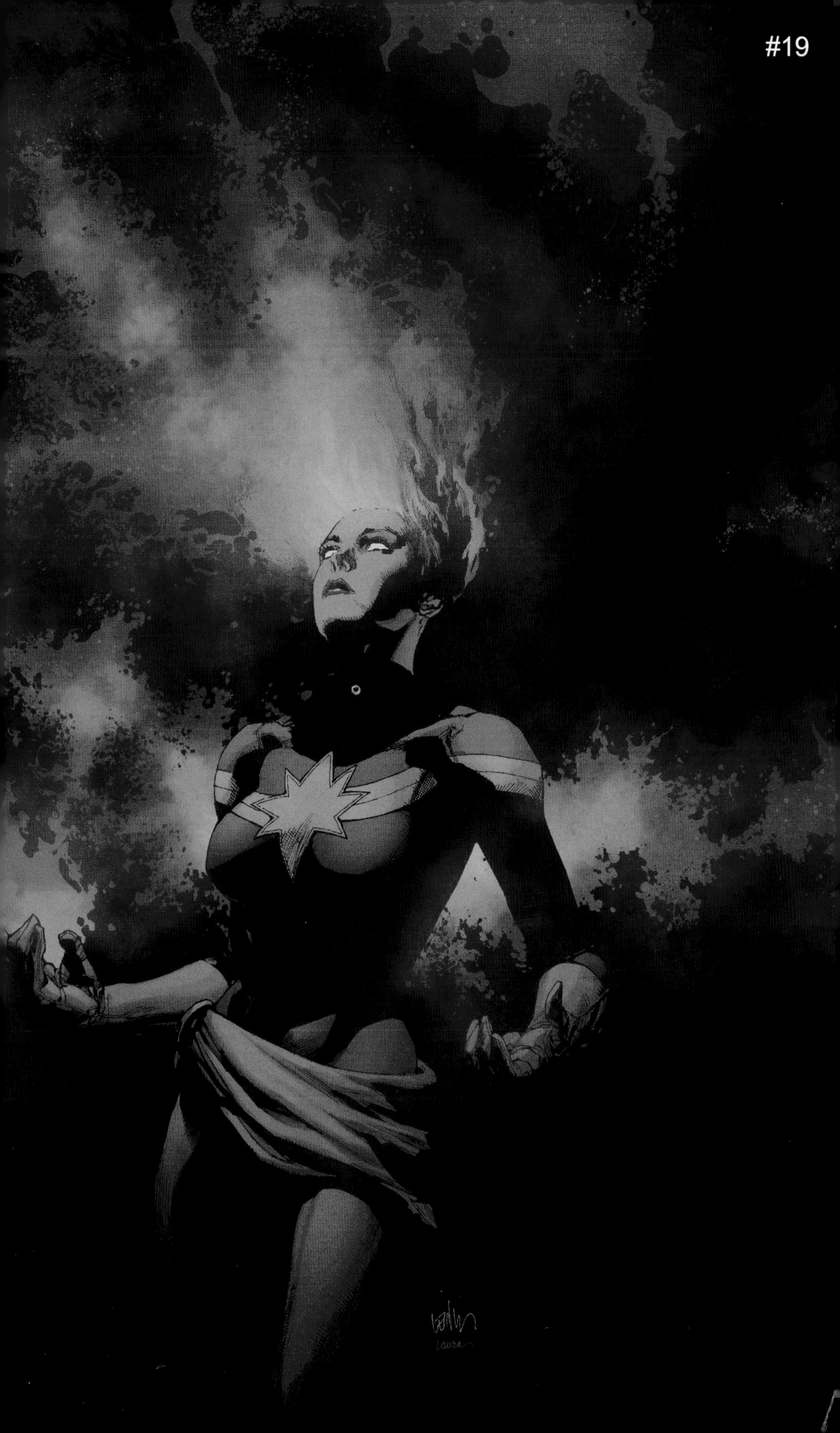

#20

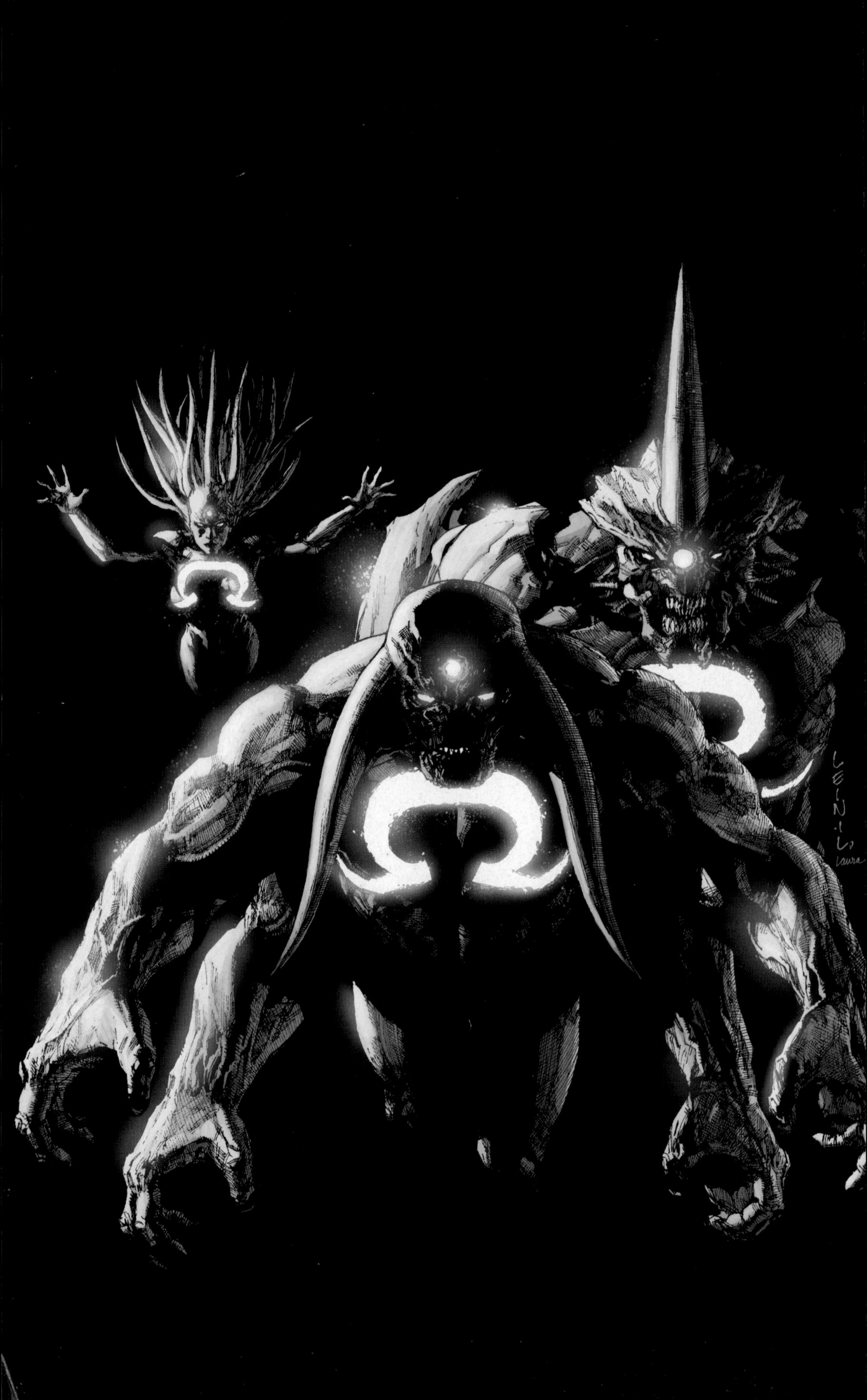

#21

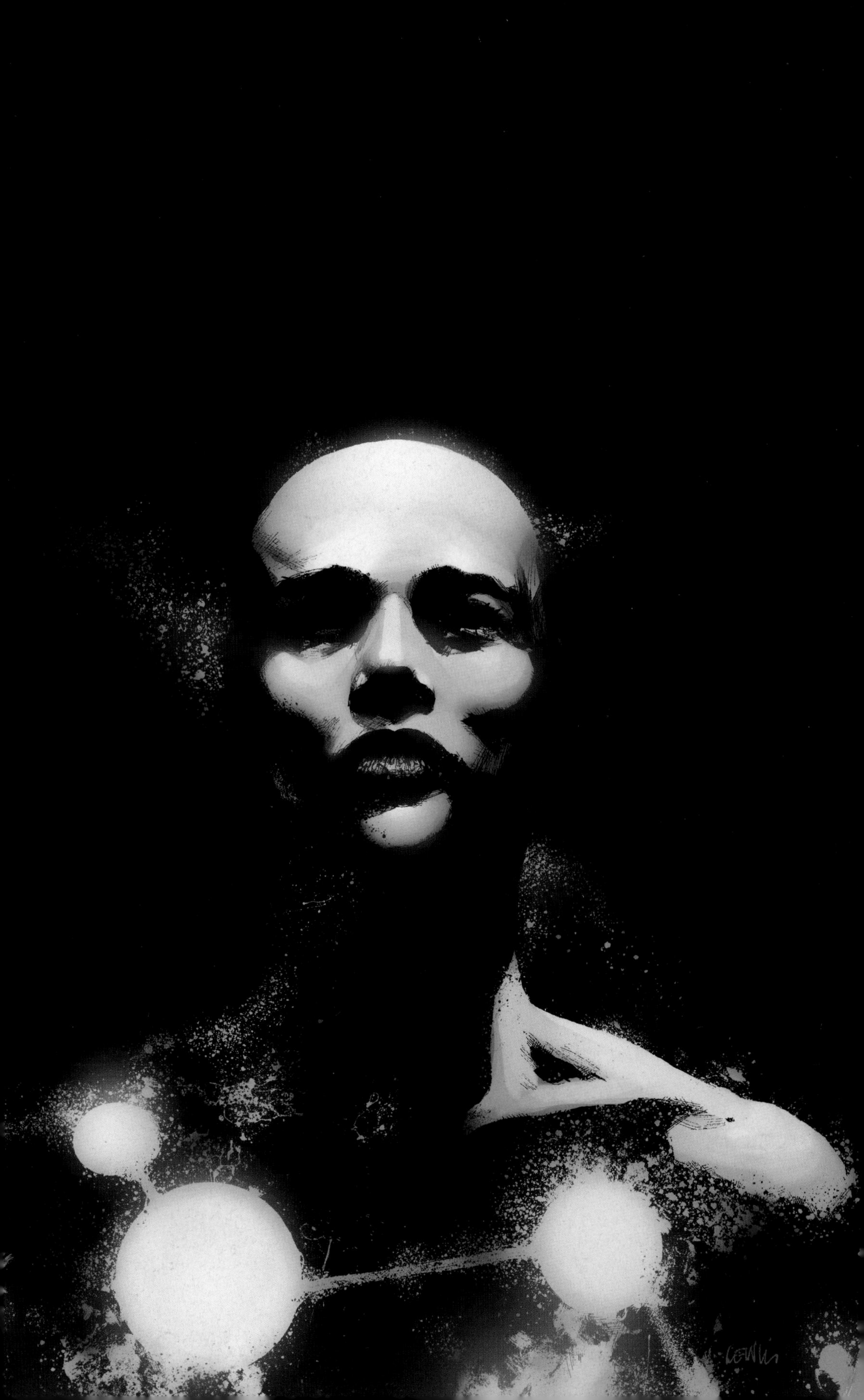

#22

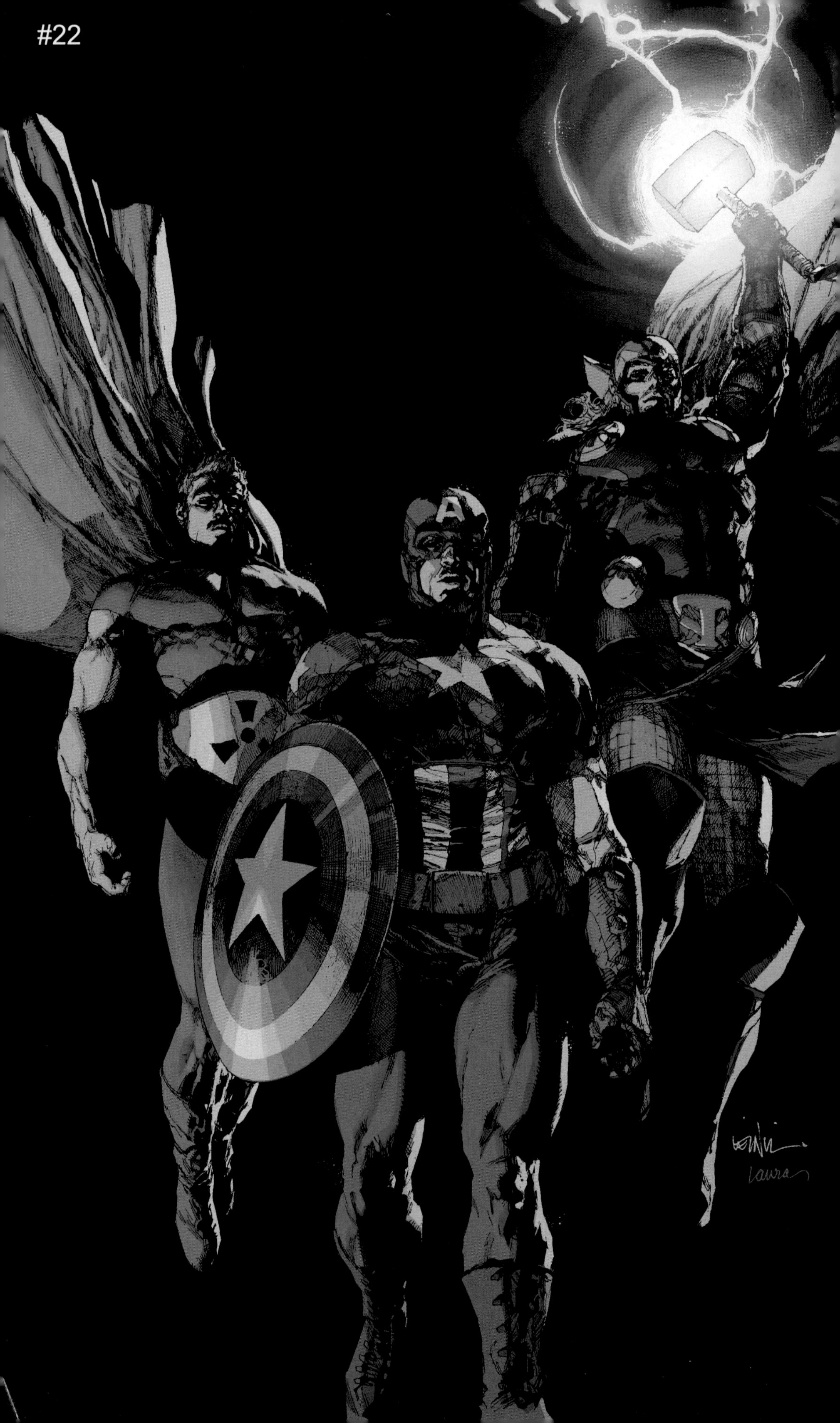

#23

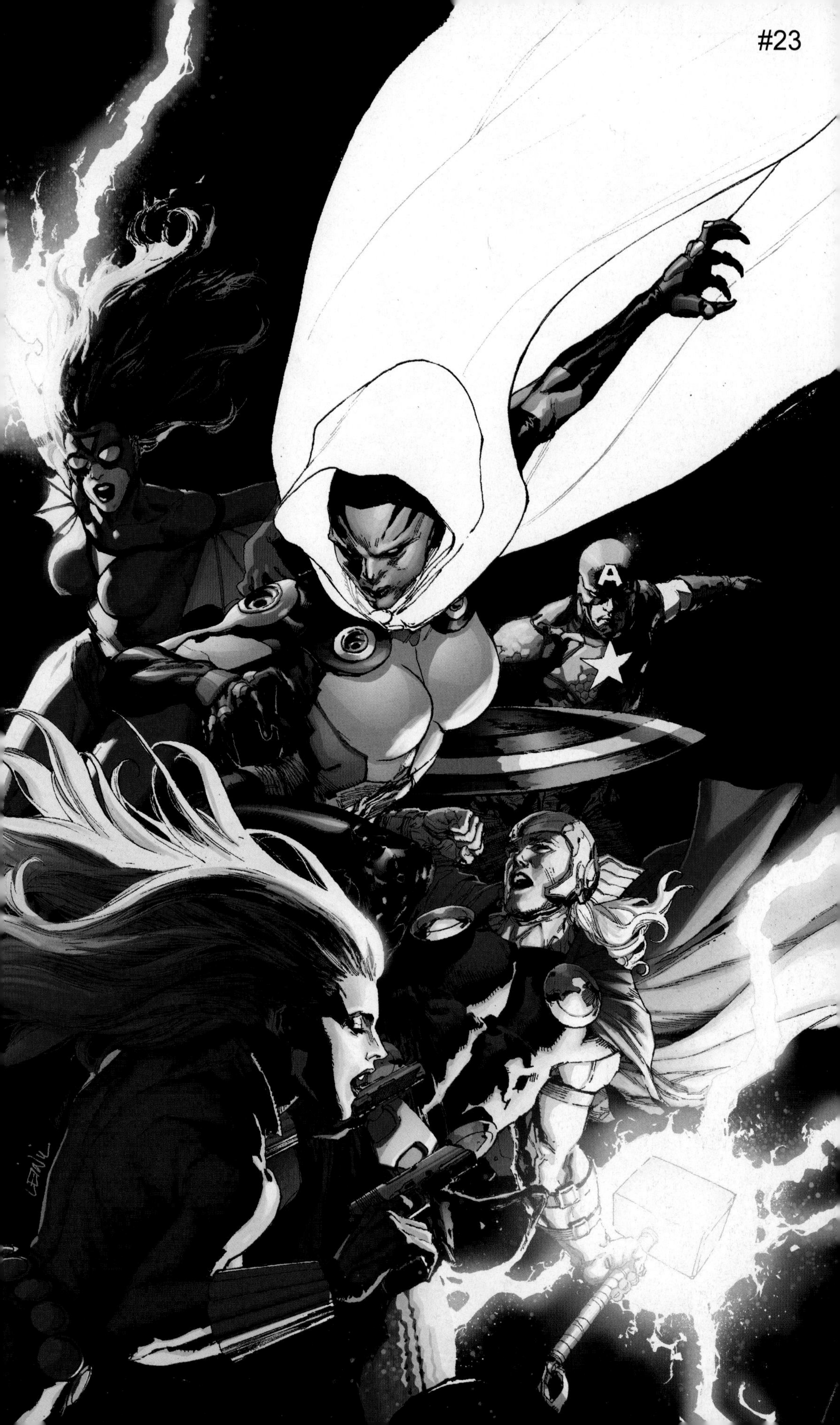

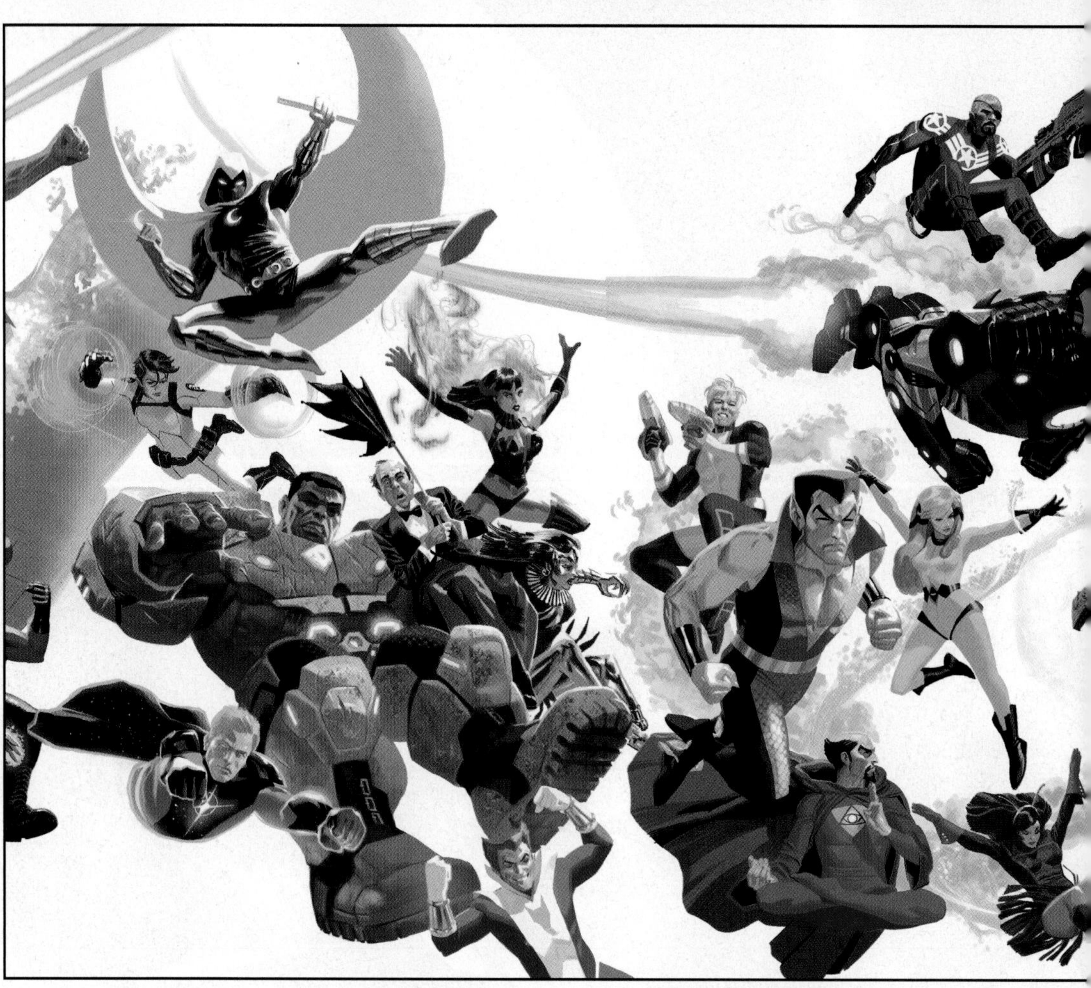

#18, #20 & #22-23 AVENGERS 50TH ANNIVERSARY VARIANTS:
DANIEL ACUÑA

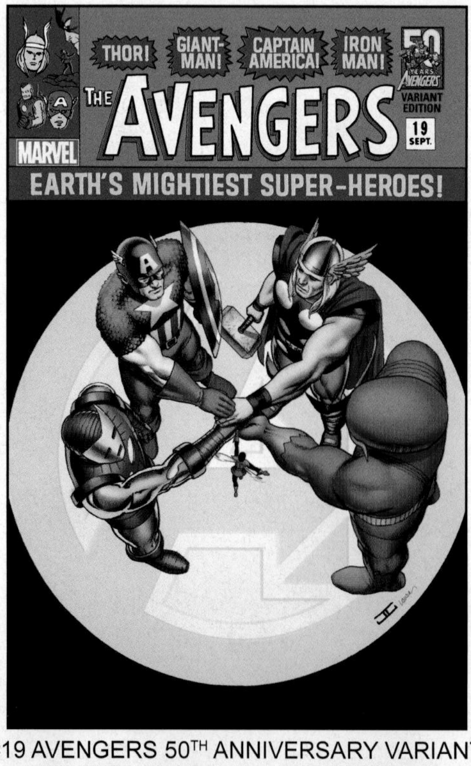
THOR!
GIANT-MAN!
CAPTAIN AMERICA!
IRON MAN!
50 YEARS AVENGERS
THE AVENGERS
VARIANT EDITION
19 SEPT.
MARVEL
EARTH'S MIGHTIEST SUPER-HEROES!

#19 AVENGERS 50TH ANNIVERSARY VARIANT:
JOHN CASSADAY & LAURA MARTIN

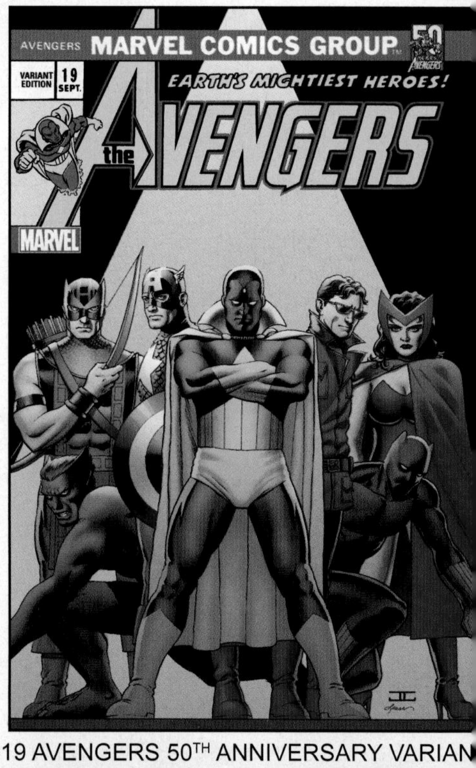
AVENGERS
MARVEL COMICS GROUP
VARIANT EDITION
19 SEPT.
EARTH'S MIGHTIEST HEROES!
the AVENGERS
MARVEL

#19 AVENGERS 50TH ANNIVERSARY VARIAN
JOHN CASSADAY & LAURA MARTIN

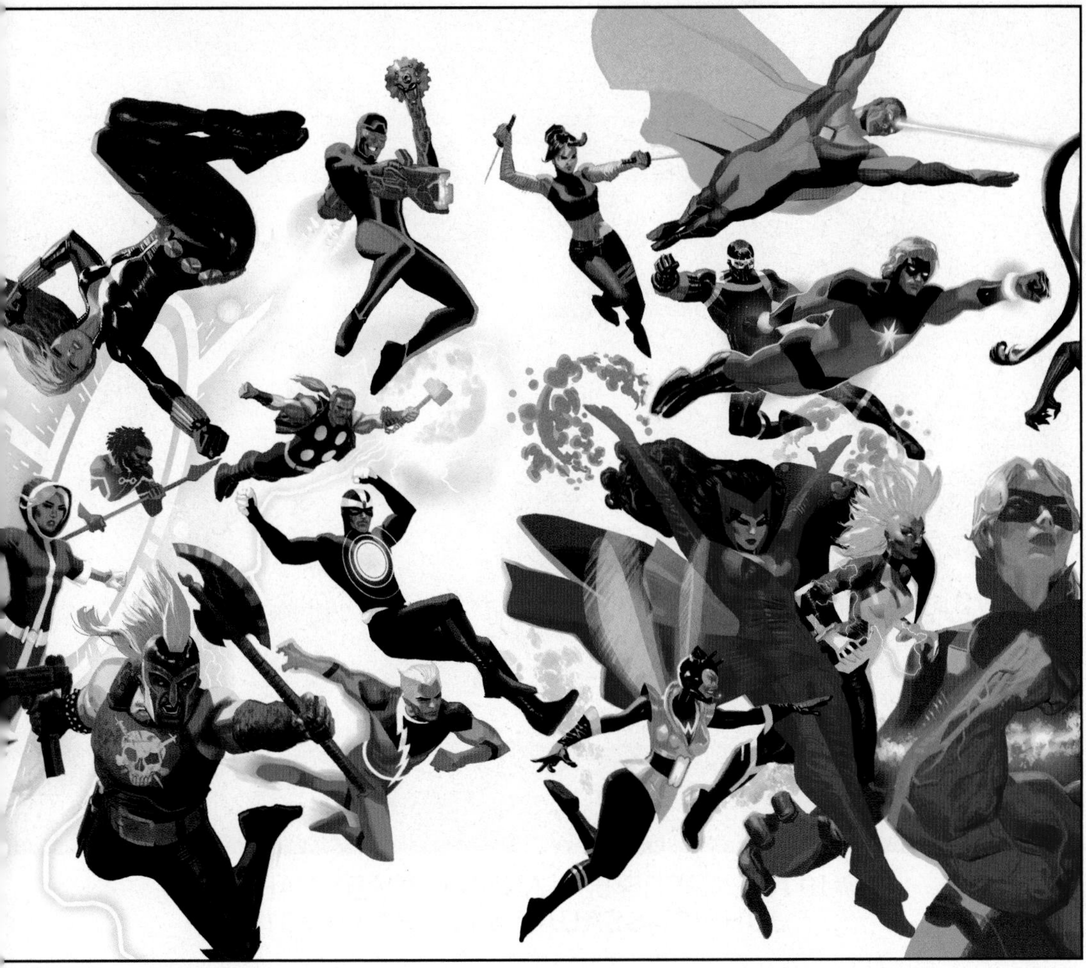

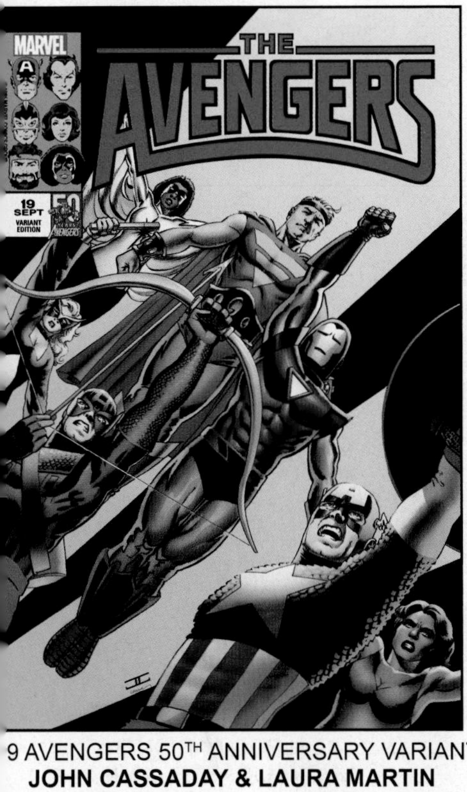
MARVEL
THE
AVENGERS
19
SEPT
VARIANT
EDITION

9 AVENGERS 50TH ANNIVERSARY VARIANT:
JOHN CASSADAY & LAURA MARTIN

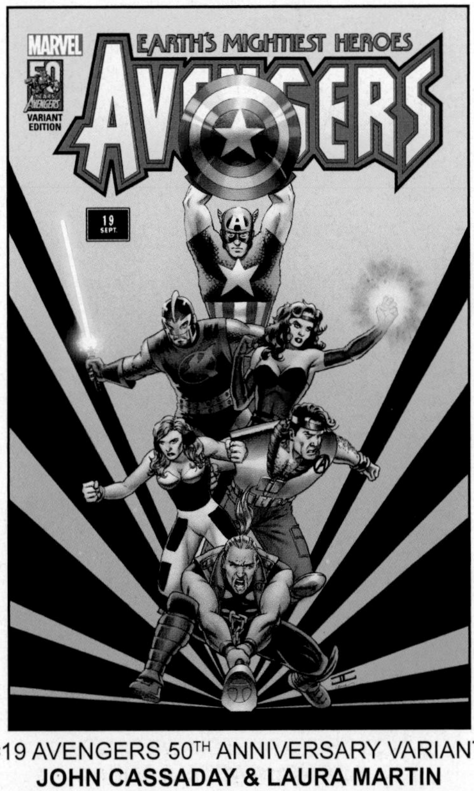
MARVEL
EARTH'S MIGHTIEST HEROES
AVENGERS
VARIANT
EDITION
19
SEPT.

#19 AVENGERS 50TH ANNIVERSARY VARIANT:
JOHN CASSADAY & LAURA MARTIN

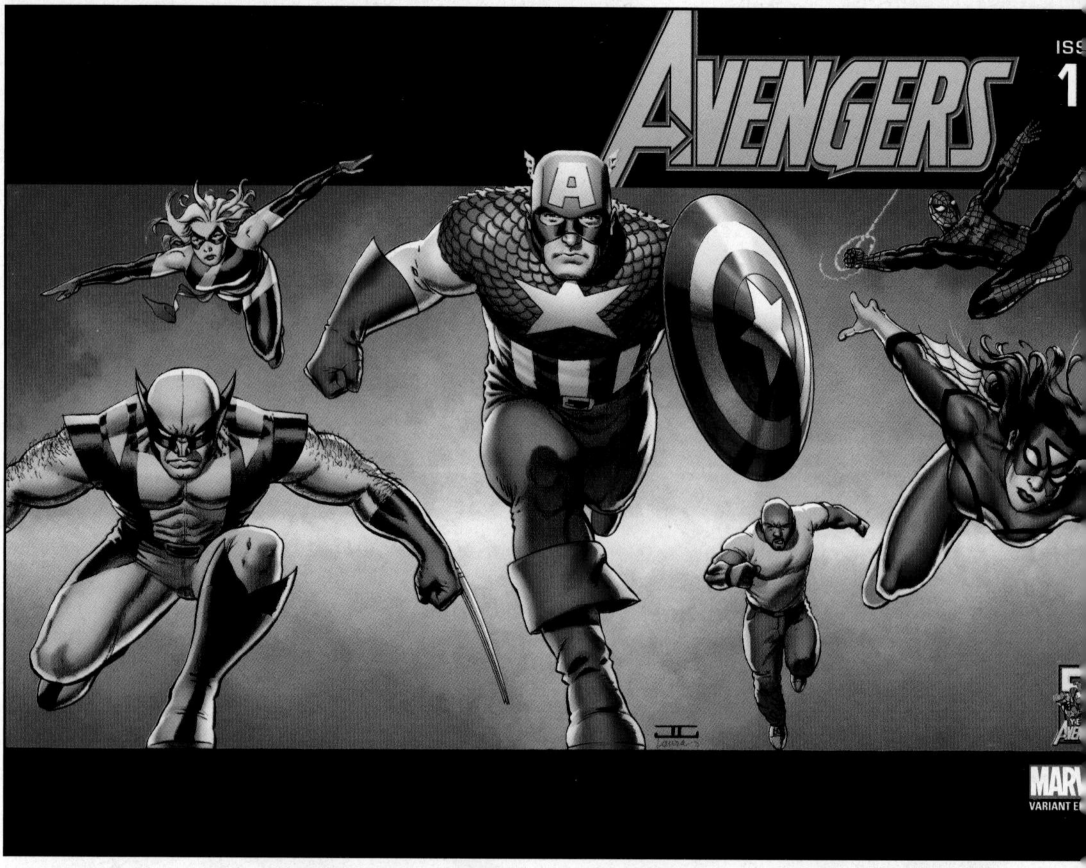
AVENGERS

#19 AVENGERS 50TH ANNIVERSARY VARIANT:
JOHN CASSADAY & LAURA MARTIN

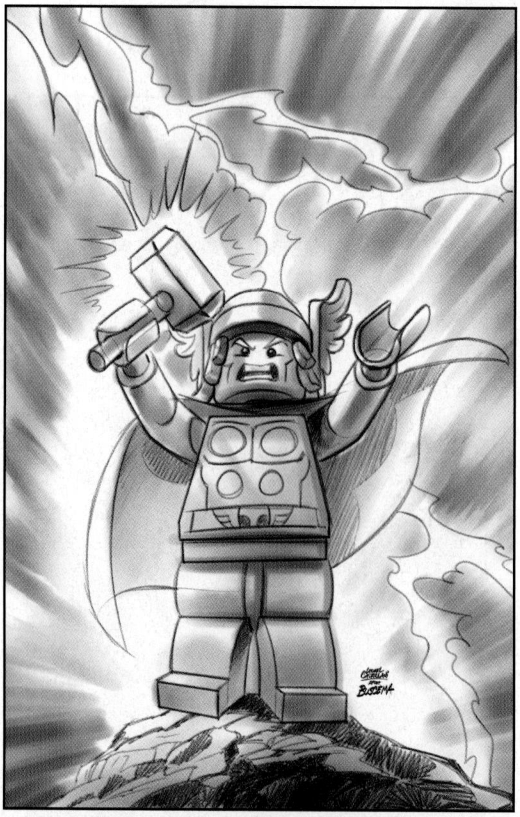

#21 LEGO SKETCH VARIANT:
LEONEL CASTELLANI

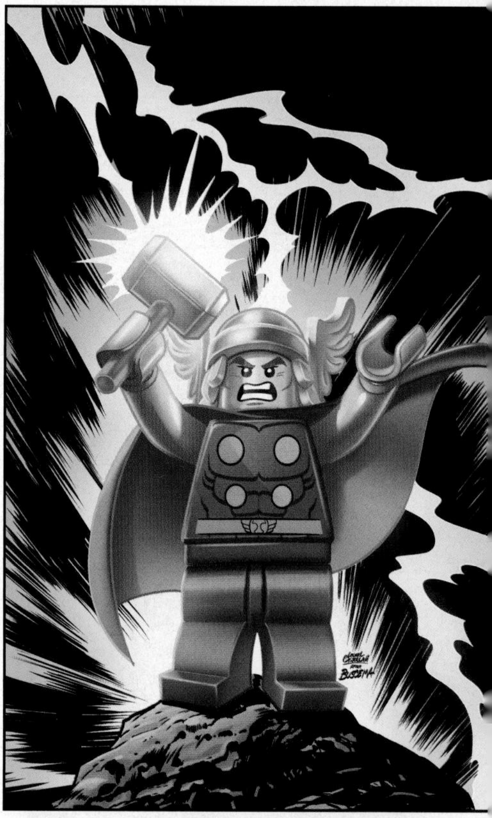

#21 LEGO VARIANT:
LEONEL CASTELLANI

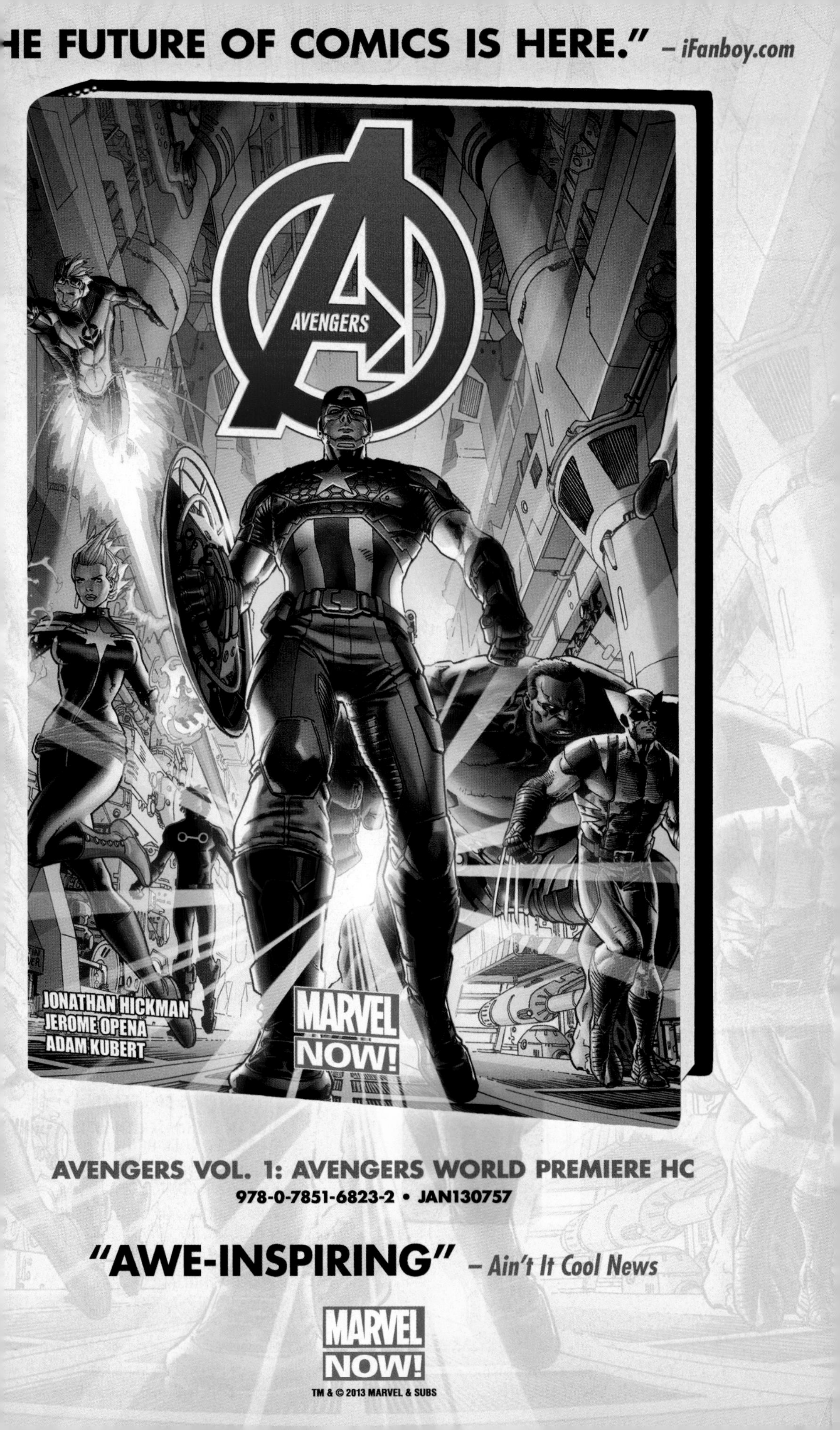

HE FUTURE OF COMICS IS HERE." – iFanboy.com
AVENGERS
JONATHAN HICKMAN
JEROME OPEÑA
ADAM KUBERT
MARVEL NOW!
AVENGERS VOL. 1: AVENGERS WORLD PREMIERE HC
978-0-7851-6823-2 • JAN130757
"AWE-INSPIRING" – Ain't It Cool News
MARVEL NOW!
TM & © 2013 MARVEL & SUBS

TO ACCESS THE FREE *MARVEL AUGMENTED REALITY APP* THAT ENHANCES AND CHANGES THE WAY YOU EXPERIENCE COM

1. Download the app for free via marvel.com/ARapp
2. Launch the app on your camera-enabled Apple iOS® or Android™ device*
3. Hold your mobile device's camera o any cover or panel with the AR gra
4. Sit back and see the future of comics in action!

*Available on most camera-enabled Apple iOS® and Android™ devices. Content subject to change and availability.

AVENGERS

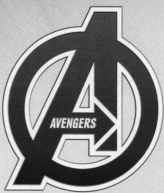

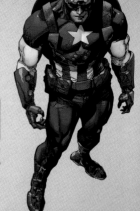

AR INDEX

TO REDEEM YOUR CODE FOR A FREE DIGITAL COPY:

1. GO TO MARVEL.COM/REDEEM. OFFER EXPIRES ON 1/15/16.
2. FOLLOW THE ON-SCREEN INSTRUCTIONS TO REDEEM YOUR DIGITAL COPY.
3. LAUNCH THE MARVEL COMICS APP TO READ YOUR COMIC NOW!
4. YOUR DIGITAL COPY WILL BE FOUND UNDER THE *MY COMICS* TAB.
5. READ & ENJOY!

YOUR FREE DIGITAL COPY WILL BE AVAILAB

MARVEL COMICS APP FOR APPLE® iOS DEVICES

MARVEL COMICS FOR ANDROID™ DE